The dominant institution in the modern economy is the large corporation. It is here that our problems and many of the solutions, lie. The large corporation is the most effective economic organization devised to date but, its potential is not being realized. Progressive corporate reform is one major alternative policy proposed by the author for the micro economy.

In the macro economy, Monetarism, supply side economics, and other recent fads are exposed for what they have become—flights into a fantasy world of unrealistic assumptions and ineffective policies. In their place, Dr. Dugger proposes fundamentally new monetary and fiscal policies based on economic realities. The new policies are fit into a democratic process of economic planning. Such planning results in wider participation in goal setting. It does not result in "The Plan", a blueprint into which everyone is forced to fit their actions. A new incomes policy is also proposed to ensure that full employment does not rekindle inflation.

In the 1980s we can continue to retrench, or we can develop new democratic alternatives. The task before us is to forge new ways to pursue democratic ideals within a reformed and revitalized economy. Within this context of choice, readers will find this book of major importance in evaluating the public policies and political platforms of the coming years. It is no coincidence that this book is first appearing in 1984, a landmark year in which the results of the U.S. Presidential elections could either drag us further into George Orwell's *1984*, or could launch us onto a new and freer path. *An Alternative to Economic Retrenchment* presents a hopeful first step onto that new path.

ABOUT THE AUTHOR

William M. Dugger is an associate professor of economics at DePaul University. Prior to this association he taught at North Texas University. He has a Ph.D. in economics from the University of Texas. Although this is his first book, he has written numerous articles which have been published in many prestigious journals.

AN ALTERNATIVE TO ECONOMIC RETRENCHMENT

AN ALTERNATIVE TO ECONOMIC RETRENCHMENT

William M. Dugger

PBI
a petrocelli
book
new york / princeton

Designed by Diane L. Backes
Typesetting by Backes Graphics

Portions of this book have appeared or will appear in a different form in the following articles by the author:

"Corporate Bureaucracy," *Journal of Economic Issues,* June, 1980.*

"Power," *Journal of Economic Issues,* December, 1980.*

"The Administered Labor Market," *Journal of Economic Issues,* June, 1981.*

"Entrenched Corporate Power and Our Options for Dealing With It," *Review of Social Economy,* October, 1981.

"The Classical Economists and the Corporation," *International Journal of Social Economics,* Vol. 10, 1983.

"An Institutionalist Critique of President Reagan's Economic Program," *Journal of Economic Issues,* September, 1982.*

"Two Twists in Economic Methodology," *American Journal of Economics and Sociology,* January, 1983.

*Reprinted from the *Journal of Economic Issues* with permission of the Association for Evolutionary Economics.

Printed in the United States of America
1 2 3 4 5 6 7 8 9 10

Library of Congress Cataloging in Publication Data

Dugger, William M.
    An Alternative to Economic Retrenchment.

    Includes bibliographical references and index.
    1. United States–Economic policy–1981-.
I. Title.
HC106.8.D83   1984   338.973   83-23692
ISBN 0-89433-231-7

*To Thorstein Veblen
Iconoclast, Humanist*

Contents

Preface   xi

Acknowledgments   xv

PART ONE
The Sick Economy and the Quacks

1 THE DISEASE   3

Introduction   3
International Comparisons   4
Stagflation in the United States   10
Reality and Apology   11

2 THE OLD REMEDY: Free Enterprise   13

Introduction   13
Reagan's Remedy   14

3 THE WRONG REMEDY   23

Introduction   23
Faulty Economic Science   23
Faulty Conceptualization of Economic Progress   28
Summary   46

4 THE NEW REALITY   49

Introduction   49
The New Social Reality   49
The New Economic Reality   61

5 DENIAL   73

In the Beginning   73
Contemporary Economic Theory   81
Conclusion   93

PART TWO
Reforming the Corporation

6 CORPORATE BUREAUCRACY   99

Introduction to Part Two   99
The Nature and Extent of Bureaucracy   100
The Bureaucratic Labor Market   114
The Personal Impact of Corporate Bureaucracy   124
Conclusion   130

7 REVITALIZATION   133

Introduction   133
Reforming Corporate Recruitment   134
Reform of Corporate Promotion and Corporate Structure   144
Conclusion   152

8 THE FEDERAL CORPORATE CHARTER   155

Introduction   155
The Federal Charter   159
Historical Perspective   165
Chapter Summary   168

9 PLANNING AND CORPORATE ADMINISTRATION   171

Introduction   171
The Administrative System Replaces the Price System   172
Unfinished Business   183

PART THREE
Reforming Economic Policies

10 WAGE-PRICE CONTROLS   201

Introduction to Part Three   201
Controls in Perspective   202
Types of Inflation   212
Effective Wage-Price Controls   215
A Wage-Price Commission   220
Concluding Remarks   225

11 MONETARY AND FISCAL POLICIES   229

   Introduction   229
   Money and History   230
   A Monetary Policy That Works   237
   The Government Budget and the Economy   242
   Toward Effective Fiscal Policy   253
   Conclusion   258

12 REVITALIZATION, NOT RETRENCHMENT   261

   America at the Close of the Twentieth Century   261
   Why We Chose Retrenchment   266
   The Significance of the Reagan Presidency   272
   Back on Course   274

Appendix   283

Notes and References   285

Index   303

Preface

This is a patriotic book. It calls for America to get back on course, to return to its historical role. This is also a subversive book. It is highly critical of the contemporary American scene, of our nostalgic retreat into individualism and privatism in the face of growing corporate collectivism. Once a revolutionary people devoted to equality and expansion, we are becoming a reactionary people practicing inequality and retrenchment. On the surface, much of the following deals with Ronald Reagan's Presidency. Yet the Reagan Presidency is more a result than a cause of a deeper-seated derangement. This book deals with that derangement: the distortions of the American economy, society, and individual character wrought by the evolution of corporate power.

Much has been written about the declining productivity of American industry. Productivity has not declined absolutely; it has declined relatively. Relative to other industrialized western economies, U.S. productivity is clearly slipping. American products have become less competitive in international markets. With the exception of agricultural products and a few special technologies, U.S. exports are meeting very stiff competition in our traditional markets in Europe, Asia, and Latin America. In our own markets at home, imports threaten entire industries. The U.S. steel industry and auto industry, mainstays of our industrial system, are struggling for survival. Japanese steel and Japanese autos are cheaper and better. But not for the reasons given by apologists for General Motors and U.S. Steel. The Japanese are not outperforming the Americans because the Japanese government subsidizes them. The American government subsidizes its own quite generously. Nor are the Japanese better because of less government regulation. Instead, they outperform us because they are better managed. The huge American corporation has become rigid, bureaucratic, and closed to new people and new ideas. The Japanese corporation has not.

Corporate bureaucracy has come to dominate much of the American economy, transforming it in the process. No longer can we call it a market economy. The market is still there, of course. Yet the market with its free give and take between supply and demand is no longer the central economic machinery. The central economic machinery is the conglomerate corporation with its vast bureaucratic administration. The American economy is now a corporate economy. Today, decisions made within corporate bureaucracies are more central to the workings of the economy than bargains struck in markets. The economy has been transformed from a market economy to a corporate economy.

American society has undergone a parallel transformation. It is no longer appropriate to call it a pluralistic society. Different institutions still exist. The church and state are still separate. The family still survives. Yet the church, state, and family are no longer self-sufficient, independent spheres of life. All three have become more and more dependent upon the corporation. Pluralism is being lost because our once pluralistic (independent) institutions are becoming dependent upon the increasingly dominant corporation. The result is a hegemonic society rather than a pluralistic one. Pluralism is highly unstable and, in historical times, quite rare. Ancient Rome was not pluralistic, at least not for long. The central state soon dominated all other institutions. State hegemony was the result. Feudal Europe was not pluralistic. At the height of church power, the church hegemony dominated all other institutions. Then came the rise of the nation state and the divine right of kings. The monarch became hegemonic. For a brief two or three centuries, the American colonies and then the United States were pluralistic. But the corporation emerged dominant at the close of the twentieth century. If we continue to acquiesce, corporate hegemony will be undeniable at the opening of the 21st century.

The emerging corporate hegemony is transforming the American character. In our nostalgia for the good old days, we still like to think of ourselves as individualists. At one time, the ideal was real, for white males of English descent. We still cling to the ideal, but the reality is very different. We want to be frontier individualists but we are really corporate careerists. For the man on the make, climbing the bureaucratic ladder has replaced taming the frontier. The bureaucratic climb, instead of the frontier struggle, now shapes the American character. Status is the essence of the bureaucratic climb and status is dependent upon the opinion and position of the other climbers. Status is never certain so the status climb is actually a status scramble and the climber is constantly in fear of losing out against others or of losing their good graces. Fear and fawning are new character traits for Americans, yet they are inherent to the bureaucratic climb of the American careerist. They are also prerequisites for authoritarianism. They represent the beginning of the hollowing out of American character and American values. That is, we still believe in certain values and character traits, but those values and traits are becoming hollow. They are rotting from within because they are not reinforced by daily experience.

The changes in the American economy, society, and character have caused a terrible malaise to fall upon the land. We are very unhappy with ourselves and very afraid. It is out of this cultural context that the Reagan Presidency has emerged. Ronald Reagan has believed for the last twenty years that he could save us from the malaise. In 1980, most of us thought he could, even though Jimmy Carter had promised the same in 1976 and we had believed him too. Both ran an anti-Washington campaign when Washington was not the problem. Carter did not destroy the federal socioeconomic programs constructed by the Progressives, the New Dealers, and the Kennedy-Johnson Liberals. He merely gestured at them. Reagan is attempting to dismantle them all, as he plays out his and our frontier fantasy to the ultimate conclusion.

Reaganomics will fail. It is based on a fantastic misdiagnosis of what ails us. Much of this book is devoted to a critique of President Reagan's program and an explanation of the misdiagnosis. A responsible social critic has a duty to offer an alternative, particularly if he cares about the subject being criticized, and I do. So the rest of the book is devoted to explaining an alternative to Reaganomics and retrenchment.

Up until now, the emerging corporate power structure has been left intact. The Progressives, New Dealers, and Kennedy-Johnson Liberals responded only in a piecemeal fashion to social and economic problems. Corporate power was often checked or reduced but never really changed. The poor were also subsidized, but were seldom given effective entry into the corporate establishment. Rather than tearing down the piecemeal programs and subsidies constructed by the reformers, as Reagan is doing, we need to coordinate them, reinforce them, and supplement them to the extent necessary to actually change the corporate establishment. In particular, we need to democratize the corporate bureaucracy, coordinate the activities of different corporations, help the poor and the excluded to push their way into the corporate establishment, and turn the corporate economy toward the public purpose. We cannot return to the frontier individualism of the nine-teenth century. But we can make the corporate economy of the 21st century a servant of the democratic process and a fit place for secure, free individuals to work.

To do so, I have proposed a sweeping reconstruction of the corporate economy as it has evolved in the twentieth century. The reconstruction involves replacing vague state charters for corporations with a uniform, explicit federal charter. The new corporate charter would dramatically change the internal workings of corporate bureaucracies, fomenting a peaceful revolution within the corporation itself. Hiring and promotion practices would be fundamentally changed and employee rights en-larged significantly. The corporation would be opened to new people and ideas. The reconstruction of the corporate economy would also involve the use of wage-price controls to keep inflation under control without depression-level unemployment rates. Furthermore, recon-struction requires the use of democratic economic planning to coor-dinate the activities of regulatory agencies and to ensure that corporate machinery is used for the public purpose. Last of all, monetary and fiscal policies must be revamped to ensure balanced economic growth within a democratic framework. Numerous alternatives to Reagano-mics and retrenchment exist. I hope my discussion will further public inquiry into them and speed up rejection of our current flirtation with frontier fantasy.

This book is arranged in three parts. Part I, THE SICK ECONOMY AND THE QUACKS, describes our relative decline and explains why a return to frontier individualism and laissez-faire economics will not work. The flight into fantasy of the American economics profession is also explained. In Part II, REFORMING THE CORPORATION, the growth and impact of corporate bureaucracy are described and reforms proposed. Part III, REFORMING ECONOMIC POLICIES, contains discussions of wage-price controls, monetary and fiscal policies, and the conclusion. Wage-price controls can be effective, efficient, and fair. Monetary policy need not strangle the economy in a vain attempt to control the money supply, and fiscal policy need not involve massive tax giveaways to the rich and funding cutbacks for the poor. The con-cluding Chapter discusses where we stand at the close of the twentieth century, why we chose Reaganomics and retrenchment, what the choice means, and how we can get back on course.

Acknowledgments

Many friends and colleagues have helped with this book, both directly and indirectly. My wife Pauly contributed the most. Dick Wiltgen, Bob Faulhaber, Bill Waters, Ken Cochran, Miles Groves, and Hugh Garnett were very supportive. Warren Samuels read the manuscript in its entirety and made many helpful suggestions. Susie Bretz and Elizabeth Johnston helped in many ways. Jim Horner of Cameron University and Lee Van Zant of Austin College allowed me to present my ideas to their colleagues and students. Brother Leo V. Ryan, C.S.V. and DePaul University provided me with the support I needed. Judge William Wayne Justice of Tyler, Texas, deserves a special thanks for his trust. Marc Tool and Will Lissner were also helpful. Peach Y. Henry Hyde and Gerre Trapper did the typing. I thank them all. Of course, none of them should be held responsible in any way for the following. The blame is mine.

Chicago
December, 1983

PART 1

The Sick Economy and the Quacks

Economic theology is the opiate of the middle classes.

THURMAN ARNOLD

1 THE DISEASE

INTRODUCTION

When founded in 1776, the United States of America was already the richest nation in the world in terms of economic resources. Perhaps we were not number one in terms of today's yardstick, real gross national product per person. Still, we started out on top with a treasure house of resources. This is not to deny that serious problems and challenges faced our new nation. We were not industrialized, communication and transportation were difficult, exploitation of native Americans was rampant, and slavery blighted the land and its people. Nevertheless, we possessed resources undreamed of by Old World countries: vigorous people, western science and technology, immense agricultural areas, timber, fuel and other energy sources, minerals, and freedom from both foreign domination and the constraints of outmoded feudal traditions.

The United States was never a poor nation. Perhaps, for us, it was too easy. We were spared overpopulation, critical scarcities of food and fuel, the absence of western science and technology, and the dead hand of ancient tradition. All of these burden the poor nations of today, and many burdened the poor nations of yesterday. We went a long way with what we had. Given our head start, a continent was tamed and settled. Transportation and communication links were forged, an industrial economy was constructed, and millions of immigrants from all over the world participated in the American dream, for the dream was real.

Those were accomplishments to be proud of and to celebrate. But what are we doing now, in the close of the twentieth century? The dream is over and the time for sober reflection is at hand; we are becoming second rate.

This is not to say that we have lost the frontier spirit, far from it. Rugged individualism is still the American ideal. That is part of the problem, because rugged individualism is the frontier spirit, yet the frontier closed in the last century. So here we are, at the close of this century, a frontier people with no frontier.[1] We work in huge corporate, government, or educational bureaucracies, not in loose-knit frontier settlements. When we get sick or old, medical bureaucracies, not our families, care for us. When we get in trouble, we no longer move to a new settlement for a new start. Now, we are institutionalized in prisons and mental "hospitals" for punishment and rehabilitation. And yet, in spite of our traditional individualism being frustrated at every turn, we cling more obstinately to it.

In economics, this means we believe ever more fervently in free enterprise and laissez-faire, in individual competition in the free market. We do so in spite of the fact that giant corporations have replaced individual competitors in most of our economy. Even though corporate planning and managerial discretion have replaced "supply and demand" and the free market, we still believe in free enterprise and laissez-faire.

The American dream was real at one time. It no longer is. But we dream on. And that is what is fundamentally wrong with us. Even though the force of events pushes us forward into increased complexity and increased social organization, we continue to look backward at a simple time and a simple society. In economics this has meant the growth of an incredible gap between theory and reality. Theory deals with the simple days of free markets and limited government. But the reality is corporation-administered markets and complex webs of government regulation and control. Both the modern corporation and the modern state have sprung up in a higgledy-piggledy fashion. They are unplanned, uncoordinated growths; knee-jerk responses to particular problems and opportunities. Unrecognized by economic theory, they dominate economic reality. Part of our disease is an inability to face this reality.

Our continued failure to deal with reality is beginning to show. Our economy is breaking down, not in an absolute sense, but in a relative sense. We are not collapsing, not just yet. But economies with far less going for them than our own are beginning to outperform us. We should take these signs of relative decline for what they are: warnings of far more serious consequences in the future. For if the gap between economic reality and our perception of it continues to widen, our problems will intensify to crisis proportions.

INTERNATIONAL COMPARISONS

International comparisons often bring out the worst in us. Sputnik and the alleged missile gap brought on an orgy of military spending and a decade of punishing school children with the New Math. The following is not intended as a chauvinistic appeal but as a sobering reassessment. I do not propose that we compete with the rest of the world. Rather, I propose that we reform ourselves. A comparison with the rest of the world can teach us about ourselves. Three dimensions of social and economic life will be used for comparison: (1) equality, (2) growth, (3) social indicators.

In all three, the United States should stand head and shoulders above other countries. Given what the country started with and our past achievements, we should be an example to the rest of the world of what an economy and society can be, not in a chauvinistic sense, but in a humanistic sense. Ours should be the great society. Given our head start, poverty, inequality, and social pathology in general are inexcusable. And yet, how do we really shape up against other countries, most of which were once far worse off than the United States?

EQUALITY

The United States is a huge multiracial nation with great geographical diversity. Equality comparisons between it and smaller, more homogeneous nations are simply unfair. So at least goes the refrain of the American Apologia. But no other nation began with a slate wiped as clean as ours. Feudal traditions of rank and status, huge landed estates, moneyed aristocracies, limited access to resources, military castes; none of these hindered Americans. Slavery was a blight, but we were spared the rest. Other nations were not. So why should we expect inequality naturally to be greater in the U.S. than elsewhere? We should expect quite the reverse.

Malcolm Sawyer, in a special study for The Organization for Economic Co-operation and Development, investigated the degree of inequality in developed countries during the late 1960s and early 1970s. Making the available data as comparable as possible, he calculated eight different measures of after-tax income inequality for households in eleven different countries. When ranked from the most unequal to the least unequal country, the United States was always either the third or fourth most unequal of the eleven countries. Only France and Spain ranked consistently more unequal than the United States.[2] This is shocking. By all rights, the U.S. ranking should have been the reverse. We should have been among the countries with the least degree of after-tax income inequality.

What has happened to the land of opportunity? In an economy where opportunities really are distributed equally, and where lucky bonanzas are offset by a progressive tax system, the degree of inequality actually observed in the United States could not occur unless individuals are born with large genetic differences. Since the genetic explanation of inequality simply will not hold water, we are left with an unpleasant conclusion: Our society has become inegalitarian.[3] We started off with ideals about the equality of man. We also started off with the least of restraints on individual ascent (excepting slavery and exploitation of native Americans). But here we are with a large portion of our society unable to rise into affluence. The American ideal and the American reality do not match. We can either rationalize inequality away, institutionalize it through repression and suppression, or face up to the shortcoming.

GROWTH

A traditional approach to determining how well an economy is doing is to compare the level and the rate of growth of that country's gross national product to the level and growth rate of the GNP of other countries. Such comparisons can easily lead to chauvinistic growthmanship, the attempt to prove superiority by outgrowing one's rival. This, of course, is the favorite game of the economics divisions of the KGB and the CIA. However, that is not the purpose pursued here. Rather than playing such games as "The Russians Are Going to Bury Us" because they grew faster than we did last year, or "Our System is Better Than Theirs" because we are growing faster this year, the following comparisons are made for purely internal reasons. They teach us something about ourselves, period.

Furthermore, the level and growth of GNP is only one aspect of an economy's performance. Many other aspects are important as well, principal among them is the degree of equality and the quality of individual and social life.

With these qualifications in mind, Table 1.1 presents the level and growth of GNP per person for the eleven developed countries discussed in the equality section above. Data for the Soviet Union was included gratis for cold war buffs. As Table 1.1 shows, when ranked with our peers our level of GNP is moderately high but our rate of growth is very low. We simply are not living up to our potential. Furthermore, our low growth rate means that the gap between our actual and potential performance is widening.

Of course, apologists would reply that countries with high or moderately high GNP's, like the United States, *naturally* begin to experience a slow down of growth. Hence, our slower growth is to be expected. But that explanation will not wash. The correlation between the size of GNP and its growth rate for the eleven countries displayed in Table 1.1 (USSR excluded) shows no strong tendency for growth to slow down as GNP rises.

Another piece of conventional wisdom, as false as the notion that the growth of high GNP economies has a tendency to slow down naturally, is the notion that our retarded growth is due to the expansion of government spending in recent years. Newspapers across the land have carried editorials angrily denouncing the growth of bloated public bureaucracies and spendthrift public projects. Traditional economists have cooked up elaborate theoretical models to demonstrate that public spending crowds out private investment. But in all this hubbub, few

TABLE 1.1

Gross National Product Comparisons

Country	1978 GNP per capita dollars	GNP rank	Average Annual growth of real GNP per capita (1960–1978) percent	Growth rank
Australia	7,990	8	2.9	7
Canada	9,180	5	3.5	4
France	8,260	7	4.0	3
Germany	9,580	2	3.3	6
Japan	7,280	9	7.6	1
Netherlands	8,410	6	3.4	5
Norway	9,510	3	4.0	3
Spain	3,470	11	5.0	2
Sweden	10,210	1	2.5	8
United Kingdom	5,030	10	2.1	10
United States	9,363	4	2.4	9
USSR	3,700	not ranked	4.3	not ranked

Source: World Bank, *World Development Report, 1980*, (New York: Oxford University Press, 1980), Table 1, p. 111.

have looked at the facts. Some straightforward international comparisons can teach us a lot about ourselves.

Table 1.2 shows how public spending and private investment have grown in recent years for the eleven developed countries we have been examining. "Public spending" for the countries includes all current expenditures of all levels of government on goods and services (public consumption) and all military spending. It does not include capital accumulation in the public sector. "Private investment" is gross domestic investment by the private sector.

The United States ranked sixth and then eleventh out of the eleven countries in growth of public spending. Clearly, compared with our peers, public spending has not grown rapidly in recent years. The conventional wisdom is wrong. In fact, the public sector in the United States has been comparatively tight-fisted. U.S. private investment growth ranked ninth and then sixth, an improvement in more recent years, but still a mediocre showing.

TABLE 1.2

Comparisons of Public Spending and Private Investment.

| Country | Growth of public spending | | | | Growth of private investment | | | |
| | 1960–70 | | 1970–78 | | 1960–70 | | 1970–78 | |
	percent	rank	percent	rank	percent	rank	percent	rank
Australia	6.8	1	5.8	2	6.2	5	0.7	8
Canada	6.2	3	3.3	7	5.8	6	4.7	1
France	3.4	7	3.4	6	7.3	3	1.7	5
Germany	4.1	6	3.9	5	4.1	10	-0.2	10
Japan	6.4	2	5.0	4	14.0	1	2.5	4
Netherlands	3.1	8	2.7	10	6.8	4	-0.1	9
Norway	6.4	2	5.6	3	5.1	7	4.1	2
Spain	5.5	4	6.2	1	10.5	2	3.0	3
Sweden	5.4	5	3.1	8	5.0	8	-1.3	11
United Kingdom	2.2	9	2.9	9	5.0	8	1.5	7
United States	4.1	6	1.7	11	4.8	9	1.6	6

Source: World Bank, *World Development Report, 1980* (New York: Oxford University press, 1980), Table 4, p. 117.

Table 1.2 helps us examine another piece of conventional wisdom: Does rapid growth in public spending crowd out private investment? If it did, those countries ranking high in public spending growth would rank low in private investment growth and those countries ranking low in public spending growth would rank high in private investment growth. A careful look at Table 1.2 shows that this is not the case. High public spending growth is not consistently associated with low invest- ment growth; nor is low public spending growth associated with high investment growth. The conventional wisdom that public spending crowds out private spending is not supported by the facts. However, the facts do show a mediocre performance by the U.S. on the growth front.

SOCIAL INDICATORS

Economic growth is only one indication of social and economic well-being. The health and educational experiences of individuals are other very important indicators. Table 1.3 presents four indicators of social and economic well-being in the eleven developed countries we have been using for comparative purposes. A glance through Table 1.3 shows that the United States does not stand head and shoulders above other countries, even though it should. The one exception to our me- diocre showing, is higher education where the U.S. ranked much more highly than the second-ranked Canada. In spite of the conventional wisdom of the day, higher education in the United States is very healthy, at least as measured by comparative enrollment.

Our individual health leaves something to be desired. We rank sev- enth in infant mortality, only Germany and Spain are worse. Our life expectancy is somewhat better, we are in a five-way tie for fourth with United Kingdom, France, Australia, and Spain. In physician avail- ability, we tie for fourth with The Netherlands.[4] Assuming that our potential is higher than the other countries, we come close to realizing that potential only in higher education.

To sum up, the degree of equality, the level and growth of GNP, and the general level of individual health in the United States are all me- diocre when compared with the conditions of countries less-favored than ourselves. This should tell us a great deal more about ourselves

TABLE 1.3

Social Indicator Comparisons

Country	Infant mortality rate[a] number	rank	Life expectancy at birth in 1978 years	rank	People per physician in 1977 number	rank	Youth in higher education[b] percent	rank
Australia	13	6	73	4	650	6	24	6
Canada	12	5	74	3	560	3	37	2
France	11	4	73	4	610	5	24	6
Germany	15	8	72	5	490	1	25	5
Japan	10	3	76	1	850	8	29	4
The Netherlands	10	3	74	3	580	4	29	4
Norway	9	2	75	2	540	2	24	6
Spain	16	9	73	4	560	3	22	7
Sweden	8	1	75	2	560	3	30	3
United Kingdom	14	7	73	4	750	7	19	8
United States	14	7	73	4	580	4	56	1

a. the number of infants who died before age 1 per thousand live births in 1978

b. the percentage of the population aged 20-24 in 1976

Source: World Bank, *World Development Report, 1980* (New York: Oxford University Press, 1980), Tables 21, 22, and 23, pp. 150-155. (In some cases, the World Bank had to use data for years other than the ones indicated in these and other tables.)

than about others. Nevertheless, a more detailed look at the United States itself is in order. Particular attention will be focused on our actual economic performance versus our potential.

STAGFLATION IN THE UNITED STATES

The U.S. economy in the 1970s and 1980s is stagnant. It has not grown fast enough to provide jobs for all who sought them and still seek them. Rising unemployment is a fact, but much is made of the new entrants into the work force. Women are moving out of the house and into the labor force in massive numbers. Many of them are unskilled, "marginal" workers. Hence, the labor market is slow to absorb them and this has pushed up the unemployment rate giving an exaggerated indication of the real severity of unemployment. At least that is the accepted apologia for our poor performance. But once again, conventional wisdom has to be brought face to face with reality.

First of all, why is it that the U.S. economy was once able to absorb a huge flow of European immigrants into the labor force while now it gets indigestion on American housewives? Most of the European immigrants were unskilled. They did not even speak English. Housewives may be unskilled but at least they speak the language. Why are they so different? The fact is, they are not. The unemployment rate even for men has gone up in the 1970s and into the 1980s. In the decade of the 60s the average unemployment rate was 3.6 percent for men over 19 years of age. In the 70s the average rose to 4.5 percent. In 1982 the rate was 8.8 and rising.[5]

Not only is a larger and larger portion of our labor force going unutilized, a larger and larger portion of our capital stock is suffering the same fate. Slowly but surely the capacity utilization rate has been falling in U.S. manufacturing. In the 1960s we used an average of 85 percent of our manufacturing capacity; in the 1970s the average was down to 82 percent; in 1982 it fell to just below 70 percent.[6] In short, our economy is stagnating. Both labor and capital are increasingly underutilizes. The actual lags behind the potential.

We suffer not only from increasing stagnation but also from increasing inflation. *Stagflation*, a new phenomenon, combines inflation of prices with stagnation of jobs. We have never experienced it before. In the past, when prices were rising, unemployment was falling; then when prices fell, unemployment rose. There appeared to be a kind of trade off between the two. Now we suffer from both inflation and unemployment at the same time. We can no longer trade one for the other. Instead, we often get more of both. Unless we are willing to drive the unemployment rate up to depression levels, as President Reagan appears willing to do, we seem to be unable to stop inflation.

REALITY AND APOLOGY

This is our reality in the close of the twentieth century: Our economy possesses tremendous potential but it is falling increasingly below that potential. Comparing the degree of inequality in the U.S. with the degree of inequality in other countries gives the lie to our equality ideal.

The U.S. growth record is mediocre as is our general level of individual health. And we suffer increasingly from stagflation.

Rationalizing away our shortcomings is easy — too easy. Our growth problems are "natural" for a developed economy; besides, public bureaucrats voraciously spend our national income and crowd out private investment. But reality and apology conflict: (1) The record shows no pronounced tendency for growth to decelerate naturally among the eleven peer economies of Table 1.1. (2) The record from Table 1.2 shows no tendency for high public spending growth to be accompanied by low private investment growth. The relations between private investment, public spending, and the growth process are far more complex than suggested by such simplistic reasoning.[7]

Nor is the rising level of unemployment in the U.S. to be explained away by the influx of women into the work force. Rather, the entire economy is slowing down, making it impossible to use all of our labor (female and male) *and* all of our capital. Then there is inflation. Are we to take seriously the old cliche that "too much money chasing too few goods" is causing our inflation? If we really have too much money to spend then why isn't the spending of it driving up both the demand for goods and the demand for labor and capital to produce those goods? In the past, inflation was often caused by an excessive money supply. But such inflationary episodes saw unemployment drop. Today's inflation is different. Unemployment is rising. The new phenomenon is stagflation, not just inflation, and it is not caused by an excessive money supply, elaborate apologia to the contrary not withstanding. It is time to stop the apologies and deal with the realities.

Even so, we are not ready to do so, not just yet. Instead of reforming our economy and using more effective public policies to deal with our problems, we want one more fling, one more flight into frontier fantasy and free enterprise.

2 THE OLD REMEDY: Free Enterprise

INTRODUCTION

Enter President Ronald Reagan on the scene of our relative decline and outright stagnation. His proposed economic program is a bold implementation of American conservatism, a whole-hearted return to frontier individualism. The President is attempting a complete revival of American free enterprise, and he is showing real and unexpected political courage and ability in doing so. Nevertheless, the Reagan free enterprise remedy will not revitalize the U.S. economy. Quite the reverse will be the case. After a brief shot in the arm from tax cuts, the long-run effects of the Reagan remedy will be to frustrate even further the immense developmental potential of the American people. This is because of the very high socioeconomic costs of the Reagan remedy, costs often overlooked by economists and policymakers. In short, President Reagan's courage and ability in implementing his conservative philosophy will work to the detriment of the economy and society he seeks so boldly to revive.

The following chapter contains a critique of President Reagan's free enterprise program. The substance of the program and the general philosophy behind it will be explored. With the substance and philosophy of the return to the free enterprise program laid out, we can then proceed in Chapter 3 to its faults: the faulty use of economic science, the faulty conceptualization, and the resulting heavy socioeconomic costs of "free enterprise."

REAGAN'S REMEDY

President Reagan's remedy has four major parts: fiscal policy, monetary policy, federal deregulation, and political decentralization. The parts form a cohesive whole. They amount to a major dismantling of the New Deal, a return to frontier individualism, and a remilitarization of the country. President Reagan's program is not being implemented in haste. It is the end product of nearly two decades of development and intellectual ferment on the "New Right." A careful examination of each part of the program and discussion of the program's "new right" philosophical foundation will follow.[1]

Fiscal Policy

The three major features of President Reagan's fiscal policy are: (1) Major tax cuts, (2) Federal expenditure reduction and reallocation, and (3) Supply-side economics stressing the replacement of social programs and social controls with individual initiative and responsibility. First, the Reagan administration cut taxes by roughly $54 billion in fiscal 1982.[2] The cuts were heavily skewed toward business and higher-income individuals. Nevertheless, with the exception of their leaning toward the affluent, the substance of the President's tax cuts really was not new at all. Instead, though very large, they basically were a technical correction of "fiscal drag," similar to the frequent tax cuts of the 1970s.

Fiscal drag is often referred to as "bracket creep." As incomes rise, generally because of inflation, we are all pushed into higher income tax brackets. Our tax bills rise even though our inflation-adjusted incomes do not. The result is a decline in after-inflation, after-tax income. This decline leads to lower spending. The Reagan tax cuts are standard medicine for a stagnating economy. Tax cuts mean more disposable income, which results in more spending. The spending injection into the private sector then provides at least a temporary stimulus to a stagnant economy. Since our economy is very stagnant, the tax cuts must be large enough to provide a strong jolt of new spending.

What makes the tax cuts controversial and the political response to them bizarre is the fact that they are supported by a conservative Republican administration espousing a "new theory" which resulted in a huge budget deficit (supply-side economics), and the fact that they are opposed by a small liberal minority in Congress espousing the need for balancing the budget. Only a few years ago, liberal Democrats were defending budget deficits and conservative Republicans were opposing them. Now they appear to have changed sides.

The second major feature of the Reagan fiscal program is reduction and reallocation of public expenditures. Social spending is going down. Military spending is going up. In fiscal 1982 nonmilitary projected spending is being reduced by about $49 billion below the old Carter budget. Military spending will go up by $1 billion over the already-increased Carter military budget for fiscal 1982. But much larger military spending hikes are proposed by President Reagan for fiscal years beyond 1982. A truly massive military buildup is in the making. From Carter's total 1982 budget with projected outlays of $739 and receipts of $712 billion, Reagan has projected total outlays of $695 and total receipts of $650 billion for his fiscal 1982 budget. The projected Reagan deficit of $45 billion for 1982 was nearly twice the projected Carter deficit of $27 billion. The actual Reagan deficits, throughout his term of office, will be the highest peacetime deficits in American history.

Of the roughly $49 billion in nonmilitary budget cuts, a large portion of the 1982 cuts fell on programs for the poor and disadvantaged. This is the case in spite of the promises not to cut so-called "safety net" programs. According to the Brookings Institution's study of the 1982 budget, the cuts include $4.6 billion less for employment and training, $3.5 billion less for foodstamps and nutrition, $3.0 billion less for social security, $2.4 billion less for health, and $1.1 billion less for education. Each of these cuts hurts the poor or the disadvantaged. Additional cuts hurt the cities, the impoverished of the third world, and various politically unorganized groups. Further cuts will force unemployment up even higher. A liquidation of the welfare state has begun.

The third major feature of President Reagan's fiscal policy is a reliance on so-called "supply-side economics." The practical result of applying supply-side economics is Reagan's bold move to replace the social programs and controls of the welfare state with the individual incentives and responsibilities of the unbridled market. Yet, when combined with increased military spending, supply-side tax cuts mean a sizable federal deficit and this has introduced considerable controversy into the otherwise unified conservative Reagan administration.

The controversy can be summed-up with the "Laffer curve," a curve depicting tax revenue as first a rising and then a falling function of the tax rate. Is the U.S. economy on the rising or on the falling portion of the curve? The original supply-side argument put the economy on the falling portion of the curve: Higher tax rates caused lower tax revenues and vice versa. If true, the Reagan tax cuts will increase aggregate supply so much that higher tax revenues eventually will be collected even at the lower tax rates because the higher after-tax incentives will bring forth more tax revenues and tax-law compliance, more work effort, and more capital accumulation. Also, if true, this means that in the past there has been far too much emphasis on creating equality through progressive taxes and far too little emphasis on creating individual opportunity through proportional or even regressive taxes. Obviously, supply-siders stress the need for more individual opportunity (higher incomes for the affluent) even if this means that the tax cuts, when combined with higher military spending, result in larger near-term budget deficits. More traditional conservatives disagree, finding even short-term deficits against their beliefs in the balanced budget. Yet, they cannot have their cake and eat it too. They cannot cut income taxes on the affluent, reduce social programs for the poor, and fund a massive military buildup without running into a budget deficit or perhaps into a social upheaval.

Nevertheless, most members of the Reagan administration, unlike more orthodox conservatives, appreciate the practical value of budget deficits. Deficits increase spending and spending stimulates the economy. Furthermore, politicians riding the crest of an expanding economy are reelected. Hence, even after further changes, President Reagan's tax cuts should still be considerably greater than his expenditure cuts (net of increased military expenditures). If so, his fiscal policy will be stimulative but also inegalitarian and militaristic. If the economy is to be stimulated, Reagan's traditional conservative supporters simply will have to live with the resulting deficits. One can rest assured, however, that the deficits will be easier to live with than the poor find the cuts in social programs.

Monetary Policy

President Reagan's monetary policy is much simpler than his fiscal policy. He has the instincts of a monetarist, believing that control of the money stock will control inflation. Accordingly, President Reagan has urged Paul Volcker of the Federal Reserve to continue his efforts begun during the Carter administration to strictly control the money stock in spite of higher interest rates. Volcker appears more than happy to oblige.

And yet, obvious conflict between the Reagan administration's stimulative fiscal policy and the Federal Reserve's restrictive monetary policy will intensify if interest rates remain so high that private sector expansion is limited. If fiscal policy's stimulus were offset by monetary policy's restriction, the net effect of Reagan's program would be zero. Budget deficits would stimulate spending while tight money would retard it. It remains to be seen how far this nullification is allowed to occur. The signs coming from the Federal Reserve are mixed. The central bankers continue to reiterate their wish to tightly control the money supply and interest rates remain at high levels. Nevertheless the Reagan administration may begin attacking the Federal Reserve's independence, since Ronald Reagan's people clearly want interest rates to decline.

Federal Deregulation

By the 1970s many of the federal regulations which had been adopted willy-nilly over the last several decades appeared to be either outmoded or favorable to the industry being regulated. The movement to dismantle these regulations began in earnest during the Carter administration. Attention was focused on deregulating oil and natural gas, transportation, and financial institutions. The Carter administration held the line on environmental and workplace regulations. Regulations ensuring environmental quality and worker safety were not eliminated. These regulations were not outmoded, nor were they favorable to the industries regulated. Rather, they were new and stringent responses to the increased public awareness of and outcry against environmental degradation and occupational disease.

But officials of the Reagan administration call for a much more thorough "regulatory ventilation." The leading ventilators are Florida businessman Thorne G. Auchter and anti-environmentalist James Watt. Auchter heads the Occupational Safety and Health Administration and Watt was Secretary of the Interior. Under their lead, the Reagan administration began to push deregulation much further into the areas left intact or even strengthened by the Carter administration.

Although the Reagan deregulation push has just begun, Auchter's plans for OSHA serve as an example of things to come. He is moving to curtail and revise OSHA's activities on four fronts: (1) New rules (such as warning labels on hazardous materials) will be revoked, revised, or delayed. (2) Plant inspections will be cut back significantly. (3) Dual enforcement will be eliminated by allowing states with their own OSHA plans to handle their own enforcement. (4) Reliance on personal safety devices will be emphasized (safety glasses, protective clothing, ear protectors, etc.) rather than workplace re-engineering.

The expanded range of federal deregulation will place greater responsibilities on states and individuals. This is in keeping with the return to free enterprise for it involves a return to states' rights and to individual responsibilities as well as a corresponding decentralization of political power. We now turn to decentralization, the fourth major part of President Reagan's overall program. Although President Reagan labels it the "New Federalism," it is really decentralization. The latter, correct label, will be used here.

Decentralization

Under the Reagan administration not only is the federal government continuing to divest itself of more and more of its regulative functions, it is also divesting itself of many of the allocative functions previously performed at the federal level. The federal funding and accompanying federal overseeing of numerous social and educational programs are being pushed down to the state level by the Reagan administration. As a first step, categorical aid to state and local government is being replaced by block grant aid. In the process, federal funding is being cut back and federal guidelines are being eliminated. The funds contained in a block grant are allocated according to criteria to be developed at the state level; not so with the former categorical aid programs where the funds were allocated according to criteria developed at the federal level.

President Reagan's 1982 budget calls for consolidating about forty specific social service and health programs into just four block grants to the states. In addition, program funding was reduced by 25 percent (about $1.8 billion).[3] The Reagan administration argues that replacing categorical grants with block grants will eliminate redundant bureaucracy at the federal level. Nevertheless, it will also create a new set of bureaucracies at the state level. Moving bureaucracy to the state level may represent a step closer to grassroots democracy but it also places a heavy burden on the already straining technical and financial resources of the fifty states. Government aid programs must be carefully administered to avoid corruption and inefficiency. Whether we like it or not, this appears to require competent, career civil servants at *some* level of government. It remains to be seen whether that level should be the state. If Reagan's "New Federalism" can be sold to the states, either the states will liquidate nearly all social programs or they will build formidable bureaucracies to administer them at the state level. The former is more likely.

Passing the responsibility for program administration down to the state level may or may not decrease total program costs, particularly when the increased likelihood of corruption at the weaker state level is figured into the bill. But saving total government cost (federal and state) is not the major objective of the block grant program or of the "New Federalism." Rather, the major objective is political decentralization, and this the block grant program achieves to some extent. Yet why stop at pushing administrative responsibilities down to the state level? Why not push them all the way down to the local-municipal level? The answer may be simple politics. Many of our major cities are staunchly Democratic while many of our statehouses are just as staunchly Republican. (The 1983 mayor of Chicago and governor of Illinois are examples.) Administration of major social programs, funded by the federal government, would give a real boost to the Democratic party.

Supply-Side Economics and Free Enterprise

The fiscal policy, monetary policy, deregulation, and decentralization parts of President Reagan's program constitute a masterful implementation of conservative economic theory, of supply-side economics and free enterprise to be specific. A kind of free enterprise counter-revolution is occurring and it is difficult not to admire the political expertise of its major promoter. From doing personal endorsements for Barry Goldwater in the 1964 Presidential race, Ronald Reagan has risen first to the statehouse of California and now to the White House of the United States. Beginning in his movie days, he has lived his dream of frontier individualism and free enterprise to its ultimate climax. Now we are all in his economic script, written by economists who proclaim themselves to be "supply-side economists."

Technically, supply-side economics is the study of the ways and means of increasing aggregate supply. To economists, aggregate supply means the flow of goods and services from producers to consumers. In the contemporary political arena, supply-side economics has come to mean tax cuts that increase the monetary incentives to work, save, and invest. Supply-side economics also means freedom from the limits socially imposed on producers and enforced by federal regulators.

When shaped into a program of action, supply-side economics has become a politically potent mixture of rugged American frontier individualism and three technical economic doctrines — Keynesianism, Monetarism, and the Rational Expectations Hypothesis.

Keynesianism comes from John Maynard Keynes who argued during the Great Depression that modern market economies do not automatically create enough jobs to fully employ the work force. Of course, even the men in the street knew that in 1936. Keynes went beyond their common sense and explained why, and what to do about it. The reason full employment was not automatic was simple. Insufficient total spending caused production cutbacks, lay offs, and unemployment. Aggregate demand (the total spending flowing to the producers of goods and services) needed to be boosted by government in times of unemployment. Otherwise, the unemployment would drag on. It could not correct itself. To boost spending, government had to either increase its own spending or cut its taxes so taxpayers increased theirs. The result of either was a large government deficit. But the financial burden of the resulting deficit paled in comparison with the social burden of the unemployment. Besides, a temporary deficit could restore the economy to full employment by generating a large increase in tax revenues. "Pump-priming" through a government deficit was born.

Monetarism is a doctrine stating that inflation is purely a monetary problem. Inflation cannot occur, the Monetarists argue, unless an economy's stock of money increases. Inflation occurs because too much money chases too few goods. Inflation stops, after enough time for adjustments to take place, when the money stock is controlled.

The *Rational Expectations Hypothesis* is an economic adaptation of the old adage "you cannot fool all of the people all of the time." Applied to the issues here, the hypothesis argues that if the government allows the money supply to outstrip the goods supply by 10 percent a year, the "rational" man will immediately expect inflation of 10 percent a year and will take the appropriate defensive action. In particular, if he were lending money at 6 percent interest, he would immediately demand 16 percent to compensate for the expected 10 percent inflation. Later on, if the government stopped allowing the money supply to outstrip the goods supply, the "rational" man would immediately expect inflation to stop and he would take the appropriate action. If he had borrowed money from the "rational" man above at 16 percent, he would immediately demand 6 percent.

Now we return to "supply-side economics" and see how all of these doctrines fit together. From Monetarism, supply-siders argue that reducing the growth rate of the money stock will bring down the rate of inflation and also the rate of interest. From the Rational Expectations Hypothesis comes the argument that inflation and interest rates will fall, not after a long period of lagging adjustment but right away because the "perfect" knowledge and effortless adjustment of "rational" decisionmakers takes very little time. With inflationary expectations—the assumed cause of high interest rates—broken so quickly, fiscal policy will be freed from the constraints of inflation and high interest rates. Then from Keynesianism the supply-siders borrow the argument that tax cuts can stimulate spending very significantly so that a cut in tax rates does not have such a catastrophic effect on tax revenues. Last, but not least, from the American tradition of frontier individualism comes the argument that what people need is more individual incentive. Just a little more individual incentive (tax cuts) and the supply of effort and, therefore, of goods and services will increase dramatically.

This makes up a very heady brew of assumptions and doctrines. But, supply-siders "pragmatically" explain that the real test of their thought is not the validity of their assumptions. Instead, the test is how well their program works when implemented, and President Reagan is now providing us with that test. We have an economic scientist's dream come true – a decisive test of a theory. Or do we? Even if the unemployment and inflation rates finally fall, should we impute the cause of such success to the implementation of supply-side economics? Or should we question the assumptions behind a program as well as insist that the program temporarily work? And, what will be the long-run impact of the Reagan master plan? What are the social costs of a return to free enterprise? Will the old remedy work in these new times? Can we realize the ideals of frontier individualism when most of us are now corporate careerists?

3

THE
WRONG REMEDY

INTRODUCTION

For the problems of the American economy President Reagan is prescribing a fiscal policy composed of tax cuts for the affluent, higher military spending for the fearful, and lower social spending for the poor. President Reagan is also prescribing a monetary policy of tight money and high interest rates for the big bankers, a policy of further deregulation for the regulated, and a strong dose of political "decentralization" for Republican controlled statehouses. All of this reliance on frontier individualism, all of this return to free enterprise, is supported by a hodgepodge of economic doctrines and assumptions labeled "supply-side economics." Furthermore, the whole experiment in economic counterrevolution appears to be some kind of a mandate from the American people. But the mandate, the faith in free enterprise and the supply-side economics hodgepodge all need to be reevaluated in the context of our corporate-dominated economy and society.

We should all hope that Reagan's remedy really works, in both the short term and the long term. But I fear that it will not. The economic counterrevolution is doomed to failure because it is based on faulty economic science, a faulty conceptualization of social and economic progress, and a blindness to the heavy socioeconomic costs of the remedy. The free enterprise remedy, the return to the frontier individualism of frontier America, is tragically inappropriate for the closing of the twentieth century. Yet old ideas die hard.

FAULTY ECONOMIC SCIENCE

Suppose our hopes come true and the rates of inflation and unemployment continue falling in the next few years. Should we attribute the improvement to the wisdom of President Reagan's economic advisers? Would we be correct to conclude that supply-side economics, hodgepodge though it may be, is sound economic science? The answer to both questions is no. The program may work in the short term. But if it does work temporarily, it will not be for the reasons given by supply-side economics.[1] Instead, we may experience a temporary improvement because President Reagan's program increased demand, not supply.

According to the traditional "laws of supply and demand," an increase in demand for a product resulted in an increase in the quantity of the product supplied but only at a higher price. Producers of the product, the traditional argument stated, had to be compensated for the higher cost of producing more. Price rose because of the increasing costs of producing more to meet the demands of the overly eager buyers. This meant that higher demand caused higher prices, at least in the near term. But, behind the back of traditional economists, the economic world has changed. Practical men and women of affairs understand the changes, but traditional economists do not. Perhaps this is why people find most economics books so boring and irrelevant.

What has happened is remarkably simple. The individual owners of small-scale businesses have been replaced by the corporate conglomerate and its managerial experts. The replacement is not complete. Some areas of our economy are resistant to corporate take over and corporate management. But most are not. So the corporate manager and large-scale operation have replaced the individual owner and small business in most areas of our economy.[2] This replacement has revolutionized the methods and the costs of production of goods and services, the corporate managers have transformed the production process. Furthermore, the costs of production have been transformed. Once a large-scale, mass production operation is in place, the per unit cost of production declines as more units are produced. The small-scale, individual owner of economic theory found his per unit cost of production rising as he produced more units. The reverse is true for the corporate managers of today's economy. For most ranges of operation, per unit costs now fall as more units are produced.

In most of today's economy, higher rates of production result in lower per unit costs of the product. Now back to the traditional "laws of supply and demand." No longer is it true that higher demand causes higher prices as individual owners try to recoup their higher costs of producing more. Today, in our large-scale, corporate economy, higher demand can mean lower prices as per unit costs of production decline with larger production runs. But since our economy has suffered serious inflation for a decade, higher demand does not mean lower prices but it does mean lower increases in prices.

In this changed economic environment, fiscal policies that increase demand in a stagnant economy actually reduce the rate of inflation. Price increases are reduced because the per unit costs of production decline with higher production runs. This means that President Reagan's fiscal application of supply-side economics, as long as it increases total demand in our economy, might reduce the rate of inflation in the near term. But such an improvement will come about because of the demand effect, not the supply effect of his fiscal policy. Paradoxically, the program may work, but for the wrong reason.

This paradox is due to the faulty economic science behind supply-side economics. While traditional economics was not watching, the economy (the supposed subject of economic science) changed in such a way that the old "laws" of the science no longer hold. Economic science has lost touch with economic reality.

Further evidence of this loss of touch with reality is the idea that tax cuts for individual taxpayers, particularly cuts for affluent ones, will result in a wave of new saving and investing. The reality is that the saving of individual taxpayers is a small proportion of total saving and investing in today's economy. The vast majority of saving and investing is financed out of business revenues, not individual incomes. In the postwar era, the savings of individuals have amounted to an average of only 28 percent of private sector saving. The other 72 percent has come from business saving.[3]

Just as only a small proportion of saving depends on individual income, only a small proportion of the investment in plants and equipment depends on individual income. Instead, most investment, outside of new home ownership, depends on business sales revenues, particularly corporate sales revenues. Since investment depends on sales, the Reagan tax cuts will not stimulate investment if the higher after-tax incomes are saved rather than rechanneled into spending. It is spending, not saving, that increases sales revenues. In short, investment will increase only to the extent that the tax cuts increase demand which will increase sales revenues.

In the stagnant 1970s capital accumulation or investment has not been hindered by a lack of personal savings. Instead, investment has been sluggish because of sluggish growth in sales. What is needed is

more sales, not more personal savings. Given an increase in sales revenue, most investment can be financed through business saving out of
the higher sales revenues. Furthermore, that small portion of investment which businesses cannot finance internally is financed through
various forms of bank credit expansion, not through personal savings.
So if business has difficulty acquiring finance, it is because the Federal
Reserve has driven up the cost of bank credit and because of declining sales revenues, not a lack of personal savings.

Yet supply-siders do not understand the crucial relation between
business sales revenues and business investment. Instead, they continue
to be misguided by an old fallacy from classical economics. The fallacy is associated with French economist Jean-Baptiste Say, a proponent of laissez-faire in the early nineteenth century. Say's Law or
Say's Law of markets claims that supply creates its own demand; excess production for the economy at large simply cannot exist. The
demand will be there when the supply is. If supply does create its own
demand then the fear that higher consumer savings will lead to lower
business sales revenues which, in turn, will lead to unemployment and
recession, is unfounded. Instead, higher consumer savings lead to
higher business investment which, in turn, will lead to more jobs and
higher incomes. Unfortunately for the supply-siders, Say's Law was
disproved by John Maynard Keynes in 1936. Rather than admit that
Say's Law is incorrect, supply-siders ignore Keynes. Their ignorance
is convenient but confuses them, no end.

As a result of their confusion, the supply-siders argue along the
following plausible, but incorrect, lines: To make the economy grow
and generate more income and more jobs requires more investment
spending. However, to bring forth more investment spending, supply-
siders incorrectly argue, requires more saving. Therefore, we should
cut taxes for the saving classes, for those with high incomes. Furthermore, we should cut federal spending on social programs to reduce the
federal deficit because the deficit diverts private savings away from
private investors. The supply-siders are incorrect because an increase
in saving and a decrease in the federal budget deficit would actually
make the economy shrink, generating fewer jobs and lower incomes
in the process.

To explain why the supply-siders are wrong requires a step-by-step
examination of what happens to our economy when consumer saving
increases. To increase consumer saving, the Reagan program gives substantial tax breaks to savers. As consumers who can afford to take ad-

vantage of the tax incentives do so, their saving rises. But consumer saving can only rise if overall consumer spending falls. The Reagan program ensures the needed decline in overall consumer spending by cutting back on the social programs that subsidized the consumption of the poor. Hence, the poor spend less so the rich can save more, causing a rise in overall saving and a decline in overall spending from consumers. The fall in consumer spending results in an equal decline in corporate sales revenues, forcing corporations to borrow short-term funds in order to cover the unexpected shortfall in their cash budgets. The corporate borrowing goes to finance the carrying costs of unexpectedly large finished goods inventories. And this "forced" corporate borrowing from financial intermediaries absorbs the new savings supplied by affluent consumers to financial intermediaries, leaving the interest rates of those intermediaries unchanged. However, corporations are still left with unwanted inventories of unsold finished goods so they cut back production by laying off workers. As a result, the unemployment rate rises and the unemployed are forced to "dis-save"by selling off their cars, houses, and other goods or by borrowing against their life insurance or home equity. This is the paradox of thrift: *The higher saving of the wealthy leads to unemployment and "dis-saving" on the part of the poor.* It does not lead to new investment in plants and equipment by business. Quite the contrary; it leads to excess capacity and unsold inventories. To repeat, an increase in saving does not result in higher investing; it results in higher unemployment.

The logical question to ask at this point is, "If higher saving does not lead to higher investing, what does?" Higher investing is caused by higher expected profits. If businesses expect higher profits in new investment projects, investment will increase. The projects will be financed through a combination of bank credit, trade credit, and retained earnings. In a pinch, long-term bonds or shares of stock will be sold to raise the funds. Business comes to expect higher profits if sales are rising or if a new technology opens up new markets, hence a rise in consumer saving has a deadening effect on investment because higher saving means declining sales and fewer new markets opening up. Investment activity also expands if monetary policy is loosened up to drive down the cost of credit, but the most important factor in investment is the expected rate of profit on new investment projects.

The supply-side view that investment depends on saving is not only wrong in theory but pernicious in practice. Giving tax breaks to the rich to save more will cause unemployment, not higher investment, if they really save all their tax bonanza. If they spend it on new consumer frivolities, we will be better off in the short run because demand for goods will not collapse, so unemployment will not get much worse. Furthermore, if government spending remains high because of Reagan's defense buildup, demand for goods will be shored up by the military spending. On the other hand, continued tight monetary policy will keep demand down because investment funds will remain very costly.

To conclude, if President Reagan's application of supply-side economics works, it will work because of its impact on demand, not on supply. Even if the program works, it will do so in the short term only. Its long-term impact will be disastrous. In the long term, the poor will harden further into an underclass of uneducated, unemployed, malnourished, excluded discontents concentrated in increasingly dilapidated housing served by increasingly underfunded schools, hospitals, courts, and jails. If they ever become aware as a class that they were deprived of their necessities so that the rich could have their frivolities, open class conflict will be unavoidable. Then the chance for reform will have passed.

FAULTY CONCEPTUALIZATION OF ECONOMIC PROGRESS

President Reagan's remedy is based on an economic theory so divorced from reality that though it might work in the near term, the theory supporting it gives the wrong reasons for the remedy's potential success. Supply-side economics is riddled with misconceptions about the nature of social and economic progress. However, an alternative view is available from the economics underground, a motley group of economists held together by their attempts to go beyond the old misconceptions.[4] From my view as a member of that underground, economic progress is a result of two propelling forces: (1) the drive for full participation in the economy and (2) the march of modern science and technology.

Full Participation for All

The first drive can be seen in the contemporary struggles of Polish workers against Soviet domination, in the struggles of "coloreds" in South Africa against apartheid, in the struggles of the NAACP against racism, of NOW against sexism, and of concerned Catholics against authoritarianism in Central America. The same drive was evident in the American, French, Mexican, and yes, even in the Russian, Chinese, and Cuban revolutions. Although revolutions usually misfire, the titanic force I speak of is the common man's drive for full participation in the life process. Full participation in social, cultural, spiritual, and political affairs. It is a drive against second class status in all walks of life. The drive is usually focused on full participation in the economy because economic well-being has always provided the wherewithall for the rest of the things that we value. The rich have always been full participators and the poor have always wanted equal status. Before Reagan, they were slowly getting it. And that, very simply, is a precondition for continued economic progress,[5] a precondition ignored by the New Right and by the Reaganites.

In eighteenth century England, Adam Smith wrote the Magna Charta for the small-scale merchants, millowners, and mechanics who were struggling against the restrictions placed on them by the Crown. Adam Smith called for laissez-faire, for removing state control of markets. Freed markets served England well because, at that time, they were a means to an end. Freed markets allowed more participation. Freed markets removed barriers to entry. Most importantly, freed markets broke down organized resistance to wider participation in the industrial revolution.

As the industrial revolution continued, the markets and the production processes in mine, mill, factory, store, and warehouse all changed beyond what anyone had envisioned. Today's markets and today's production processes would amaze even Adam Smith. Laissez-faire, which once served to increase participation in economic activities, no longer does so. Now, because of revolutionary changes in the economy, it does the reverse.

When the Crown stopped restricting the economic participation of minorities in eighteenth century England, even a humble Scotsman or two could become textile manufacturers. In the eighteenth century, minorities and the powerless had been excluded primarily by law. When the law was removed, the primary restriction was lifted. Today the primary restrictions are no longer legal ones; they are socioeconomic ones. The evolving economy has erected new barriers to participation because markets and production technologies have changed.

Most of today's markets are oligopolistic. That is, they are dominated by a handful of very large, very strong corporations. Little room is left for the individual proprietor of the eighteenth century. Furthermore, most of today's production technologies are very sophisticated and operate on a mass scale. Little room is left for the indivdual inventor, the unskilled worker, or the frontiersman.

Even in our advanced economy there is room for *a few* individual proprietors. A few unskilled jobs can always be found by a few eager but untrained workers. Furthermore, a few legal restrictions still provide state protection of vested interests. Nevertheless, the continued drive from below for more participation is now running up against a different set of barriers than the laws of the eighteenth century. The barriers are not of government construction so weakening government will not weaken the barriers. Nor will freeing the creative genius of a few "great men" or "captains of industry" from the fetters of the state controls which existed in the eighteenth century revive economic progress in the close of the twentieth century. Continued economic progress in the twentieth century requires reforms of the socioeconomic conditions hindering the further advance of millions of excluded minorities, not the deregulation of a few swashbuckling entrepreneurs.

Science and Technology

Along with the drive from below for full participation has been the vast advance of modern science and technology. In fact, the two have moved in tandem, one complementing the other. As the drive from below has emancipated more and more people from the formerly excluded lower strata, scientific and technological enlightenment have also spread among the formerly illiterate and ignorant. This enlightenment has been cumulative. As the formerly excluded gain access to modern science and technology, their awakened minds and spirits make further contributions to the march of science and technology. The more people participating in our scientific-technological age, the more new ideas and skills are incorporated into the scientific-technological advance.

This scientific-technological advance is a social process of discovery and use based on the accumulation and dissemination of a joint stock of knowledge and skill. This joint stock has been accumulating since before recorded history. It has been passed from generation to generation and from culture to culture in a number of ways. First it was passed orally and informally, perhaps for several hundred thousand years, as Homo sapiens and his/her joint stocks spread from their birthplace in Africa to the four corners of the globe. With the advent of writing and formal schooling, the pace accelerated. Then printing and later mass education resulted in a veritable explosion.

The point is, each advance in science and skill is based on former advances, on the joint stock inherited from previous generations. The reasons that we advance so quickly today are that we have inherited so much from yesterday and so many of us now share in that common inheritance. If we are to advance even faster tomorrow, we will do so for the same reasons: The ever more inclusive sharing of an ever enlarging joint stock. The process requires more participation from all strata, and as it cumulates, more participation is demanded by all strata. It is a social process par excellence. It is not dependent upon the genius of a few great men nor a product of an elite group. In fact, where access to the joint stock is available only to a favored few, the process stagnates for its essence is inclusion, not exclusion.

When applied to the more mundane world of economics, this process results in the invention and innovation of new processes and products. These, in turn, raise productivity and the level of living as the new processes are adopted in production and the new products are adopted in consumption. Specific new processes and products are always associated with a specific inventor and innovator: The lightbulb with Edison, the moving assembly line with Ford. As a result, we learn to think of invention and innovation as due to the creative genius of a few great men. But, clearly, we are incorrect. First of all, many discoveries are made independently by two or more people. Had Edison not come up with the lightbulb, someone else would have; the same with Ford and the moving assembly line. Second, every discovery builds on the vast accumulation of our joint stock. Where would Ford have been without the previous accumulation of the centuries? In short, invention and innovation are not due to the existence of select individuals but to the advance of social accumulation and the ever wider dissemination of its fruits, both material and immaterial.

The Supply-Side Confusion

Economic progress is conceptualized by the supply-siders to be a result of the market freedom of select individuals and the monetary rewards of those individuals. Supply-siders hold a variant of the great man theory of economic progress.[6] Our current stagnation, it follows, must be due to the overregulation and overtaxation of the upper strata. Overregulation has stifled that strata's innovative freedom and over-taxation has siphoned off their rewards. To revive our stagnant economy we must cut back on those regulations and taxes. Doing so not only will give a bonanza to the upper strata whose after-tax incomes will rise and to the regulated whose socially-imposed constraints will be lifted, but economic progress will speed up for everyone (the Trickle Down Theory).

More freedom from government and more rewards from the market are preconditions to renewed economic progress, according to supply-side economics, which misconceives progress as a trickle down process dependent upon the actions of the higher strata.

Economic progress however, is not driven by the larger rewards, the additional saving, or the freedom from social constraint of those who already are fully participating, not by more for the upper strata. Rather, economic progress is propelled by the drive from those below and by the accumulation and dissemination of the joint stock of knowledge and skill. Broader, more effective access to the joint stock is the key to long-term improvement. This can be secured for those excluded from participation in the closing of the twentieth century only when their access is supported by public action. Laissez-faire sufficed for eigtheenth century England, the first country to industrialize; it no longer suffices. In summary, supply-side economics misconceives the nature of progress in the twentieth century. Implementing the out-moded supply-side policies will impose heavy unintended costs on society in the long term.

The Heavy Social Costs

President Reagan's bold plan to revitalize the U.S. economy through tax cuts, expenditure reductions and reallocations, control of the money stock, and deregulation might work in the short run. The gnashing of teeth on the part of liberals and big labor not withstanding, the rate of inflation might just moderate and the rate of unemployment might just fall. These improvements may not be for the reasons given, but the improvements may be forthcoming nonetheless, as long as spending is stimulated so that total demand rises and brings into active use both more of our existing labor force and more of our existing industrial capacity.

An increase in total demand is necessary not only to increase employment but also to increase the capacity utilitzation rate. The latter is crucial for two reasons: (1) higher capacity utilization will help offset the current spiraling upward pressure on costs by moving the operating position of plants out into the declining range of their per unit production costs.[7] (2) Higher capacity utilization and the accompanying greater throughput will help provide the large corporate cash flow needed to finance expansion in the face of the extraordinarily high costs of external financing. Yet this fillip, provided by tax cuts, social program cuts, and military spending will yield a short-run improvement at exorbitant long-run costs. We now turn to the heavy socioeconomic costs of the Reagan program.

Three major socioeconomic costs or distortions will be felt in the long-run from President Reagan's plan: (1) Increased inequality will hinder the drive from below for more participation. (2) The economy and society will be further militarized. (3) Deregulation and decentralization will weaken the public's ability to act. These long-term impacts will more than reverse the temporary gains – potential at best – which might be felt in the next year or two.

Increased income inequality will be the first result of the President's tax cuts and social program cuts. The affluent will receive the bulk of the tax cuts while the poor and near-poor will bear the brunt of the social program cuts. In addition, cuts in the areas of education and training will make it much harder for the disadvantaged to acquire job skills and general education. This, in turn, will make it more difficult for them to participate as workers in plant and mine, let alone as scientists and technicians in lab and office. In this day and age it takes more than a quick mind for a poor girl or boy to get ahead. It also takes a degree and the education that supposedly goes with it.

In a program with a stated objective of increasing individual incentives, program cutbacks which reduce the opportunities of disadvantaged people to learn and to earn are cruelly contradictory. Yet supply-side economists are not overly concerned about the resulting inequalities. To most economists, not just to the supply-siders, inequality is not a distortion or a social cost in the first place. In fact, quite the contrary is argued. The views of Arthur M. Okun, a most humane economist, are representative of the best the orthodox profession has to offer us on this point. In his *Equality and Efficiency: The Big Tradeoff* Okun argues that as a general rule increasing equality is bought at the expense of reducing efficiency.[8] Hence, equality is a cost, an economic burden. Okun supports this argument with an analogy drawn between a leaky bucket and an income redistribution program. The analogy deserves extended discussion for Okun represents the conventional wisdom when he warns us that we cannot have the efficiency of free markets (those glorious institutions Adam Smith championed in the eighteenth century) and equality at the same time. In fairness to equality, Okun recognizes that some egalitarian programs might promote both free market efficiency and equality. Nevertheless, these are the exceptions that prove the rule, and the rule, according to conventional wisdom, is that equality reduces efficiency. This rule – rather, this assumption – is the starting point for Okun's argument.

From this assumption he proceeds to develop his leaky bucket analogy whereby any kind of egalitarian or income redistribution plan encounters the assumed leaky bucket problem: The income must be taken from the rich and then carried to the poor in a leaky bucket. So, of course, only a part of the money taken from the rich will get to the poor. The other part leaks out of the bucket and is lost through inefficiency. This leaky bucket analogy views the rich as the source of production and the poor as just so many hungry mouths. Furthermore, it views egalitarians as right-hearted but wrong-headed, so anxious about the hungry mouths that the leaks in the bucket go unnoticed. But Okun is so intent upon the leaks that the potential productivity of well-trained healthy minds and bodies pushing their way up from poverty is ignored.

Okun discusses four kinds of leaks. First are administrative costs. Redistributive taxes and programs to aid the poor must be administered. Okun stresses that the costs of doing so are inefficiencies. Yet the costs of maintaining glaring inequalities are reduced if the inequalities themselves are dismantled. Redistributive programs must be administered but the costs of other programs can be reduced. In particular, the costs of maintaining law and order and protecting concentrated wealth are reduced. The blatant police state that we see in South Africa could be dismantled, for example. And less blatant but still costly methods of controlling the poor in the U.S. could go the same way.

Okun's second leak is reduced or misplaced work effort. Yet, Okun concludes that this leak is not a large one. The tax system before the Reagan cuts had virtually no effect on the work effort of the well-to-do themselves, according to Okun. The rich did not work less because of high taxes. Nevertheless, considerable work effort is misallocated into the growing occupations of tax accounting and tax law. Although the well-to-do have not changed their work efforts, they have hired others to work hard for them reducing their taxes. This distorted work effort of the tax experts has taken many of our most ingenious minds away from productive work and has directed that ingenuity into tax avoidance. Okun argues that this distortion is a cost of our efforts to redistribute income through taxes. But surely he is in error. The number of tax experts is increasing because of the number and complexity of the loopholes for the rich written into the tax code by those very same experts. We have legions of unproductive tax experts because of the loopholes created to avoid income redistribution, not because of the redistribution itself.

Okun's third leak is the impact of high tax rates on saving and investing. But again, even Okun in his leaky bucket analogy admits that the impact certainly is hard to find in the empirical evidence. High tax rates simply have not affected investing and saving in the twentieth century, even Okun concurs.

Okun's fourth and final leak from the redistribution bucket has to do with the possibly adverse effects on attitudes. But in this case also of the not-so-leaky-leak, Okun does not find any gaping holes in the bucket. Rather, he falls back on the old Horatio Alger myth by arguing in favor of lower taxes so that the route from rags to riches remains open. At this point, Okun balks and admits that social programs which allow the poor to rise out of poverty are important avenues to advancement.

These are all the leaks that Okun can muster, minor dribbles when compared with the gushing currents of equality that have been flowing from below since the Industrial Revolution. Equality is a technological necessity, a requirement of an industrial society. It is not a cost. Achieving it may reduce the technical market efficiency of static economic theory. Equality opens and keeps open the floodgates of technological advance because it allows more and more people to participate in, and therefore to further, the advance. The static efficiency criteria of orthodox economic theory, based on the eighteenth century free market, tells us nothing about progress. It yields no directions for the long run, it does not answer the crucial question of the evolution of man's economy in society.

To determine which way is forward we must go beyond Okun's concern with static efficiency. We must go all the way to underground economist Marc Tool's instrumental value principle. Tool states,

> ... "that direction is forward which provides for *the continuity of human life and the noninvidious re-creation of community through the instrumental use of knowledge.* "[9]

This is a far cry from Okun's static market concern over alleged leaks in his redistribution bucket. The source of productivity is the communal and instrumental use of knowledge which continuously pays the costs and reaps the benefits of drawing more people into the developmental process. It is not in the market institution, even though the free market served us well in the eighteenth century. It does not lie in the savings of the rich. The source of productivity lies in the continued creation of a nonexclusionary, egalitarian, and technologically-advanced society. Development of the modern economy, Clarence Ayres argued, "... has all along been coincident with the expansion of the powers of a continually larger part of the community."[10]

Supply-side economists would argue that Ayres and other underground economists (Ayres and many others would prefer to be labeled "institutional economists") do not understand the free market system. Supply-siders argue that the market system itself is the greatest eliminator of poverty the world has ever experienced. They claim that the free market causes growth and the trickle down effect spreads its benefits. But the market institution did not cause the growth experienced since the first Industrial Revolution in England. Rather, the free market of Adam Smith allowed that growth to occur by lifting the mercantile remnants of feudal restraints. Here is where an understanding of our economy as a technological system first, a market system second, is of crucial significance. The sources of long-run growth and development are advancing technology and the push for full participation from below, not the market institution and the touted trickle down effect from above.

Although the free market was a facilitator in the eighteenth and nineteenth centuries, growth through the twentieth century market no longer has the same effect. For one thing, it no longer eliminates poverty. The incidence of poverty in the United States has declined significantly since the early 1960s. But the decline has not been because the poor have been earning more through the market (the trickle down effect). Summarizing their intensive investigation, Sheldon Danziger and Robert Haveman conclude that the incidence of poverty would have declined since the 1960s from 21 to 20 percent had it not been for nonmarket programs for the poor. This was a pittance. Most of the substantial reduction in poverty that actually occurred was due to increased federal transfer programs. The incidence of poverty, when the benefits to the poor of all the various social programs are calculated, dropped from 15.6 in 1965 to 11.4 percent in 1978.[11]

Two implications follow: First, the trickle down effect is far too slow. Second, remove all poverty programs and the incidence of poverty will return to unacceptable levels. The social costs of the latter will be immense, for the continued inclusion of more and more formerly disadvantaged people into active participation as producers and consumers will come to a stop. Rather than paying the costs of including them (Okun's not-so-leaky-leaks) and receiving the benefits of the full participation of all, our society will bear the costs of excluding them. At first these costs will be moral. As President Reagan's supply-side medicine drives more people back into poverty, affluent Americans will turn a deaf ear to the protests. As we tell each other more anecdotes about welfare cheats, a hardening of the American heart can be perceived already. The human capacity to rationalize morally unacceptable behavior is substantial, particularly when the rationalizations are provided by opinion leaders at the highest political and social levels. Next the costs will be economic. The vitality that the poor and the excluded could have provided will be lost to the economy. In spite of a fillip to the economy from military spending, American productivity will continue its relative decline because the new people and new ideas needed by the corporate world will be excluded from that world. The costs will be profoundly individual and irrevocable as the poor sink down into the ghettos and jails. If the Reagan retrenchment goes far enough and lasts long enough, the costs may be political. Class conflict may bubble up from the excluded if the push from below takes that turn. In the ensuing rebellion and repression, democracy would be lost. Surely, we will not let it go that far.

Inequality is a burden on modern society. This burden will not be lifted automatically by President Reagan's dose of free enterprise. But it is only one of three heavy socioeconomic burdens placed on our economy and society by President Reagan's program.

The effect of militarization is the second major socioeconomic cost of the Reagan program. The obvious drain on the federal budget and the increased likelihood of global war need not be emphasized here.[12] The national and global distortions of militarization and the accelerated arms race are important issues.

Remilitarization does not provide for "the continuity of human life," but for its destruction. Remilitarization does not provide for "the noninvidious recreation of community." Rather, it means that invidious distinctions between people born "here" versus people born "over there" gain strength as we look for foreign enemies and security risks. Committees on terrorism and internal security or on un-American activities will open for business and do a brisk trade in fear. Demagogues will cash in on the spreading paranoia and civil liberties will be weakened as they do.

Furthermore, neighboring or opposing nations will become increasingly alarmed or threatened by our bellicosity and rearmament. Then they will reciprocate in kind. Their reciprocation will vindicate our original fear, leading us to pile up more arms, alarming them even further. In this way we will speed up the arms race and provide the justification for doing so, all in one step. Furthermore, each escalation in the arms race drains off more resources and causes more fear and distrust.

The resulting sets of garrison states, each set clustered around each superpower, will reinforce the division of the earth into three worlds:

the free world, by implication the unfree world, and then the third world. The first two worlds will then try harder and harder to pluck off pieces of the third world as if third-world nations were pieces of pie to be eaten up before someone else gets them. If one is born into the world dominated by the United States then the world dominated by the Soviet Union is the unfree world. On the other hand, if one is born into the world dominated by the Soviet Union then, of course, just change the labels: the U.S.S.R. becomes the free world, the U.S.A unfree. Those unfortunates born into the third world become pawns in the global struggle. Either they can help keep the world safe for free enterprise (American trade) or they can join the liberation forces (and the Soviet empire).

Perhaps this is overdrawn but surely militarization is not the foundation for a peaceful development of the U.S. economy and of our place in the emerging global economy. Rather, under the pressure of militarization, the global order will increasingly become a conflict arena where distrust and discontinuity will be heightened.

In terms of Marc Tool's instrumental value principle, the Reagan administration's speeding-up of the arms race – and the almost certain Soviet reciprocation – are the wrong ways to bring more people permanently into active economic participation. This is a step backward, even though in the short run military spending will drive down the rate of unemployment in the U.S. In the short run an increase in effective demand for military hardware will boost employment in the military-industrial complex but in the long run we will suffer from war at the most, lower productive abilities at the least.

It takes very little analysis to conclude that militarism is cumulative, materially destructive, and culturally regressive. Militarism is cumulative because of two related processes. The first process is the arms race itself, which is cumulative because it escalates. No country can allow itself to be out-armed lest the other(s) attack. The second process is similar to the panic or rage that spreads through a mob. Thorstein Veblen referred to the result as *"dementia praecox."* It occurs because fear and anger are contagious, particularly among people who are ignorant of the feared/hated object. Such fear and anger can quickly build to a fever pitch. In a mob it leads to a lynching or a riot. In a nation it leads to war. Militarism is materially destructive for obvious reasons. It is culturally regressive because it leads to the repression of internal dissent, to the suppression of "foreign" ideas, and to a generalized intolerance and rigidity.

None of these effects are conducive to the push from below since such a drive is misinterpreted in militaristic times as being due to "outside agitators" and is dealt with accordingly. (Remember the fear and suspicion that Martin Luther King, Jr. was a Communist?) Nor are the effects of militarism conducive to scientific and technological advance. Despite much technological fallout from military research, the benefits would be larger by far if all the scientific and technical minds currently working directly or indirectly for military purposes were working for civilian ones. What we are experiencing is a vast diversion of talent away from the general advance of knowledge and skill and into a very specialized applied field. The general advance cannot help but be distorted and slowed down as a consequence.

In addition to the first costs of inequality and the second costs of militarization, President Reagan's program will impose on society a third set of costs: the costs of political decentralization and federal deregulation. Granted, decentralization and deregulation can bestow benefits in the form of lower prices and greater political responsiveness to grassroots pressure. But decentralization also significantly reduces the political ability and motivation to plan for the meeting of many social needs. Furthermore, President Reagan's deregulation push will put the unsuspecting victims of pollution more at the mercy of polluters and it will alter significantly the nature of safety programs in plant and office. First a look at the costs of political decentralization.

In the United States, far more is involved in decentralization than meets the eye. Moving power from the federal to the state and local levels not only moves political power closer to the grassroots level; it also fractionates and weakens government. The old maxim "divide and conquer" applies here with particular force. As the scale and geographical range of economic activities continue expanding, the trend in business toward larger, more centralized organizations follows suit. Today's business organizations are multinational corporations employing thousands and hundreds of thousands and doing business in scores of nations. The revenues of these megacorps run into the billions. In terms of revenues, the largest megacorps now are larger than the majority of nations. In such a world of giant business enterprise, it is foolhardy to return to reliance on state and local government for regulating possi-

ble business abuses. State and local governments are simply not up to
the task. A mini case study will illustrate the point.[13]

Hilton Hotels Corporation, a giant in its field, negotiated with the
City of Chicago for property tax concessions on a new Hilton Hotel in
Chicago. The negotiations began in 1980 and all seemed to go well between the City and Hilton. However, the planned site lies in Cook
County and the County Assessor, Thomas C. Hines, questioned the
need for the huge concessions granted the hotel chain. Furthermore,
a group of downtown Chicago real estate owners banded together to
argue against the Hilton concessions. Up until that point, the whole
episode sounded like Chicago politics as usual. But then Hilton delivered what amounted to an ultimatum to the city: unless the tax break
was delivered on or before December 15, 1981, Hilton would not build
the new hotel in Chicago. The city did not deliver so Hilton backed
out. Opponents of the plan claimed that the total costs to the city for
Hilton's new $250 million hotel would surpass $300 million. Opponents also pointed out that those costs would have to be paid by somebody, and, you know who that would be – either the other taxpayers
who lack the clout to bargain for their own tax concessions, or those
people dependent upon the city services which would be cut to make
up for the reduction in tax revenues.

The crux of the matter is simple. A municipal government, desperately in need of new jobs and new facilities, has very little bargaining
power when it faces a large corporation. The megacorp can easily build
elsewhere so it can play one powerless city off against another. The
resulting power imbalance can be used by astute corporate planners to
keep local and even state taxes and regulations at a minimum. This is
not to say that corporate planners are evil men, for they clearly are
not. But they are trying to serve the interests of their own corporation.
Unfortunately, as they do so in our environment of numerous separate
state and local governments, state and local interests are badly eroded.

So we have a paradox: Reliance on the separate, decentralized state
and local governments closest to the grassroot interests, reduces the
protection and furtherance of those very interests. The paradox is due
to the power imbalance between large corporations and small government units. As big business gave rise to the need for big labor, it also
gave rise to the need for big government. But the latter need has not
been recognized very clearly.

In short, local and even state government are just not able to meet the needs of our modern urban society. The federal government has repeatedly bailed out financially distressed state and local governments. Most of this federal aid has been in the form of categorical grants to the local-municipal level where the funds are spent under the watchful eye of federal agencies applying federal guidelines to keep racism, sexism, incompetency, and corruption – often rife at the weakened, decentralized local-municipal level – at a minimum. Federal funding aid is needed because at the lowest level of decentralization the tax base is either too narrow, or simply inadequate, or has been eroded away. But, except for President Nixon's revenue sharing experiment, federal funders have not been willing to fund activities at the local-municipal level without making sure that certain guidelines were followed. This federal reluctance seems well-founded.

The Reagan administration is de-federalizing much of this. In addition to the combined block grant consolidations and funding cutbacks discussed above under fiscal policy, the same thing has been done in federal aid to education. Over forty categorical grant programs have been consolidated into just two block grant programs with a 25% cutback in federal funding.

By and large, the new block grants are administered by the various affected state-level agencies rather than federal-level agencies. Hence, guidelines are set by a semi-decentralized level of government – the state, but not the local municipal level nor the federal level. If adopted, the "New Federalism" proposed by Reagan will push the majority of political decisions to the state level. Wags point out, of course, that President Reagan, a Republican, is redirecting federal monies and powers to statehouses, likely to be Republican, and away from courthouses and municipalities, likely to be Democratic.

Of course, there is more to the difference between the levels of government than partisan politics. James O'Connor, in his *The Fiscal Crisis of the State*, elaborates on the differences among federal, state, and local levels of government.[14] In general, the influence of business special interest groups on government is much stronger at both the local and state levels than at the federal level. However, the situation is somewhat better at the level of the very large city where organized labor has obtained a degree of political influence and other diverse groups have a voice. In large cities with a diversity of organized interests and classes the city's major function becomes that of managing the conflict of interests. Such cities are "arbiter cities." The large "arbiter city" is often run by a Democratic mayor. In smaller cities, however, this "arbiter city" becomes the "investor city" where government caters to the needs of local and national investors, providing subsidized industrial parks, property tax concessions and a myriad of other subsidies. At the state level, the smaller population "investor state" does the same kind of thing except that it often can deliver right-to-work legislation which the "investor city" cannot. Furthermore, at the state level, very little is budgeted for health and welfare by the "investor state." Instead, priority is given to "economic development programs" (statewide boosterism) and to the highway lobby or to the state's major industry. In addition, state aid to education, in the absence of federal guidelines, is often more interested in educating productive corporate employees than in educating healthy community citizens.

Federal funds and the power to set guidelines for their use are being rechanneled by the Reagan administration to the state level where the long-run needs of local people and communities usually take a backseat to the short-run needs of state boosters and corporate employers. In short, President Reagan's decentralization probably will reduce local-level government's meeting of community needs and increase the meeting of corporate needs. The local communities of our land need schools that help wipe out prejudice. They need improved social and health services for the poor, free libraries, museums, and day-care centers, nutritional programs, adult education and community jobs. They are likely to get schools that specialize in real education for a select few and mass incarceration for the rest, strict zoning laws and freeways for the affluent, and above all, subsidies and concessions for potential corporate investors. The right community environment is not necessarily the same thing as the right business climate. But it is the latter which will be provided.

President Reagan's "New Federalism" will be a dismal failure for the poor, for the excluded, and for the communities. While Reagan has offered to pick up the tab for the states' share of Medicaid, he offers to do so only after cutting Medicaid back considerably. In exchange, his "New Federalism" will burden the states with virtually every federal social program initiated since FDR. The "New Federalism" goes far beyond the conversion of federal programs to block grants, yet it is neither new nor federalist. It is not new because most of it was proposed over thirty years ago by the Old Dixiecrats. It is not federalist because it is not based on a concern for the health of state and local governments. It is based on a desire to dismantle programs that benefit the poor, the excluded, and the communities.

In 1948 Strom Thurmond, conservative southern Democrat, broke ranks with the Democratic Party and formed the States Rights Democratic Party, better known as the Dixiecrats. In 1982 Ronald Reagan broke ranks with Abraham Lincoln's Party, better known as the Republicans, and formed the "New Federalists." In 1948 the Dixiecrats opposed federal activism in civil rights, income redistribution, and national health insurance. The Dixiecrats justified their opposition to federal programs on the constitutional basis of states' right. But the truth is, they were reactionary segregationists, not defenders of the constitution. In 1982 the New Federalists justify turning federal programs back to the states on the basis of strengthening grassroots democracy. The truth, of course, is something else again. In the 1948 Presidential election Thurmond and the Dixiecrats received only 39 out of 531 electoral votes, a crushing political defeat. Nearly 35 years later, Ronald Reagan and his supporters proclaim that what we need is a New Federalism. The New Federalists, like the Old Dixiecrats before them, want none of the federal government's activism in civil rights, income redistribution, and welfare. In fact, the New Federalism is remarkably similar to the stand taken by the Old Dixiecrats, a reactionary and racist stand repudiated at the polls in 1948.

Nevertheless, Ronald Reagan is the most amiable President since FDR. He radiates charm, not bigotry. Yet a President must be judged by his actions. President Reagan's actions are appallingly similar to those called for by the Old Dixiecrats. In 1948 the Old Dixiecrats opposed President Truman's activist Fair Employment Practices Commission, designed to reduce racial discrimination. In 1982 Reagan opposed the Equal Employment Opportunity Commission's affirmative action plans. In 1948 the Dixiecrats opposed federal support of black voting rights in the South. In 1982 Reagan opposed strengthening the Voting Rights Act. In 1948 the Dixiecrats opposed virtually any kind of federal social program that interfered with their states' "right." In 1982 Reagan proposed dumping on the states virtually every federal social program.

In theory, the idea that the fifty separate states can handle social problems better than the federal government can is very appealing.

The separate states are closer to the people, closer to the grassroots level of democracy, than the more centralized federal government. But in practice, both political will and financial ability are often lacking at the state level. This is not to say that our state governments are corrupt or ineffective. Rather, many of our states simply lack the tax base to support the needed social programs. Poor people are often concentrated in poor states. So, unfortunately, poor states lack the resources to lift their poor out of poverty. Furthermore, effective solutions to social and economic problems often involve reducing the power or privilege of regionally-based vested interests. Unfortunately, many state governments are not powerful or independent enough to do so. As a practical result, only the financial capacity and political power of the federal government are sufficient to deal with the difficult problems of poverty, discrimination, and environmental degradation. Turning these problems back to the states will fail. The Old Dixiecrats wanted federal social programs, particularly integration, to fail. What of the New Federalists?

Decentralization will also heighten the conflict, inherent in federalism, between the state and federal levels of government, leading to a significant reduction in the federal government's ability to engage in coordinated planning. The planning function is essential to perform even the minimal role of offsetting cyclical swings in private spending, let alone the more ambiitous functions of long-term guidance of the market economy or of indicative planning.[15]

Not only is planning at the federal level essential for the offset function and for the reduction of sexism, racism, and incompetence frequently encountered at the lower levels of government, it is also essential for the coordination of government efforts at all levels. It is the only way to avoid the competition in regulatory laxity often encountered at lower jurisdictional levels as, for example, states vie with each other to attract investment through reducing corporate taxes, passing right-to-work laws, and easing environmental standards. Furthermore, at least some degree of centrism is required for effective redistribution. Economic anthropologist Karl Polanyi emphasized that the need for centrism and redistribution existed even in primitive societies and the need is far greater in our complex one.[16]

In addition to decentralization, President Reagan plans a deregulation sweep which goes far beyond the deregulation sweep of the Carter administration. Under President Carter, deregulation was pushed into transportation, communication, financial intermediation and energy, but regulation in the occupational health and safety and environmental fields was simplified and streamlined rather than cut back. Under President Reagan the health, safety, and environment fields will experience major cutbacks in federal regulation.

One of the most criticized federal agancies to remain intact after the Carter deregulation push is the Occupational Safety and Health Administration, created in 1970 and loudly condemned ever since in the business press for overregulating the workplace. OSHA standards and inspections gradually have been pushing laggard industries to redesign safer workplaces. However, the Reagan administration is redirecting the basic thrust of OSHA away from workplace redesign and toward protective devices for workers. This change in orientation represents a reversal of decades of safety reform in the workplace. Rather than placing the burden of providing a safe workplace for the worker on the employer the change will place the burden on the worker.

This shift will involve heavy reliance on such devices as earmuffs and plugs to protect against hearing loss and respirators to protect against gas poisoning. However, ear-protecting devices can lead to fungus infections. Such devices make it hard to tell from which directions a sound is coming, increasing the risk of accident and disease as a cost of protecting hearing. Similar kinds of problems are encountered with the reliance on respirators. Placing the burden of protection on the worker can be compared with the reasoning of a race car owner who, because he gives the driver a crash helmet, thinks it is all right to skimp on safety features in the car. Such reasoning is in line with the individualistic misconceptions of supply-side economics, but not with the realities of workplace hazards. Individual workers are simply incapable of detecting all the complex hazards of modern work. Exotic chemicals and radiation are not hazards easily understood even by "experts," let alone by individual workers. Placing the burden of protection on the worker instead of the employer is placing it on the party least able to cope with it. Employer prevention is superior by far to employee protection.[17]

SUMMARY

Free enterprise and rugged frontier individualism are no longer realistic approaches to our problems. Supply-side economics is faulty economic science; it has lost touch with twentieth century conditions.

Economic progress now and in the past is a result of the push from below for full participatory status and of the spread of accumulated knowledge and skill to more and more people. Further progress will not be promoted by giving higher rewards to those already participating in the process. It will come by bringing the excluded into active participation.

"Free enterprise," deregulation, decentralization, and militarization of the economy will not put us back on the track. Rather, these steps will distort our society and economy, imposing heavy long-run costs on us all. This counterrevolution that we are experiencing is a step into unreason and unreality.

4 THE NEW REALITY

INTRODUCTION

Policies based on free enterprise and frontier individualism take us into unreason and unreality because the social and economic conditions in which such policies used to be appropriate have long since passed into history. Frontier America, where individual entrepreneurs tamed a continent and built economic empires, *was* the world of free enterprise. Mature America where corporations administer those empires is the world of managerial planning. Frontier America where meaningful family life, moralistic churches, poor but independent schools, and robust democracy all prospered *was* a pluralistic society. Mature America of the fragmented family, timid church, rich but compliant school, and moribund democracy is no longer that same pluralistic society. For lack of a better word, society has become hegemonic. That is, formerly independent institutions (family, church, state, proprietor) have lost their independence. They have fallen under a "hegemony." And the economy has passed from free (individual) enterprise to corporate enterprise.

This chapter contains a discussion of the new social and economic reality, and why we don't understand them. Emphasis will shift away from President Reagan's program for, even after Reagan passes from the scene, the problems of the new reality will remain.

THE NEW SOCIAL REALITY

The social reality of the late twentieth century is bureaucratic life in the giant corporation, not individualistic life in the frontier settlement. As the twentieth century progressed, most individuals became increasingly hemmed in by huge corporations led by smaller and smaller numbers of very powerful men. In the process, most individuals and most noncorporate institutions have become powerless. The problems

49

of power, individuality, and pluralistic institutions are intertwined in such a complex fashion that one cannot be understood without understanding the others.

Let me preview my approach to these problems by asking two questions. Why do individuals, often physically and mentally stronger than their rulers or leaders, willingly obey instructions? That question leads to another: How do individuals acquire motives, goals, ideals, and means? The answer to this takes us down to bedrock, the institutional structure in which the individual is embedded. Institutional structure is the source of power, for individuals learn motives, goals, ideals, and means from their participation in our society's institutions. In the family, church, school, military, corporation, and government, we learn what is expected of us and we learn how to do it. Some of us also learn how to exercise power, and how to back it up if the need arises. Some of us are institutionally supported in our exercise of power. The rest of us are not.

Any discussion of power should first define it. *Power is the ability to tell other people what to do with some degree of certainty that they will do it.* When power wielders must coerce others, power is tenuous and obvious. When coercion is unnecessary, power is secure and unnoticed. In twentieth-century America, coercion is minimal. This is because power is relatively secure, except during times of overt crisis and war. Twentieth-century Americans, usually, submit to power voluntarily. Individuals often do not even consider their behavior as submissive. Rather, they "choose" to do what is expected of them. They do not even notice power. Instead, they consider themselves as free, as exercising their individual initiative. These illusions of individual choice and individual autonomy make it very difficult to see, let alone analyze, power. So the following discussion will place great emphasis on the institutional structure and the individuals that structure produces. Only after grasping the relation between institutional structure and individuality can power itself be analyzed.

INSTITUTIONAL STRUCTURE

A society is a structure of institutions, each institution linked more or less tightly to other institutions. An institution is two things. First, it is an organized pattern of roles, often enforced with both positive and negative sanctions. Second, it is the patterned habits of thought learned by individuals performing those roles.

Institutions, as both these patterns, are clustered around general functions. In a pluralistic society, as existed in nineteenth century America, no single institution and no single cluster of institutions was dominant. Family, church, state, and economic institutions all competed for prestige and power. As a result, each was more or less independent of the others. Each was able to claim prestige and to excercise power within its own sphere of life and none was able to extend its prestige claim or its exercise of power much beyond its own sphere. An equilibrium of give and take was maintained. In twentieth-century America, the rough and ready equilibrium is no longer maintained. Each functional cluster of institutions has become linked to a dominant cluster. Pluralism has been lost. The institutional cluster to which the others have become linked is the economic cluster, and within that cluster the corporation is dominant. Economic (corporate) values and functions reign supreme. The social importance of other functions has declined.

The corporation, labor union, and regulatory state agency are the major institutions within the economic cluster. Most of the regulatory bodies surviving the recent deregulation drive are corrupt, coopted, or largely impotent (OSHA, EEOC, and EPA partially excepted). Also, with organized labor representing a smaller and smaller proportion of the work force, and with internal dissension, corruption, and apathy plaguing most unions, the corporation has been left with an open field. It forces increasing rigidity into the American institutional structure by linking the other institutions and other institutional clusters ever more tightly to itself.

American society contains six clusters of institutions: (1) Economic institutions produce and distribute commodities, (2) Educational institutions produce and distribute knowledge, (3) Military institutions prepare for and conduct war, (4) Kinship institutions produce children, (5) Political institutions make and enforce laws with recourse to the ultimate sanction — violence, and (6) Religious institutions instill faith in a system of supernatural doctrines.[1] Each of the noneconomic clusters of institutions in the U.S. are linked to the dominant economic institution, the corporation, in a kind of means-ends relationship. That is, the corporation uses other institutions as means for its own ends.

This is important because it provides the first glimpse at the true source of power and at the nature of our nonpluralistic or hegemonic society.

Educational institutions, particularly public schools and state universities, produce an ample supply of trained and disciplined specialists for corporate employment. In addition to serving their "educational" function, high schools, junior colleges, and universities often are extensions of the corporate personnel office, grading the human capital for easier processing. Most high school drop-outs become either human drudges, criminals, or unemployables. High school graduates are earmarked for blue collar jobs. Junior college graduates are slated for clerical use. University graduates become either management material or specially-trained corporate experts in this or that technique.

Hence, compliant educational institutions produce the human means for pursuit of corporate ends. Of course, some less compliant educational institutions can exercise a degree of autonomy and pursue their own ends. Nevertheless, the main thrust of education is not education, but the production of suitably graded employees with specialized knowledge. Educational institutions can ignore this corporate imperative, but only at their own risk and expense.

The military occupies a unique position within our institutional structure. During a cold war it protects corporate interests at home and abroad by underwriting corporate research and development, by buying corporate commodities, and by insuring a receptive investment climate in developing nations. But during a hot war, military institutions become dominant. Instead of being means for corporate ends, they become the ends and corporations temporarily become the means. Yet hot wars are infrequent and are the occasional price paid by the lower strata for the more useful periods of cold war, useful to the upper strata that is.

The major kinship institution in twentieth century America is the family. It serves two major functions for the corporation. First, as a household, it is the major outlet for corporate commodities. It is the terminal point in the Galbraithian "revised sequence." According to this revised sequence, salesmanship has replaced craftsmanship in our economy because it is far harder to sell produced goods to the sated affluent consumer than it is to actually produce goods. In the past, producing enough *for* the consumer was the problem. In the present, selling enough *to* the consumer is the problem.[2] Constantly larger sales must be forthcoming in order to ensure corporate jobs and profits. The consumer must absorb larger and larger amounts of corporate commodities. If the revised sequence breaks down, as it occasionally does, the fault often lies within the household for failing to follow the corporate imperative: "Thou Shalt Consume." Because it is the weak link in the revised sequence, tremendous corporate pressure (in the form of advertising) and corporate investigation (in the form of market research) is directed at the household. Second, as a family, the major kinship institution produces the semiprocessed materials used as inputs into educational institutions. Children must be instilled with respect for authority lest school officials find them unduly active and irreverant. Children whose ultimate destination is corporate management (future technocrats) must also be instilled with a desire to succeed. If families fail in this general child-molding function, resort is often made to psychotherapy (drug abuse, either professionally-applied or self-administered), corporal punishment, or incarceration.

Political institutions – parties, state and federal legislatures, executive and judiciary branches -- are, in a sense, the most unruly of all twentieth century American institutions. This is because they sometimes pursue ends which are not corporate means. The roles of persons in political institutions are of very ancient origin. They evolved long before the corporation. The people performing these roles often acquire motives, goals, ideals, and means which took concrete form in the Age of Enlightenment rather than in the Age of Corporate Capital. Some judges seek justice. Some legislators seek equality, liberty, and fraternity. Some presidents seek basic social reforms. The institutional roles they perform not only teach them these noncorporate habits of thought, but also provide them with the means to follow them. Such political individuals possess power, that is, they can tell others what to do with some degree of certainty that it will be done. But most political officials exercise their power in the service of corporate ends. After all, corporations usually fund or corporate officials usually direct the higher educational institutions attended by future political officials. Corporations usually employ their fathers, give them their first jobs, finance their political campaigns, provide them with the information they need to perform their public duties, and hire them back when they tire of "public" service. In short, the habits of thought of most political officials are those learned in performing, or in preparing to perform, corporate roles. Compliant political officials are not corrupt. They are not conspirators. They do not have to be. They simply follow the motives, goals, ideals they have learned, and in doing so they use political means for corporate ends.

The last major cluster of American institutions are those that pursue religious ends. But they employ economic means, and there is the rub. Most American religious denominations employ various functionaries and officials. These employees must be paid, or at least fed, clothed, and sheltered. Most denominations also use various and assorted houses of worship. These must be paid for and maintained. In short, religious institutions must be financed, and without the power to tax, financing comes from voluntary contributions. If a religious institution pushes too hard against the sensibilities of its financiers, it loses their support. Sad, perhaps, but the bottom line is brutally clear. Most religious institutions cannot aggressively attempt to change thought patterns of their lay supporters for fear of losing their support. This means that most religious institutions have little autonomy. Even if religious leaders want to instill certain habits of thought in their lay supporters, the best they can do is legitimate or reinforce those habits of thought already held. If they preach against them, they may lose the means necessary to do so.

In summary, at the close of the twentieth century, a structure of institutional hegemony clearly can be discerned in the United States. With a few exceptions, noneconomic institutions are either ineffective or perform functions linked to the corporation, the dominant economic institution. Most institutions are means to corporate ends. People performing roles in these subordinate institutions may possess power, but it is usually exercised in such a way that it serves corporate ends. Their power is not autonomous. Rather, it is literally and figuratively incorporated into an institutional structure of corporate hegemony. Pluralism has died. Yet few academic writers, outside of a few renegade sociologists and outside of the underground of "institutional economics," have taken note of the passing.

INSTRUMENTS OF HEGEMONY

This corporate hegemony is not held together by a conspiracy. Several social mechanisms simply operate in such a way that they become instruments of hegemony, means of corporate domination, and, ultimately, the social cement which holds the edifice together. These social mechanisms may be called the superstructure, but the name is unimportant. Four of them are important to an understanding of power: subordination, contamination, emulation, and mystification.

Subordination occurs when the function performed by one cluster of institutions becomes the means of another cluster of institutions. Thorstein Veblen's *Higher Learning in America* is perhaps the best study of subordination ever written. According to Veblen, higher learning has its own means and ends: the increase and dissemination of knowledge. The major institution performing this function is the university, but American universities are not autonomous. Most are run by and for corporate businessmen. As a result, the end of higher learning has become subordinated into a business means. Universities became "practical" and began producing practical knowledge (how to get ahead in the corporate world) and practical men. Knowledge for knowledge's sake faded into the background.[3]

It is through subordination that the formerly autonomous clusters of American institutions have become linked to one dominant institution, the corporation. Subordination is one of the least studied social phenomena of the twentieth century. The reason is simple. Subordination destroys the foundation of a pluralistic society. That is, it replaces institutional autonomy, a former truth so near and dear to the hearts of mainstream liberals, with institutional hegemony, the foundation of corporate power and the reality of twentieth century America. It is through subordination that the functions (ends) of our major institutions have become incorporated as the means of one dominant institution. In the process, the power of the subordinated institutions has either declined or has become an extension of corporate power. "Eat your breakfast, Johnny, or you won't grow up to be a successful businessman like your father."

Contamination occurs when the motives appropriate for the roles of one institution spread to the roles of others. Religious institutions in the United States are contaminated with corporate (pecuniary) motives to the extent that the acquisition and display of wealth (conspicuous consumption) has become *the* motive of religious officials. To the extent that they are judged by and judge themselves by their moral and theological stature, they are free of contamination. To the extent that they judge themselves and are judged by the stature of their real estate, they are contaminated. That is, their motives are those of the corporation rather than the church.

The same applies to people in other institutional roles. "Vote for John Doe and put sound business practices to work in city government." "This university should be run according to sound business principles." "What this family needs is a business manager!" Although obvious, it seldom consciously occurs to people in their roles as political officials, university administrators, or parents that governments, universities, and families are not business corporations. As a result, motives appropriate for corporate roles have contaminated the roles performed in other institutions, giving corporate roles and those performing them far more weight in society than noncorporate ones.

Contamination is akin to emulation. Emulation, as used here, occurs when one institution or institutional cluster successfully denies the prestige claims of other institutions and successfully realizes its own claims, becoming the fountainhead of social value. That is, emulation occurs when one institution becomes the source of status. Acquisition of status then comes from performing the top roles of the dominant institution and from displaying that successful performance. In our society, one must earn and then spend big money or emulate those that do.

One earns it performing a top corporate role of one form or another. And one spends it, not just in conspicuous consumption, which is a bit gauche, but also in "public service." A choice ambassador post is an excellent way to turn corporate cash to public account (acclaim). Philanthropy is also a suitable activity, for educational and religious institutions are always in need of the businessman's pocket *and* the businessman's animus. Furthermore, he who throws his bread upon the water receives it back a thousandfold.

Through emulation, two things happen. First, corporate leaders cash in their corporate status by becoming leaders of other institutions. Second, and more important, people performing roles in other institutions usually do not object to the usurpers. Instead, they wish to be like their corporate benefactors. Through emulation, strong and proud men willingly accept the status claims of others and willingly denigrate their own. After all, if you have never met a payroll....

Mystification is the emulation and distortion of symbols. It occurs when one institution produces the most important or the most valued symbols of a society and other institutions attempt to emulate or support them. Such symbols as "free (corporate) enterprise," "private (corporate) property," and "individual (corporate) initiative" are examples of two things. First, they are very important symbols to most Americans. These symbols all originate in the corporate sphere of life and are actively disseminated by that sphere and by its outlyers. They represent or purport to represent things of great value to Americans in *all* walks of life. Second, these symbols are mystifications, distortions. In the twentieth century, free enterprise, private property, and individual initiative no longer mean what they purport to mean. Instead, they are mysteries or talismans of immense emotional potency. These symbols are used as weapons, both offensive and defensive. When used defensively, such symbols rally public support for free enterprise (that is, corporate power to administer prices) in the oil industry and elsewhere. When used offensively, they rally support for individual initiative (that is, union busting and right-to-work laws) in the southern textile mills. And, of course, the symbol "private property" is so powerful that its potency even protects corporate property from abuse at the hands of the profane federal regulators.

In short, corporate hegemony is maintained, not through a conspiracy, but through four social mechanisms. Subordination ties all institutions together so that noncorporate institutions are used as means to corporate ends. Contamination puts corporate role motives into noncorporate roles. Emulation allows corporate leaders to gain acceptance, even respect, in noncorporate leadership roles. And mystification covers the corporate hegemony with a protective (magic) cloak of the most valued American symbols. No wonder most social commentators leave well enough alone.

INDIVIDUALITY

The source or foundation of power in the twentieth century should now be clear. It is institutional position, not individual strength, will, or cunning as it was in frontier America. But this statement may simply beg the question, for do not strong, willful, and cunning individuals still rise to high positions and then use those positions for their own ends? The answer is no because the question contains a false premise. The question assumes, incorrectly, that powerful individuals acquire their ends independently of the institutional roles they performed on their way to the top. This is not true. Prefabricated individuals simply are not selected to perform certain roles. Instead, as individuals perform certain roles, they are shaped by the roles they play. And the easier they are shaped, the faster they rise to higher roles.

An institution is an organized set of roles and the habits of thought people learn as they perform those roles. Furthermore, our current institutional structure is one of corporate hegemony, which means that in the family, the school, and in the corporation proper, individuals are shaped by the roles they play in each institution, and each institution is itself linked to the corporation. For the individual who passes through the family and school on his/her way to the corporation, this institutional shaping produces the motives, goals, ideals, and means of the individual. It shapes their character.

The shaping process makes us fit into our new corporate way of life and shapes a new American character in the process. Individuals who pass through this habituation process and find themselves chief executives for the largest corporations are very powerful men. But they do not exercise individual power. They may idealize themselves as frontier individualists but they are really corporate careerists.

POWER

Their power is not individual but corporate, in both its source and in its direction. In other words, both the ends and the means of individuals who exercise power are institutionally determined. The ends of power are institutionally determined because the motives, goals, and ideals of the powerful have been learned in their role-by-role climb to the corporate top. From the role of father's little man, through teacher's star pupil, to chief executive's protege, the powerful corporate executive learns how and why to act, how and why to think. He has become a corporado, a person who is as much a product of the corporation as the goods it sells.

Furthermore, if the corporado is religious, then his god provides him with the ultimate sanction. If he has been in the military, then as chief executive of XYZ corporation, he performs his patriotic duty. If he has served in government, then political doors and regulatory rules are open to him. Such access helps him prevent unreasonable regulation and unbusiness-like principles in government. In short, other institutions are his means. But the corporado's ends are corporate, not religious, not military, not political.

The means of power are also institutionally determined because as a corporate executive, religious, military (outside of hot war), educational, and political ends are all available to him as means. The leaders and followers of the other institutions depend on him for material and immaterial support. He is not depended upon as an individual, but as head of an institution. His power, and the willing obedience to it, are institutionally determined. Another can easily fill his shoes. This is because both individual power and what individuals do with it are determined by the institutional roles performed. Institutional roles, then, and the "superstructure" supporting them, are the ultimate source of power. The corporado, as an individual, is powerless. Witness the fate of executives who lose their positions due to merger. Their fall is precipitous and painful, unless broken by a "golden parachute."

The top roles in the top institutions of any institutional structure (society) are supported by certain social mechanisms. This reinforces the power of a top role, whether that role be in second-century Rome or twentieth-century America. But in the former case, power is easy to see and to analyze because it was tenuous and based on coercion. In the latter case, power is hard to see and to analyze because it is secure and based on voluntary compliance. Institutional analysis is the key to understanding power based on obedience or compliance. It is from institutionally organized roles that we, in twentieth-century America, learn the habits of thought conducive to getting along in the institutional structure into which we are born.

Getting along means adjusting to our position in life. We are aided in this adjustment process (Veblen's habituation) by four social mechanisms. These mechanisms not only support and reinforce the top roles in our top institutions. They also help all of us, including the performers of the top roles, accept the situation, maybe even enjoy it. Through subordination, the ends of teachers and students, parents and children, military officers and enlisted men, elected officials and bureaucratic staff, nicely mesh into a means-ends continuum. They provide the means, the corporation the ends. And he who serves best is happiest. Through contamination, a churchman can work for a huge building fund and feel good about it; a student and her teacher can work for a good job offer and feel the same. In short, people in all walks of life can acquire and follow a corporate animus, even though in doing so they are borrowing corporate motives and applying them to noncorporate activities. Nevertheless, they do so willingly. They individually and freely want to, therefore it is right and good; or so they think.

Being contaminated with the motives of corporate business, very few people notice that the values and prestige claims of corporate life are emulated in *all* walks of life, allowing successful performers of top corporate roles to "cash-in" their claims by becoming leaders of noncorporate institutions. All this is done, not in the name of the corporation, but in the name of free enterprise, or private property, or individual initiative. Mystification allows (some of) us to think that individual initiative is served by union busting, to believe that private property is protected by the corporate attacks on the Environmental Protection Agency and the Occupational Safety and Health Administration, and to believe that free enterprise is served by dismantling government regulation of corporate power in general. And we cling to our myths very tenaciously, even to the exclusion of reality.

By now the reader may be quite upset. Perhaps my picture of the new social reality has been overdrawn. People, after all, are not puppets. Individuals possess free will. They can choose their own careers and their own lifestyles. Quite true. Each individual is precious. Each is divine. But each is born into a particular family, a particular time, a particular society. It is within those particular structures that we each try to achieve and to exercise our individuality. We make choices, we exercise our free wills, but within limits imposed upon us by family, by time, and by society. We choose, but we choose from a predetermined set of alternatives. We strive, but for goals that already exist. In the process, we may redefine the alternatives and the goals, but we start out with the limits imposed upon us by the social reality into which we are born.[4]

We can deny that such limits exist. In fact, that is what we have been doing. We nostalgically cling to the rugged individualism of frontier America with its pluralistic society and open competition. We even elect a President who, after playing it on the screen, does it for real. But the consequences will be catastrophic because we no longer are frontiersmen living in a pluralist society. We are corporate men living in a corporate society. Like it or not, we are corporados.

THE NEW ECONOMIC REALITY

Now that the broad outlines of contemporary social reality have been sketched, we can narrow our focus to the changes that have occurred in our economy as it evolved from free market capitalism to corporate capitalism. Three roles in our economy have undergone dramatic change. The consumer, the producer, and the regulator have become different from what they once were. The new reality of our corporate economy is such that our denial of how these roles have changed leads to poor overall performance. We pretend that the economic world works one way, while it in fact works increasingly in another way. In a sense, economic evolution has been very cruel to us. It has turned many truths of the eighteenth and nineteenth centuries into the myths of the twentieth.

THE CONSUMER

In preindustrial America most of the things that most of us consumed were necessities. We had to have them to live. Consumer demand was very real. The demand for food, clothing, and shelter were absolute because a minimum of each was, and still is, absolutely necessary. When most consumption is of necessities, the consumer is necessarily king. Then, consumer demand determines what is produced. Otherwise, blood flows in the streets. This is just as true in a tightly controlled economy as it is in a free market economy. Bread riots are fearful to behold whether in Leningrad or London.

But when consumer demand for absolute necessities is easily met, things begin to change. The consumer remains king, but he becomes fickle. With the important exception of those still trapped in poverty, millions of U.S. consumers today are spending discretionary income. That is, after easily affording the necessities of life, they can choose *not* to spend the rest of their income. Or they can quickly change their spending pattern. And when they do, the corporations, forsaken by the fickle consumer, must lay off workers, cut dividends, maybe even terminate managerial personnel. The latter is very painful. Hence, tremendous effort is put into salesmanship[5] and diversification. The affluent consumer must be sold, again and again. The status anxieties and personal insecurities of affluent consumers must be turned to corporate account. Doing so is not that difficult. Caught up in career games played out in corporate bureaucracies, affluent corporados and their families are constantly searching for ways of assuring themselves of their status and for ways of displaying that status to the other game players. The properly exclusive winter vacation and the properly displayed winter tan, the rustic second home and dropped references to it in office conversation, the properly selected stimulants, depressants, and hallucinogens and discreet evidences of dissipation, are all fairly recent additions to the art of conspicuous consumption. Old standbys are still important, of course. The proper wardrobe, automobile, suburban home, private club, and hobby are still mandatory in the game of status scramble. The affluent consumer is still king and marketers still pander to his/her wants. But the affluent consumers no longer demand goods. They demand status objects. Furthermore, from the seller's point of view, the consumer is no longer a demander of a particular product. Now, he/she is a supplier of corporate revenues. The subtle shift from eager demander of particular goods to fickle supplier of general revenues is of crucial significance. Affluent consumers have gained discretionary income to spend in the status scramble but they have lost the organic relation to production that they once had.

On their part, producers have shifted their emphasis from making useful things for people to making people into "useful" things, sources of revenue to be tapped rather than customer needs to be met. At one time, personal consumer loyalty to a particular product was extremely valuable; maintaining it worked as a constraint on seller behavior. That old constraint is far less operative today. Consumers in a particular market can now be milked for all they are worth because the conglomerate is always moving on to new consumers in new markets with new products under new brand names managed by new subsidiaries. Most consumers do not know or care what conglomerate makes the products they buy. Not only has the affluent consumer become fickle because of his/her discretionary income and because of his/her entrapment in the status scramble, but the producer has become fickle as well.

At their discretion, the conglomerate producers easily move into lucrative new markets and out of old dried-up ones. No longer operating in one market, the old market constraints no longer limit their discretion. If they ruin one market, there is always another. If they ruin one brand name, there is always another. Even if they ruin one community with plant shut downs or pollution, there is always another.

Affluent consumers, drawn deeper and deeper into competition for status through conspicuous consumption, are finding that their discretionary incomes must be stretched to the limit to keep up in the game. The level of spending required just to maintain appearances, let alone improve them, keeps rising. Status gets more expensive every day, fear of failure spreads among the affluent. With that fear comes greed, a new trait in the American character. As a frontier people we were ambitious, short-sighted, and insensitive to the rights of native Americans and blacks. But the American character of the time was seldom described as greedy, not even by our detractors. But caught in the status scramble, and fearful of falling behind, affluent Americans have become greedy. Although the federal tax burden has actually declined for the typical affluent tax payer (see Chapter 11), and although tax loopholes have proliferated, the outrage against taxes has mounted steadily among the affluent. Tax revolt spreads at both the federal and state levels, and many of us cheer President Reagan on as he cuts aid to the poor, the aged, the young, the sick, and the disabled. Affluent consumers find it harder and harder to keep up in the status scramble so they have deprived poor consumers of their subsidies. The result is more spending on consumer frivolities and less spending on consumer necessities. The affluent are allowed to overindulge themselves on status objects while the poor are deprived of adequate nutrition, education, health care, and housing. Who knows, perhaps the current revolt of the affluent will be followed by a revolt of the deprived? Will the counterrevolution of the corporados spark a real revolt of the desperados?

THE PRODUCER

Production of goods is a three-stage process. In the primary stage the producer interacts directly with nature in the extraction of minerals or the harvesting of plants and animals. Forestry, fishing, mining (or drilling), and agriculture begin the production process. In the secondary stage the producer turns raw materials into finished or semi-finished goods. In the third stage of production, goods are delivered to their final users and financed and serviced, if need be. Wholesalers, retailers, insurers, bankers, service centers and so forth all perform this third step.

In the eighteenth century all three steps in the production process of just about everything were performed by independent businessmen. For example, a planter grew cotton and sold it to a local buyer. Then it was sold at a major market to a spinner who sold it to a weaver who sold it to a textile wholesaler who sold it to a retailer who sold it to a final consumer, who made it into a dress.

But after the Civil War the independent businessman, particularly in manufacturing, began to be replaced by the vertically integrated producer. From the lowest stage of production to the highest, vertical integration forged industrial systems in oil and steel, and in other industries. All that former buying and selling in the market was replaced by planning within the firm. Huge industrial combines and the expertise of their corporate management replaced the higgling of the market and the rule of thumb of the independent businessman. Production soared; costs plummeted; prices often collapsed. Furthermore, at each stage of production, Adam Smith's invisible hand of the market was replaced increasingly by the visible hand of management.[6]

Producer and consumer still face each other in the market, but independent producers at different stages of production seldom do. They have been brought under the same corporate roof and the role of the market in our market system has been reduced accordingly, at least within the production process itself. The cause was cost-reducing, production-expanding, vertical integration, but the result was a diminution of the market system. The invisible hand of the market no longer coordinates the production activities of independent businessmen in all stages of production.

A further shrinking of the market's discipline has occurred through horizontal integration. Vertical integration comes about when a wholesaler acquires a retailer or manufacturer in a given line. Horizontal integration occurs when the wholesaler acquires a competing wholesaler. Horizontal integration in an industry, if carried out completely, results in monopoly. Vertical integration was carried out far more thoroughly than horizontal — *monopoly* is an illegal restraint of trade in most instances. Horizontal mergers were taken only to the point of oligopoly; a few competitors have dominated most industries for years, but they have not merged further into monopolies.

This latter fact has lulled most economists into complacency about market competition. In the postwar period, there has been little trend toward increased integration, either horizontal or vertical, so many economists conclude that the competitive market system is still flourishing. But they miss the point. The gate has closed on vertical and horizontal integration, true. But the cows got out over fifty years ago! By the close of the 1920s both vertical and horizontal integration had become the rule in much of the economy. Just because the extent of integration has changed little since then is no reason to conclude that the free market still thrives. The correct conclusion is quite the reverse: The free market has been moribund in much of our economy since before the Great Depression.

Although moribund and no longer completely "free," the market still functioned. Workable competition still existed. Vertically integrated oligopolies were forced to coexist in the same market.

But in the 1960s, the conglomerate movement revolutionized the market system to such an extent that it became something else. Now we have corporate capitalism rather than market capitalism. The conglomerate movement allowed vertically integrated oligopolies to escape the constraints of any single market because they discovered that they could move into several different markets simultaneously. This development is truly revolutionary and it is no coincidence that stagflation first reared its ugly head during the conglomerate movement of the 1960s, for freed from the constraints of any single market, the corporate production system came of age. Finally, with the evolution of the conglomerate corporation, all the pieces of corporate capitalism were in place.[7] So too were all the causes of stagflation.

In a vertically integrated production system managerial planning coordinates each stage of production, reducing the total cost of production. Former market frictions, the lags and bottlenecks inherent in market coordination, are reduced because the product no longer passes through the market at each stage of production on its way to the consumer. But, with the product no longer passing through the open market during the production process, the actual costs of production at each stage of the process are buried deep within the internal accounting system of the corporation. What does a fully integrated producer really pay for its raw materials and semi-finished goods? They no longer are bought and sold at arms-length so we know only what the producer tells us. Nevertheless, vertical integration put in place the first piece of the corporate system — the ability to coordinate each stage of production.

Horizontal integration brought into play the second piece of the corporate system — the economies of scale of mass production for a mass market. As the scale of production increased the per unit costs of production declined, so the formation of large oligopolies provided substantial cost savings. Unfortunately for consumers, the formation of oligopolies also provided the huge producers with the market power to drive up prices. But as long as an oligopoly produced for one market only, great hesitance was exercised in raising the oligopoly's price. To understand the reason for this price restraint we must make a brief foray into technical economics.

Two things occur when the price of a product rises. On one hand, the seller receives more per unit sold. On the other hand, fewer units are sold. Buyers of the product reduce the quantity they purchase by finding substitute products and/or by learning how to get along without the product, however, it takes time for them to cut back. Therefore, when the price of a product rises, the seller immediately receives higher total revenues on the output sold before buyers have time to significantly reduce the amount of the product they purchase.

In the short term, a higher price means higher revenue and higher profit for the seller. But in the long term, revenues and profits may fall as buyers adjust by reducing their use of the higher priced product. This means that a seller dependent upon one market for his profit and revenue is quite cautious about raising his price because, in the long run, his market will be "spoiled" by the higher price. That is, a higher price eventually reduced his profits.[8]

If a firm can easily move into new markets, the firm's pricing strategy is no longer constrained by the fear of "spoiling" any single market. There are always new markets to tap should old ones run dry. The large oligopoly, a product of horizontal integration, possessed the market power to push up its price. But, being dependent upon one market, exercising that market power was just too costly in the long run because the market became "spoiled." That is, revenue and profit eventually fell and this market eventually constrained the use of oligopoly power. The conglomerate movement, begun in the 1960s and continuing today, broke that market constraint as oligopolies learned how to move into numerous new markets by simply buying into them. The final piece of the corporate system is now in place. With the advent of the conglomerate, corporate capitalism is rapidly replacing market capitalism in most of our economy.

OPEC price increases are a dramatic example of how the new system works. By the time drastic decline sets in on the petroleum industry, the maximum profits will have been earned and used to finance the movement of oil conglomerates into other markets. The process already is occurring. Thanks to OPEC the oil giants are acquiring toeholds in many new markets, just waiting to be tapped. Other industries do not have an OPEC godfather so the process outside of the petroleum industry is less dramatic. But it is still going on in areas outside of oil.

The conglomerate movement is the root of rising prices, rising unemployment, and the soaring federal deficit. As a conglomerate begins tapping out new markets, it drives up prices in those markets. Then as production cut backs set in, workers in the affected industries are laid off. Overall unemployment rises. The laid off workers find few job opportunities in other industries because the conglomerate is moving into them as well, in order to tap them as additional revenue sources. Conglomerate management means no harm to anyone in this process. Management is merely pursuing the corporate interest as management sees it. But local communities are devastated by plant closings, and the unemployed find no new jobs. Futhermore, the federal budget deficit soars as the local communities and the unemployed turn to the federal government for the only aid available. Prices, plant closings, and federal deficits keep rising as more markets are tapped.

The American public, seeing unemployment, inflation, and federal red ink flowing over the land, is frightened, and for good reason. But without good reason, the public believes that the rising prices and plant closings are due to the federal deficit, spawned, we are told, by spendthrift bureaucrats and logrolling liberal Congressmen. Some members of the public even believe the ambitious young supply-side economists who eagerly explain that the poor, the unemployed, and the devastated communities would all be better off if the hemorrhaging federal social programs that keep the affected afloat were slashed and the taxes which are already inadequate sources of financing were reduced. The unreason of it all boggles the mind. It conjures up images of Marie Antoinette saying "If the people have no bread, let them eat cake." Our current inflation and high unemployment is not caused by the federal government. Savaging it will not bring back full employment and price stability, supply-side economists to the contrary. The cause is the completion of the corporate system. Once vertically integrated oligopolies freed themselves from the constraint of single markets, the inflation-unemployment problems were generated as side-effects of the conglomerate's exercise of its newly found freedom. Yet savaging the conglomerate is no more justified than savaging the federal government.

The conglomerate corporation is the most advanced production planning mechanism evolved to date. Soviet planners are not even in its league. It represents an incredible achievement in organizational technology. Nothing surpasses it in planning effectiveness. But nothing surpasses it in avarice, either. It taps out people as well as markets. Nevertheless, it guides the production process better than the old market. Reform and reshape it we must, but in the process care must be taken not to lose efficiency and effectiveness, for it can outproduce any available alternative. The trick is to rein in the avarice without losing the productive potential.

THE REGULATOR

The dramatic changes in the consumer and the producer, wrought by the twentieth century, have been matched by dramatic changes in the regulator. All three economic roles have undergone considerable evolution since the nineteenth century.

The regulation of our economy has never been left exclusively to the market. Legal restraint and public policy guidance have always played significant regulatory roles. However, it was not until the Progressive Era and more forcefully during the Great Depression, that federal regulatory agencies became the most important forms of government regulation. The Interstate Commerce Commission, the Federal Reserve System, the Securities and Exchange Commission, and the Civil Aeronautics Board were the most important of these early regulatory agencies.

Though at first resisted by conservative business groups, these early regulators, like the defunct Agricultural Adjustment Administration, were not really protectors of the public interest. The Federal Trade Commission is a possible exception. Yet the FTC was, in some respects, an early example of a function-specific rather than industry-specific regulator. The distinction as explained below, is an important one. As Gabriel Kolko explains, most early regulators were captured easily by the industries they were supposed to regulate.[9] The early business resistance to regulation faded as regulation was turned to account by the regulated. Larry Reynolds explains why the cooptation of these early regulators occurred so naturally.[10] Except for the FTC, they were all industry-specific regulators functioning to stabilize or augment the revenues of a single industry. Being concerned with one specific industry, the single-minded interest of all members of that industry always focused on the regulator. The regulator, constantly dealing with this concentrated attention, naturally began to accept the views and interests which were constantly surrounding it. The result was special interest regulation, a result worse than no regulation at all. To make matters worse, the major concern of these early regulators quickly became the stabilization or, even better, the increase of industry revenues. Attention was focused on the need to eliminate "cut throat competition." That is, the regulator quickly established rate-fixing procedures and barriers to unfair competition (price cutting or new firms entering the industry). The SEC, ICC and CAB were very effective in fixing prices; other regulators were less so. Hence, the first attempt to regulate business in the public interest clearly backfired. Finally, during the Carter administration, most of the surviving price-fixing schemes were either removed or reformed. Good riddance to them; shippers, airline passengers, securities investors, and many bank customers have benefitted greatly from the deregulation which has allowed price competition to return to the formerly protected industries.

But Larry Reynolds also points out that a second generation of regulator has emerged. The most important of the new regulators are the Environmental Protection Agency, the Occupational Safety and Health Administration, and the Equal Employment Opportunity Commission. These regulators are not captured so easily by the industries they are supposed to regulate. The second-generation regulator is no longer industry-specific. Instead, EPA, OSHA, and EEOC are function-specific. They concentrate on specific functions which cut across industry lines. As a result, no single industry is able to monopolize the views presented to the regulator. The new regulatory process is more open, making the new regulator more resistant to capture by the regulated. To the outrage of conservative business groups, EPA, OSHA, and EEOC actually implemented public-interest regulation rather than special-interest regulation. That is, they were doing so before they were "ventilated" by Reagan and his ambitious young men and women who responded so quickly to the cries of pain from the regulated. (An aside: The ambitious need not wait long for reward, if the past pattern of revolving door "public service" tours is repeated by the current crop of political appointees.)

No longer easily coopted from below, by the industry being regulated, the new regulators must be coopted from above, by political appointment and budget cutting. Otherwise, we are in danger of having the new regulatory agencies implementing regulation in the public interest. If this were to happen, rather than augmenting or stabilizing the revenues of the regulated, the new agencies might force business and industry to bear the full cost of their activities. Rather than the consuming public bearing the cost of a polluted environment and an unhealthy and an unsafe workplace, industry might have to pay for installing pollution abatement equipment and designing a safe and healthy workplace. But as long as the ambitious young Reagan appointees protect us from "radical environmentalists" and "bleeding-heart liberals," we are safe. The new regulators will not do the job they can do.

In regulation, the old reality was of coopted regulators staffed by dispirited incompetents. Deregulation made sense because a coopted regulator was worse than none at all, but the new reality is of independent regulators. The new regulator is not restricted to one specific industry. Function-specific rather than industry-specific, the new regulator not only is resistant to cooptation but is also competent, more competent than industry. The only real vulnerability of the new regulator is the ability of opportunistic appointees to demoralize the professional staff and to defund the agency, as was done to the FTC years ago and is being done now to the other new regulators by Reagan appointees. EPA, specialized in the *one* function of environmental protection, is more competent in that function than its adversaries. The same applies to OSHA and EEOC. Deregulation made sense for the coopted and incompetent first-generation regulator. It does not for the new-generation regulator.

The twentieth-century has seen a veritable revolution in the economic roles of consumer, producer, and regulator. So why do we continue to use ideas out of step with the new economic reality? Why do we continue to cling to the pluralistic image of social reality, long after the reality of pluralism has faded? The first reason is power politics. Not facing up to the new reality benefits those with a vested interest in its maintenance. Critical voices who point out that our economy and society are no longer based on individual and institutional competition are labeled crackpots or malcontents; clearly they are unsound at best; un-American at worst. If not dismissed, criticism is simply ignored because it does not fit into the mainstream of intellectual life.

Since the pen is still mightier than the sword, it is hard to credit power politics with the contemporary denial of reality. But the critical pen is mighty only to the extent that it is grounded in an accepted intellectual-scientific tradition. The second, more important reason, that we cling to an outmoded image of reality is that the intellectual-scientific tradition which has spawned the critical voices is not accepted as legitimate. The long line of sociologists and economists stretching from Thorstein Veblen through C. Wright Mills and John Kenneth Galbraith, all of whom have questioned the conventional wisdom in economics and sociology, have been assigned by their colleagues to the underground. Their works have remained outside the pale of mainstream discourse in both the universities and the mass media. Social critics in the United States do not speak with the authority of an accepted scientific-intellectual tradition behind them. Instead, they speak out either as individuals or as members of the economics underground, not to be taken seriously. A realistic, critical tradition in economics is almost nonexistent in the universities. The best that has been mustered is institutional economics, a largely ignored, underground school of thought which exists in a kind of interdisciplinary limbo between legitimate sociology and legitimate economics. (Legitimate means published in the old, established sociology or economics academic journals.) As a result, an unquestioned, outmoded view of reality has become the conventional wisdom. It is seldom challenged and the challenge, if made, is usually ignored. This lack of critical vision, particularly in economics, has resulted in scientific stagnation. We now turn to this sorry state of economics as a science.

5 DENIAL

IN THE BEGINNING

Economics is a young science, scarcely 200 years old. It could not be called a science, really, until Adam Smith wrote *The Wealth of Nations* in 1776. Smith was the first of the classical economists, the path-breakers of economic science. Unfortunately, at the time Smith and the other classical economists set the path for later economists to follow, the institution which eventually came to dominate the modern economy was still in its infancy. In 1776, the corporation was a suspect institution, restricted to only a few activities. Furthermore, most consumers were still buying simple necessities from small shopkeepers and regulators were still enforcing the will of the Crown. In the lower North American colonies, rebellion was giving birth to a pluralistic, frontier society where rugged individualism would thrive for a century. *Pax Britannica*, enforced by British naval supremacy, soon provided the global stage upon which English individualism would play its historical role. It was this unique social and economic environment that gave birth to the science of economics and long after the environment had changed, economics still would bear its birthmark.

Adam Smith wrote about a nation of individual shopkeepers and small manufacturers who were struggling against the restrictions of mercantilism and the repugnant commercial results of the divine right of kings. One of the institutions of the English Crown's mercantile system was the joint stock company, the precursor of the modern corporation. Adam Smith had no illusions about the nature of the mercantile system. He stated,

> It is the industry which is carried on for the benefit of the rich and the powerful, that is principally encouraged by our mercantile system. That which is carried on for the benefit of the poor and the indigent, is too often, either neglected or oppressed.[1]

73

Fortunately for the English poor, the joint stock company played a minor role in the mercantilist regulation of internal trade and production. Its major role was the monopolization and regulation of external or foreign trade.

Of course, collective or joint enterprises did not spring full-grown from mercantilism.[2] Such enterprises are as old as Western civilization. One interesting medieval form was the *commenda*, in which joint investors enjoyed individually-limited liability and did not directly manage or control the venture. An ancient form was the Roman *societas;* these were treated as entities legally separate from the individual members comprising them. These joint enterprises usually conducted trading expeditions.

In medieval England, trading companies developed out of the guilds. The actual trading was usually done by the individual guild members for their own account and out of their own stock. A joint stock of goods for trade was not used. What joint stock (property) existed was confined to maintaining some kind of guild headquarters, at least in the early phases of the organizational form. The joint stock form of ownership began replacing individual ownership in ventures that involved trade over long distances. Although the exact nature of the company is disputed, the Russia Company, formed in 1553, was probably the first royally chartered joint stock company in England. By the beginning of the seventeenth century, the joint stock form of ownership had become common in England for both long-distance trade and large-scale domestic ventures. By the end of the seventeenth century, an individual could sell his share of the joint stock to another individual with no difficultly. In fact, a London market in the shares of major companies was well established by 1700. Also by that date, at least 140 joint stock companies had been formed in England. The joint stock company was beginning to resemble the twentieth-century corporation, even though it was still used only in some areas of foreign trade and in some very large domestic projects. But soon a trading company was to be formed whose fate would alter the course of British economic history and distort economic theory as well.

The South Sea Company was established in 1710 by Act of Parliament rather than Crown Charter. Nevertheless, it was a mercantilist creation. Its purpose was to expand trade with South America, and it was given an exclusive trading privilege (monopoly) to do so. The Company also conveniently relieved the government of its debt by converting government annuities into stock and using the government debt as a "fund of credit." Its ventures were not profitable and the Company began speculating in its own stock. The directors actively puffed up the profits of the Company and the value of its stock in order to keep the scheme afloat. As a result, the first corporate scandal (in England) was a big one. It became infamous in financial history as the *South Sea Bubble*. The collapse of the scheme came in 1720 and caused Parliament to pass the Bubble Act in the same year. The appropriately named Act made it very difficult to get charters for new joint stock companies and imposed exceptionally harsh penalties for trading in the stock of companies which were not chartered. The Act was poorly worded, however. Some unchartered companies continued their activities and a few new companies were able to obtain charters for semi-public activities such as canal-building. But the Act threw most businesses back to a reliance on the simple partnership form of organization. Although exceptionally ambiguous as a law, the Bubble Act as a statement of public policy was clear. Parliament was condemning the speculative excesses and fraudulent practices of both chartered and unchartered joint stock company promoters and their sales agents, "stock jobbers."

The South Sea Company and the Bubble Act were to leave an almost permanent taint on the joint stock company. Leading early economists, who favored capitalism, built their theories of laissez-faire on the "legitimate" foundation of individual firms, lest the taint of fraud poison their optimistic treatises on capitalism as the system of natural liberty. Adam Smith was no exception. He, too, wanted to build the strongest case possible for replacing mercantilism with laissez-faire. Furthermore, the joint stock company was a tool of the mercantilists in the first place. Hence, its role in laissez-faire economic theory was bound to be very limited.

As if this and the South Sea scandal were not enough, another mercantilist joint stock company was becoming equally infamous, but in a very different way. The English East India Company was created to expand and regulate trade with India. As Adam Smith knew full well, joint stock trading companies were extensions of the mercantilist state, exercising a wide range of public power. The East India Company, the most successful of its type, went so far as to become a private government. It exercised the rights to maintain armies and fortifications and to make war or sue for peace. Of course, these rights were exercised against "barbarous natives," not the English government which sanctioned them. The extent of abuse of these rights is indicated by Smith's appraisal of the actions of the East India Company's directors:

> No other sovereigns ever were, or, from the nature of things, ever could be, so perfectly indifferent about the happiness or misery of their subjects, the improvement or waste of their dominions, the glory or disgrace of their administration; as, from irresistible moral causes, the greater part of the proprietors of such a mercantile company are, and necessarily must be.[3]

No wonder Adam Smith based his laissez-faire system of natural liberty on the theorized activities of individual entrepreneurs rather than the known abuses of company directors. Smith wanted England to replace mercantilism with a system of unregulated domestic industry and free international trade; for free trade, unregulated industry, and division of labor were, he argued, the true *Wealth of Nations*. To support his proposal he constructed a theoretical system composed of unregulated individual producers and free individual international traders. This was a hypothetical system used to support a new set of public policies. However, it was close enough to eighteenth-century reality to be scientific theory. The foundation of that scientific system, its theoretical building block, was the individual entrepreneur.

Yet, as individual entrepreneurs gave way in the nineteenth century to corporate combines, the theoretical system continued using the individual entrepreneur as its foundation. However, this gap between individualistic theory and corporate fact manifested itself only after Adam Smith's passing. The Bubble Act was not repealed until after Adam Smith's death. During the period that the Act was in force, 1720-1825, joint stock companies were relatively unimportant. Those that continued operating were generally viewed as necessary evils. Adam Smith both shared and added to the views of his time. In addition to their mercantilist taint, Adam Smith believed that joint stock companies were usually mismanaged. This mismanagement, Smith reasoned, was because company directors were managing other people's money rather than their own. Company directors could not be expected to exercise the same vigilance over someone else's interests as they would exercise had they been managing their own private firm. Furthermore, Smith was convinced that the joint stock company generally did more harm than good.

Smith believed that only in unusual circumstances was the joint stock company a justifiable form of producing unit. For a joint stock company to be allowed, Smith insisted on three special circumstances: (1) the activity must be reducible to "strict rule and method"; (2) the purpose must be "of greater and more general utility than the greater part of common trades"; and (3) it must require "a greater capital than can easily be collected in a private copartnery."[4] Only banking, insurance, and some public works met these requirements in the internal or domestic economy. Smith believed that the joint stock form could be used in external trade, to open up new regions for trade. But as soon as the new trade was established, any exclusive privileges granted the company should be revoked, lest the company become strong enough to mismanage or confine the trade.

With these minor exceptions, Adam Smith placed both mainstream economic theory and the actual wealth of nations on a foundation of individual not corporate production. Economic theory is still tied to the same fountainhead, the individual entrepreneur. But contemporary economic reality is that of corporate enterprise. After Smith, the gap between theory and fact began to widen.

During the period of the Bubble Act (1720-1825), the simple partnership was adapted for use as a kind of unincorporated joint stock company. This was done by putting the joint stock of a large number of partners under the control of a smaller group of partners or trustees who then managed the joint stock for all of the partners. In this way, the captial of a large number of investors could be pooled and managed in a centralized fashion. (More than a century later, a similar trust arrangement would be used in the U.S. to pool separate corporations into unified monopolies.) If done properly, it was even possible to transfer shares in these fabricated joint stock companies to others without dissolution of what was formally a partnership. In this way, the unincorporated partnership became a vehicle for pooling capital into a joint stock form of organization. Such unincorporated joint stock companies were beginning to flourish by the early nineteenth century. Legal reform in Britain was long overdue, for these proliferating new companies were very similar to the few chartered joint stock companies, but were not subject to the formal controls placed on the latter.

Then, between 1803 and 1810, a number of test cases were brought against unincorporated partnerships operating as joint stock companies. Many of these companies had been attracting subscribers (partners) by claiming that subscribers' liability was limited to the amount subscribed. Of course, this was not formally correct because the organizations were technically simple partnerships. The cases, tried under the provisions of the Bubble Act, set no real precedents but did lead to the eventual repeal of the Act in 1825. In addition to repealing the Act, Parliament also gave the Crown more powers to grant charters on more standardized terms. Finally, led by William Gladstone, the Companies Act of 1844 provided for freedom of incorporation on standard terms. Lengthy and expensive appeals to Parliament or the Crown for a charter were no longer necessary. Corporate capitalism was born.

But interestingly enough, the Act of 1844 did not provide limited liability to shareholders. This aspect of the modern corporation requires a minor digression. In the earliest chartered joint stock companies, shareholders generally assumed that their liability was limited to the amount of their subscription. However, there was no formal provision for such limited liability. This rather tenuous state of affairs persisted until the Hamborough Company Case of 1671, in which it was decided that individual shareholders were liable to the creditors of the company. It then became common for charters to specifically limit liability to the amount subscribed. Yet, as mentioned above, the Companies Act of 1844 reinstated full personal liability for all shareholders. However, full liability proved to be both inequitable and unworkable because wealthy stockholders were always the first and often the only investors to be sued, making their risk much higher than average investors. Furthermore, determining which shareholders were personally liable and which ones were not was complicated by the fact that many of them had sold their shares before the main losses occurred and many had purchased their shares after the losses. Legally affixing and releasing liability on individual stockholders was simply not practical. As a result, in 1856 liability was formally limited for all shareholders by Act of Parliament. The corporation's essential form had been fixed, after nearly three centuries of evolution. The legal form necessary for the development of corporate capitalism had been completed.

While these organizational foundations for the transition to corporate capitalism were being laid, what did the followers of Adam Smith have to say about the rapidly evolving form? Neither Thomas Malthus nor David Ricardo added anything new to Smith's thoughts in their theoretical works on the corporation. While the corporate form was

evolving right under their noses, mainstream theorists continued explaining the actions of individual entrepreneurs and largely ignored the
seamier, yet ultimately more fruitful, schemes of "stock-jobbers." As
late as 1864, John R. McCulloch in his *Principles of Political Economy*
merely echoed Adam Smith's general condemnation of the joint stock
company.[5] John Stuart Mill, however, did pay some attention to the
evolving corporate form in his theoretical work. Writing in 1848, Mill
recognized that "The advantages of the joint stock principle are numerous and important."[6] Among them were the ability to pool a large
capital and the purifying effect of the publicity brought to bear on
company dealings by periodic meetings of shareholders. But Mill was
an exception to the rule for mainstream economic theorists. For most
of them who followed Smith, the corporate revolution swept past
them, unnoticed.

Following the Registration Act of 1856, which provided limited
liability for shareholders of registered companies, a steady expansion
in incorporation occurred in England. This expansion is shown in the
data on incorporations compiled by H.A. Shannon. Shannon estimated
the number of effective incorporations of public companies under the
provisions of the Registrations Act: For the first five years of the Act,
an average of 149 effective new corporations were formed each year.
By 1883, the last year Shannon studied, the average figure had risen
to 556.[7] The corporate revolution in Britain was in full swing.

In the United States, the corporate revolution swept the economy
after the Civil War, with the legal foundations already laid before the
War. At the turn of the nineteenth century in the U.S., corporations
could be formed only through special legislative act by either a state
legislature or the U.S. Congress. Most corporate charters in the U.S.,
as in Great Britain, were for large-scale public projects—canals, turn-
pikes, or banks. In the late 1830s, the Jacksonian democrats began
attacking the monopolistic nature of banking by proposing general
laws of incorporation to replace the special legislative act. The first
modern law providing for general incorporation was passed by Con-
necticut in 1837. After the Civil War, such general incorporation
laws became customary. States began a kind of competition in laxity,
granting ever more lenient terms of incorporation in hopes of attracting more incorporations than other states. Even before the Civil War,
the use of the corporate form was spreading beyond banking and public
enterprise. In addition to its widespread use by railroaders, textile

manufacturers also were experimenting with the new form. As early
as 1813 the Boston Manufacturing Company, a textile giant, had been
granted a charter, but not under a general incorporation law.

By 1899, two-thirds of all U.S. products were manufactured by
corporations; by 1919, 87 percent.[8] What this meant to the typical
experience of individuals in business is simple. The entrepreneurial
climb was replaced by the bureaucratic career. Reinhard Bendix estimated that the entrepreneurs among American businessmen declined
from 68 percent of all businessmen born in 1801-1830 to only 36 percent of all businessmen born in 1861-1890.[9] (Bendix defined an entrepreneur as a substantial owner of a firm who did not inherit considerable wealth.)

As the American economy became dominated by the corporation,
industry became increasingly bureaucratized. In 1899, the ratio of
administrative to production employees in U.S. industry was 8:100.
By 1923, the year Alfred Marshall published the fourth edition of his
famous *Industry and Trade,* the ratio had doubled to 16:100.[10] Seymour Melman, in his 1951 study of administrative overhead in manufacturing, and Reinhard Bendix have made more recent studies of the
spread of administrative employment, showing the bureaucratization
trend continuing.[11] Administering the corporate economy had become
a major problem, even in the 1920s. It required a larger and larger
proportion of the work force. Britain lagged behind the incorporation
and bureaucratization of the U.S. Yet Alfred Marshall, still in the classical tradition, used the individual as the representative producing unit
in economic theory rather than the corporation. In 1923, he stated
"...the partial (?) supersession of individual by joint stock enterprise
has not changed the problems of business administration very
greatly."[12] Nevertheless, Marshall argued that corporations (he called
them joint stock companies) had two weaknesses relative to the individual entrepreneur. First, Marshall reasoned, individual owners are
more aggressive and willing to take risks than salaried managers. The
latter generally prefer maintaining the old, comfortable ways rather
than taking risks in trying out the new. Second, shareholders often lack
adequate knowledge of the business while individual owners are usually
well informed through personal experience. Despite these rather limited theoretical excursions into the corporate world, Alfred Marshall
based his "representative firm" on the individual mode of production,
not the corporate. In fact, when he introduced his concept of the "re-

presentative firm," he discussed it throughout his *Principles* as if it were individually owned and managed.[13] Hence, as late as 1920, when the eighth edition of Marshall's *Principles (the* book for many years) was published, the premier mainstream economist was still weaving economic theory out of eighteenth-century thread. In 1920, the British and American economies were dominated by corporate producers. Yet Alfred Marshall constructed his theories of how that economy worked using the same building blocks that Adam Smith had used. Smith's world was actually made up of individual producers — the butcher, the brewer, and the baker. But Marshall's world, and ours, is made up of IBM, AT&T, and GMC. These are giant combines, powerful private bureaucracies. Their behavior is no longer that of individual entrepreneurs. As long as mainstream economists assume that IBM behaves *as if* it were John Smith, mainstream economics will be a denial of reality.

CONTEMPORARY ECONOMIC THEORY

Supply-Side Economics and the Mainsteam

Although contemporary economics and other social sciences are split into a number of competing schools of thought, economists in the United States are predominantly followers of Adam Smith and the classical economists. After making a few changes here and there in Adam Smith's doctrines, his contemporary followers refer to themselves as neoclassical economists. Of course, neoclassical economists disagree about many particulars. Nevertheless, a neoclassical core of agreement does exist and a neoclassical unity is evident among most U.S. economists who work in the mainstream of contemporary theory. This core of agreement is, in general terms, a faith in government non-intervention in economic processes. Markets, unless they clearly fail, should be left alone, more or less. Since our markets frequently fail to operate as theory says they should, the general faith in the market inherited from Adam Smith has taken on a new tone when applied to particular problems.

The neoclassical core of faith in the market is now composed of three major if-then propositions: (1) If government removed all forms of price and wage control, then prices and wages would adjust up or down rapidly and consistently so that markets would stabilize. The "price mechanism" can still coordinate the activities of consumer and producer, to the mutual advantage of each. (2) If formal social controls were lifted from independent entrepreneurs, then pursuit of their individual self-interest would be controlled by the competitive pressure of the market. If their actions harm others (in Economese, harm to others is referred to as a "negative externality," a sanitized euphemism for dirty air and filthy water), then private bargaining with the affected parties will minimize the harm. (3) If the federal government would stop trying to fine tune the economy, then the booms and busts of the business cycle would be less severe because the market system could stabilize itself. This is the modern version of "Say's Law of Markets," a principle of classical economics. According to Say's Law, supply creates its own demand. That is, general overproduction for the economy as a whole will not occur because as we produce goods we earn enough income to purchase all that we produce. Overproduction may occur in one industry, but if it does, another industry is underproducing because the buyers that left the first industry left it for the second. As workers move from the overproducing industry to the underproducing one in accordance with the change in buyers' preferences, the economy stabilizes itself. With general overproduction not a problem, general unemployment is not a problem either.

Not all neoclassical economists believe in all three if-then propositions to the same degree. A few entertain doubts about proposition (1) or proposition (2); a few more are downright skeptical of proposition (3). But most neoclassical economists believe in most of them. Underground economists believe in none of them. The U.S. underground began taking shape at the turn of this century when men like John R. Commons, Thorstein Veblen, and a long line of other institutional economists, not to mention the few Marxists who were able to survive, began to argue that neoclassical theory just does not fit modern conditions. By and large, their critique has been deflected from the core of neoclassical theory so basic faith in government nonintervention was only slightly weakened by their growing attack.[14]

In addition to surviving the institutionalist attack, faith in neoclassical teachings also survived, in attenuated form, the Keynesian revolution. Keynes questioned the faith in Say's Law by introducing the instability of investment and saving into economic theory. Nevertheless, this Keynesian heresy was merely grafted onto the old neoclassical core, sans Say's Law of course. The Keynesians argued that the total amount of spending, particularly investment, should be stabilized by government. Everything else, government should leave alone. But the Keynesian graft and the neoclassical core were incompatible from the very beginning. Now with memory of the Great Depression fading (the crash occurred more than half a century ago) and with a rebirth of political conservatism, the neoclasssical core is giving rise to an anti-Keynesian counterrevolution. The counterrevolution is a revival of the faith, a return to belief in complete nonintervention by government in the economic process: Not even investment should be stabilized. The resurrected neoclassical core is the new economics and Keynesianism the old.

Supply-side economists are in the forefront of this neoclassical resurrection. Supply-side economics *is* the old core, just in new, pinstriped clothing. It is not a new development in economics, in spite of the fact that the young supply-siders make much to do about their "new" economics. It is quite old, going back to Adam Smith. It is not a rebel movement inside economics, in spite of the rebellious poses struck by the young supply-siders. Instead of a rebel movement, supply-side economics is a reactionary movement pulling wayward economists back to the faith, back to the narrow core of neoclassical economics and away from temporary flirtation with the realities of corporate captialism. These "new" economists seem as unable as the "old" ones to make our economy produce more, or to maintain full employment, without rampant inflation crippling the effort. Economists, at least those listened to by decision makers, do not seem to be finding out how to beat inflation and unemployment at the same time. As a result, our economy wobbles along from one crisis to another. And yet the revival of faith in the neoclassical core of U.S. economic theory gathers momentum, unaffected by the lack of progress in economic policy. Why the regression?

Rumblings from the Underground

If we outline developments in the economics underground with an eye on their ideological implications and then survey the countermoves of those who purvey the conventional wisdom, the reader will find the answer.

From the writings of anthropologists, sociologists, and others who have worked in the broad research area of "social control,"[15] institutional economists have distilled the concept of "economic institution." They have used this concept to criticize contemporary economic theory. An economic institution is concerned with the production, consumption, and regulation of the economic process. An institution is also a duality: First, an institution is an organized pattern of roles. Second, it is the habits of thought people learn as they perform the prescribed roles. In twentieth century America the corporation is the most important economic institution. In the broader traditions of sociology and anthropology, an institution is only one form of social control and economic institutions are only one kind of institution. For our purposes, attention will be focused on economic institutions and economic social controls. Social control is all pervasive in the modern economy. Three kinds of social control are exercised: (1) Institutional control of individual behavior, (2) Corporate control of markets, and (3) Uncoordinated political control of the economy.

To Thorstein Veblen, control of individual behavior was exercised through the habits of thought learned by individuals as they worked for a living. To John R. Commons, such control was exercised through the evolving working rules of the going concerns in which people worked. Although the isolated individual human organism (abstract economic man) has impulses and reacts to physical stimuli, the actual content or meaning of these impulses and the acceptable reactions to them are learned from other human beings and from the institutionally-determined role-demands they place on each other. Social controls teach us society's norms and how to conform to them. In short, social controls enter into even the most simple individual act. But social controls do not control us like strings control puppets. Rather, for individuals, they are guides to what is acceptable or unacceptable behavior under the circumstances.

Social controls cannot be avoided for we are all members of institutions, voluntarily or involuntarily. We all must perform an institutional role of some kind and it is through performing institutionally-determined roles that we learn how and why to act. As members of a family, students in school, corporate employees, church members, soldiers and citizens, we learn what to do, how to do it, and why. As we do so, we internalize these norms, and develop our own consciences. In short, social control of individual behavior is exercised through institutions, whether or not these institutions are humane and consciously planned or inhumane and traditional. Yet this is only one kind of social control.

Another kind of social control is exercised by the market, not the "free" market of the nineteenth century but the imperfect, monopolistic, administered market of the twentieth. The institutionalist literature on administered markets has become massive, but a brief outline of the most recent work will suffice.[16]

John Kenneth Galbraith explains that our economy is now a dual economy. One part still approximates the "free" market system; the other part is a planning system. In the planning system, markets are administered by the managerial hierarchies of conglomerate corporations possessing the market power necessary to supplant or manipulate the "free" give and take of supply and demand. The result is, among other things, a serious social imbalance. Too many resources are devoted to private production in the planning sector; too few resources devoted to the provision of public goods and production in the unplanned sector.

Alfred Eichner explains, very carefully and analytically, how these huge corporations, "the megacorp," actually administer markets in such a way as to maintain a high "corporate levy." The unintended result of this private corporate planning is *stagflation* — high unemployment and high inflation. Eichner's theory provides a substitute for the old laws of supply and demand which applied to the individual competition of a former era.

The political implications of Galbraith and Eichner are quite apparent. The modern economy is in need of democratically coordinated economic planning within the market system to direct the actions of corporate power centers (the megacorps) in the private planning system toward the public purpose. Since much of the economy is already planned privately, it is essential that public planning bring the activities and interests of the small competitive sector into the democratic planning process. Furthermore, the private interests and plans of geographical regions, industrial sectors, and individual firms all need to be coordinated by the public planning process where attention can be constantly focused, democratically, on the general public interest. In this way, the existing private planning processes can be raised above the disparate private interests they now serve to the service of the general public interest.

So in addition to the institutional control of individual behavior and the megacorp control of markets, a third kind of soical control is needed and is painfully being born – the political control of the

economy. Federal, state, and local government regulation is now pervasive, but it is also unplanned. That is, political controls are largely
uncoordinated. Different federal programs and agencies often contradict each other and contradictions among levels of government also
occur. J. Ron Stanfield refers to the chaotic nature of contemporary
political controls as "interventionist drift." This interventionist drift
must develop into democratic, coordinated planning if the modern
economy is to serve the public purpose. At least that is the conclusion
of those economists, most of whom call themselves institutional economists, who have become disenchanted with the neoclassical core and
who have taken seriously the progress made by sociologists and anthropologists working in the broad area of social control. Institutionalists
begin with the instrumentalist view that people can and should democratically determine their own fate. Next they add two facts: First,
extensive social control of individuals is exerted already through the
institutionalized roles they must play in the modern economy; second,
extensive control of markets already is exerted in the planning sector
through the power of megacorps. Then they draw the *institutionalist
planning imperative* — democratic, coordinated planning must be the
next evolutionary stage of our economy if we are to bend the private
purpose of the megacorp to the public purpose of democratic society.[17]

Although ignored by the mainstream, institutionalists continue forg-
ing new insights into how the modern economy actually works and
how it could work. A notable example is Adolph Lowe who has been
probing the problem of how to achieve individual freedom in our complex society with its need for coordination of individual actions and
restraint of concentrated power. According to Lowe, we need to learn
how to replace the "irrational constraints" of our corporate capitalism
with "rational constraints" of a planned society responsive to the
democratic process.[18] The unmistakable thrust of institutional economics is toward democratic planning.

Yet this new thrust in economics runs counter to the neoclassical
core of mainstream economics. The institutionalist's view even runs
counter to the half-hearted Keynesian revolution. Institutionalist's
and Keynesians agree that Say's Law does not hold. But from there
the two schools of thought begin to part company. Most Keynesians
argue that aggregate demand management by the state is sufficient to
remedy the unemployment flaw of modern capitalism. Some Keynesians go a bit further and suggest the need for antitrust policy; a few

"wayward institutionalists" even agree. But Keynesian demand management never gets at the entrenched power of the megacorps to administer markets and prices, so more aggregate demand usually means more inflation, less aggregate demand means less employment. The Keynesian "trust-busters" mean well but will cost the industrial economy dearly, by reducing economies of scale and economies of planning, if they succeed in dispersing corporate power by breaking up our planned industrial system. The institutionalists would keep the industrial plant intact but turn it to account; make it serve the public purpose through democratic comprehensive planning.

With the shortcomings of Keynesian aggregate demand management becoming increasingly evident, more and more citizens and economists are taking the institutionalist planning imperative seriously. In short, the need for comprehensive democratic planning has become obvious. And the old belief that planning and its required social control interfere with the exercise of man's "free will" has become very difficult to hold in view of two institutionalist conclusions: Man's "will" is shaped by the institutionally-determined roles he plays in the first place, and most of his markets now are administered by Eichner's megacorp.

Protective Responses

The need for comprehensive democratic planning is becoming increasingly urgent; however, many economists are adhering to government nonintervention even more doggedly. Along with and in support of this new conservative tone, the ancient quantity theory of money has been resurrected as the Monetarist School of economics and an old philosophy known to economists as subjective utilitarianism has been reborn as the New Austrian School of economics. These developments have served to further insulate the neoclassical core of mainstream theory from criticism. Each "new" school, both the Austrian and the Monetarist, proposes a major change in economic methodology, the effect of which protects the core of neoclassical theory from the new institutional reality.

The institutionalist attack on the mainstream has to do with assumptions, but it centers around the issue of social control. To the critic, the following assumptions are crucial. Along with their policy implications, they represent the core of neoclassical theory: If we assume that Say's Law holds, then Keynesian control of aggregate demand is not necessary to maintain full employment. If we assume that prices are freely determined by competitive supply and demand, then price controls are not necessary. If we assume that production is conducted by independent entrepreneurs maximizing their profits in perfect competition without "externalities," then market competition controls their behavior and the need for formal social control is minimized. But the need for such social control is minimized only to the extent that the assumptions hold. Furthermore, the fact that observations show that the opposite of the assumptions is the rule is becoming more evident every year as empirical research in the social sciences continues to advance.

The positivists in economics, led by Milton Friedman's new method of inquiry, tell us that "unrealistic" assumptions can be ignored. Comparison of "predictions" with empirical observations is all that really matters. On the other hand, the New Austrian Economists go even further. They support a method of inquiry which asserts that economic principles cannot be refuted by empirical observation.[19]

The methodology of the resurgent Austrians is straightforward. Economic agents make choices based on their subjective, individual evaluations of alternatives. Furthermore, due to the pervasiveness of ignorance and error in the real world of human action, the economic logic of choice cannot explain actual individual choices in concrete situations. Economics simply cannot produce "predictions" to compare with historical or empirical observations. Hence, economic theory is the logic of subjective choice and cannot be tested by comparing predictions (theoretical implications) with observations. This subjectivist position will be referred to as the S-twist.

The new method of inquiry used by the resurgent Monetarists is equally straightforward though diametrically opposed to that of the Austrians. Instead of the S-twist, the Monetarists use the F-twist, so named by Paul Samuelson. According to the F-twist, a theory can only be tested by comparing its "predictions" with observations. A theory's unrealistic assumptions about perfect competition and so forth are irrelevant. First, let us look in more detail at the F-twist followed by a detailed analysis of the S-twist.

The new twist given to economics inquiry by Milton Friedman looks deceptively like accepted scientific method. Friedman fools even himself, for he claims that his method is *the* method for testing hypotheses.

The way to test a hypothesis, Friedman explains, is to deduce a state-ment (prediction) from it and check the statement with observed re-ality. In this way, the economist should sift the valid from the invalid hypotheses. So far, so good. But now Friedman adds the twist. If a hypothesis is based on assumptions, as it is in economics, the realism of assumptions should not be subjected to the usual comparison with reality. Only the predictions should be tested, not the assumptions. Testing the assumptions for realism, Friedman claims, leads to con-fusion and impedes consensus. Testing assumptions directly to see if they are realistic does impede consensus in economics. Friedman is correct, for that is why institutional economists do not share in the neoclassical consensus that government should not intervene in eco-nomic processes. The neoclassical assumptions are unrealistic, so in-stitutional economists reject neoclassical hypotheses. Free markets where individuals compete face to face, as in Adam Smith's day, no longer exist in large areas of the American economy. To assume that they do and then to go about "testing predictions" based on unreal-istic assumptions is the height of folly.

Friedman himself is confused when he argues that testing the real-ism of assumptions leads to confusion. Quite the contrary is the case: Not testing assumptions to determine their realism is the source of confusion in neoclassical economics. Unrealistic theories are irrelevant. Economic principles which applied to Adam Smith's world can be manipulated until they "predict" correctly once in a while, even in the twentieth century, where they clearly do not apply. But why do so, when we know that the economic conditions of the eighteenth cen-tury, which made the principles realistic in the first place, have long since passed from the scene? There is no valid reason, except that doing so protects the assumptions so essential to maintaining faith in neo-classical economics.

Of course, it took Friedman some time to formulate his new method of inquiry. Its roots can be traced to his 1946 review of a Keynesian treatise by Oskar Lange (Price Flexibility and Employment).[20] In his book, Lange criticized faith in government nonintervention because he believed that the conditions favoring it had passed. In particular, Lange argued that a lower price for a factor of production would in-crease the use of that factor only under special conditions. He also argued that such conditions were not met under twentieth-century capitalism. In other words, Lange concluded that our present economy would not generate full employment without government action. At least a modicum of political control was necessary because Say's Law no longer holds. Friedman strongly objected to Lange's book, labeling it mere "taxonomic theorizing" because Lange generated no formal "predictions."

An empirical foundation is essential to a science, but Friedman's insistence that the realism of assumptions is irrelevant cuts off economic science from its empirical foundation. That empirical foundation has to do with the nature of actual competition (administered markets are replacing "free" ones) and the nature of the social controls, that is, institutionally-determined roles and social norms, that shape people. The F-twist insulates economics from the empirical observations which should form its empirical foundation and then focuses attention on prediction, when institutionalists and other critical economists have a long tradition of refusing to make positive predictions. The F-twist also protects the faith in government nonintervention from Keynesian attack and institutionalist criticism by labeling institutionalists and Keynesians (Lange) as unscientific because they do not make predictions in the first place (at least the institutionalists refrain from doing so).

Adolph Lowe argues that economics, to be useful, should reverse the prediction test entirely. That is, rather than predicting a future or unknown condition and then testing the prediction, economists should first decide on a desired future outcome and then devise ways and means of achieving it.[21] This is the method of inquiry followed by institutional economists.

If the F-twist is not sufficient to protect an unrealistic faith in the continued beneficence of the market, a much older methodology is available. The S-twist of the Austrian School provides an ironclad defense against objective facts. Ludwig von Mises provides us with the clearest explanation of Austrian subjectivism as a method of inquiry in his *Ultimate Foundation of Economic Science*. Mises prefers the phrase "methodological individualism" to subjectivism, but the essence of his Austrian position is that only the subjective feelings of individuals are "real." All else, ultimately, is fabrication. Institutions, Mises refers to them as "collectives," are particularly suspect as building blocks in any systematic explanation of human behavior. Institutions, Mises insists, simply do not exist as real objects of social inquiry. According to Mises, an institution or collective is nothing more than a group of people, each one of whom has "chosen" to participate in the institution, the institution itself ceases to exist when the individuals composing it "choose" to leave it. Hence, Mises concludes, the proper method of inquiry is to explore the subjective feelings and logic of individuals, not the objective roles people perform in institutions nor the objective norms people learn in social intercourse.

The novice in economics, following Mises's argument up to this point, will conclude that Mises wants to use psychology, the study of the individual, as the starting point in his method of inquiry: But not so! Having rejected sociology as a reality base for economics, the stalwart Mises is not about to allow the objective findings of psychologists to intrude upon his subjective economics. Instead of relying on the objective findings of sociology, anthropology, psychology, history, or any science whatsoever, Mises and the Austrian economists try to construct their own prescientific science. Mises calls it "economic praxeology." No use looking it up in the dictionary, the phrase is not there. Mises made it up. This new prescientific science is straight out of *Alice in Wonderland,* for it is a science which ignores the findings of other sciences because it is prescientific.

Before Mises straightened us out, a few economists thought that economics was related in some way to human experience through history. But economics, a branch of "praxeology," according to Mises and the other Austrians, is not historical. It is *not* derived from man's experience through time because, again according to Mises, we cannot "...interpret our concept of action as a precipitate of experience."[22] Human action is not to be understood by using history as a kind of research lab for the economist, according to Mises. The experience of man through time does not organize *itself* into categories and principles or general trends. Rather, "history" is organized by the concepts, principles, and theories brought to bear upon it by the mind of the historian. So far so good, but Mises then argues that his "economic praxeology" is the appropriate source of these unavoidable, *apriori* concepts, principles, and theories. Now, critics of mainstream economics who argue that no apriori knowledge at all need be brought to bear upon the study of economic history are simply wrong. Mises is correct on that score. Nevertheless, the apriori concepts, principles, and theories that the investigator brings to bear upon economic questions do not have to come from the Mises "economic praxeology"; nor must they come from the neoclassical core of mainstream economics. Instead, they can come from the general theory of social control as formulated by sociologists and anthropologists. But social control theory and the empirical historical findings of the other social sciences negate the neoclassical core of economics.

The positivist F-twist of Friedman and the Monetarists means that the realism of assumptions is irrelevant. But at least Friedman will accept observations about the empirical validity of predictions. The subjectivist S-twist of Mises and the Austrians, however, means that empirical observations of human behavior cannot contradict or refute propositions of economics. Experience, Mises argues, "... can never falsify any theorem ..."[23] He is correct if economics is no more than the pure logic of subjectively interpreted individual action (economic praxeology). But if it is only that, then economics is irrelevant to our current problems. The F-twist of Friedman may save assumptions from the charge that they are unrealistic but the S-twist makes them impregnable and irrelevant. Mises draws a barrier between the objective world of experience and the subjective world of the mind. He insists that no connection can be made between the objective and subjective, for all human action originates in the subjective free will of the individual, not in the objective world of institutional roles and social norms studied by other social sciences. With his refusal to allow the findings of psychologists, sociologists, anthropologists, or historians into his "economic praxeology," his study of economic problems leads nowhere. It begins and ends within the subjective mind of the hypothetical individual.

For the social scientist who dares to probe into institutional roles and social norms, with an eye toward reforming them to improve man's lot, Mises has nothing but wrath. Such meddlers, Mises argues, are driven by a "dictatorial complex." Mises believes, such people want to substitute their own personal desires for the personal desires of everyone else. Mises, clearly, has a point: The temptation is very strong for highly educated intellectuals and academics to tell others what to do. Intellectual, social, political, and financial elites have all been far more influential than their numbers would justify in our democratic society. Nevertheless, even though Mises's distaste for elitism and paternalism is justifiable as a defense of freedom and democracy, the use of that distaste to deflect empirical criticism from the neoclassical core of economic theory is not. The first use is supportive of freedom and free inquiry. The second stops free inquiry at a wall labeled "subjective individuality."

From the sociological-anthropological studies of social controls and from studies of imperfect competition, monopolistic competition, and oligopoly, institutional economists and others have forged a devastating objective attack on the assumptions supporting the neoclassical core of mainstream economics. Yet in spite of the growing empirical evidence, the core holds. More than that, it expands. Protected by the F-twist and the S-twist, an ultra-orthodox neoclassical revival is taking place. In the Monetarist School, the revival has gone far beyond the positivist's license to predict. The School's leading spokesman, Milton Friedman, is no longer satisfied with testing predictions. In his latest work with his wife Rose Friedman, he makes prescriptions, not predictions.[24] The Friedmans prescribe no less than seven constitutional amendments to limit either the federal or state government's ability to tax imports and exports, to regulate prices, wages, and occupations, to levy progressive income taxes, to finance deficits, and to issue nominal-interest rate securities. In short, in a book entitled *Free to Choose*, the leading proponent of pure positive economics in the United States proposes to dramatically reduce the freedom of the public – acting through government – to choose to regulate its economy.

The Friedmans are no longer positivists. They have become social activists. Taking the neoclassical core of mainstream theory to its practical conclusions, they have become advocates of government nonintervention.[25] As such, they can no longer retreat into pure positive economics to protect that neoclassical core when its assumptions come under empirical attack. They must stand pat and face the criticism without retreating behind the F-twist, or lose all credibility. The S-twist of the Austrians, on the other hand, leads to a know-nothing position in economics. If all phenomena of importance are purely subjective individual feelings, then economics has no handle on the external world of objective events. At least with the positivist F-twist, there exists a connection, albeit only a partial one, between theory and observation. But with the subjectivist S-twist, even that partial connection (testing predictions) is severed. Criticism need never be faced head-on.

CONCLUSION

Either make "predictions" from unrealistic assumptions or contemplate the subjective workings of a hypothetical individual. These are the two cul-de-sacs into which mainstream economists have been backed by the march of events. But if a foray is made into the real world of economic problems, all defenses are lost, and the critics must be faced. Political relevance can only be acquired if objective reality is faced. Beginning with Adam Smith, the principal classical economist, and continuing through Alfred Marshall, the principal neoclassical economist, the evolution of objective reality has been most unkind to mainstream economics. The free market where the individual consumer and producer bought and sold face to face in Adam Smith's time has been revolutionized by the evolution of the corporation.

Vertical and horizontal integration produced massive corporate bureaucracies. These organizations possessed the power to implement the new technologies of mass production on a grand scale. As they did so, the most efficient industrial system in the world was constructed and the affluent consumer could purchase the necessities of life with a fraction of his income. These organizations also possessed the power to drive up the prices of their products, but the long run loss of profits suffered in single markets constrained them. The conglomerate changed all that. Freed from the constraint of any one market, prices can be raised quickly to tap out a market because other markets also can be tapped out, as needed. The old assumptions about market competition no longer apply.

Regulation of the economy has also undergone considerable change. The heavy-handed regulation of the Crown gave way to Adam Smith's invisible hand as mercantilism was replaced by the free market system. But the golden age of the market, dynamic and exciting as it was, gave way to the age of the robber baron in railroading, petroleum, steel, and so on. Industry-specific regulation was the public response to these early corporate abuses. This regulator was easily coopted. Deregulation was called for and the Carter administration carried it out. But in the meantime, a new regulatory response was being born. Function-specific regulators rather than industry-specific ones were created. Environmentalists pushed for and got the EPA, safety advocates got OSHA, minorities EEOC. These new regulators really work because they are not coopted so easily. Nor are they servants of special interests, lest one considers clean air, clean water, a safe workplace, and equal employment opportunities to be "special interests." The new regulator is no longer the servant of the Crown nor the servant of the industry being regulated. For the first time, regulation serves the public interest, and serves it relatively well – hence the outcry from business groups against the new regulators. The old assumptions about misguided or coopted regulation no longer apply.

But, in the world of Adam Smith the assumptions applied. They were realistic then. Now they are not – hence the popularity of Milton Friedman's argument that unrealistic assumptions are irrelevant. Going even further, Mises and the Austrians would make all of economics irrelevant with their "economic praxeology." This is why mainstream economics offers so little guidance to the economic problems of the day. The social and economic changes creating those problems have left the core of mainstream economics untouched. Yet now that laissez-faire core, protected by the F and S twists, has given rise to the most wreckless of free enterprisers — the supply-side economists. Supply-siders are totally oblivious to the realities of our twentieth-century economy, dominated as it is by huge corporate bureaucracies. So, naturally, their theories and policies, when applied to the modern corporate economy, do far more harm than good.

PART 2

Reforming
the Corporation

*No place is so strongly fortified
that money cannot capture it.*

CICERO

6 CORPORATE BUREAUCRACY

INTRODUCTION

Now that the extent of our social and economic problems has been described and the fallacies of Reaganomics and of supply-side economics have been explained, the *real* source of our socioeconomic problems must be identified. Furthermore, effective ways of dealing with those problems must be explored. These are the tasks of PART II: REFORMING THE CORPORATION. The title of this part of the book should give the reader an indication of why our economy is sagging and of what we should do about it. Our economy is failing because our principal economic institution, the corporation, is failing. The failure is not due to a reduction in the efficiency of the market. The corporation is far more efficient than the market and the millions of independent businesses it would take to keep the market competitive. That is why corporate administration has replaced market bargaining: The corporation proved itself more efficient than the market in the rough and tumble world of real life. However, corporate efficiency has not been passed on to the working and consuming public. Instead, it has built huge corporate empires, bureaucratic organizations of immense size and power serving the private corporate purpose, not the public purpose. The power of corporate bureaucracy is the source of our problems. Turning that power to public account is the solution.

Of course, that is much easier said than done. Chapter 6 explains the nature and extent of bureaucracy, both public and corporate. Chapter 7 contains a proposal for revitalizing corporate bureaucracy. Chapters 8 and 9 discuss how the revitalized corporation can be guided toward the public purpose.

THE NATURE AND EXTENT OF BUREAUCRACY

Bureaucracy Explained

At the close of the twentieth century, any organization, private or public, composed of more than a few hundred people either has become bureaucratized or has remained relatively inefficient. As the scale and pace of life have picked up, more and more organizations in both the public and private sectors all over the world have come to use the bureaucratic form. One might even refer to the close of the twentieth century as The Age of Bureaucracy. This is in spite of the fact that in common usage, bureaucracy refers to the slow, routine-fixated operation of a government agency resulting from the petty application of complicated rules and procedures. Bureaucracy often connotes the labyrinthine workings of Charles Dickens's "circumlocution office."[1] As it is commonly perceived, bureaucracy is hopelessly inefficient and is found primarily in government. But that view is a partial one. Bureaucracies are found in both the public and private sectors and range from the very efficient to the very inefficient. Clearly, a more scientific view is needed to complete the common perception of bureaucracy: A *bureaucracy* is any large organization composed of hierarchically ordered departments (bureaus) run by specialists according to formal rules. It is a precision instrument designed for controlling or dominating the actions of a large group of people pursuing a common objective.[2] Of course, this precision instrument can become dulled or distorted. It can become very inefficient even though its potential effiency is considerable. Furthermore, a thoroughly bureaucratic way of life can stifle human initiative and creativity.

A statement by C. Wright Mills could easily serve as an upper bureaucrat's prayer, and as such explains the purpose of bureaucracy: "Between decision and execution, between command and obedience, let there be reflex."[3] In short, the purpose of a bureaucracy is to insure that everyone in a large organization performs specialized tasks as instructed, without personal factors entering into the duties. Bureaucracies are constructed and formal rules enforced to facilitate the application of specific rules to all cases, to coordinate the functions of diverse specialists, to maintain strict subordination to authority, and to do so with precision and efficiency. A bureaucracy's ultimate purpose is to maintain precise organizational performance. Or, from a negative perspective, to maintain standardized, day-by-day operations like a machine, even though the cogs are human beings, not metal gears. A bureaucratic machine can be applied to any immediate purpose — making goods for a profit, regulating the profit-making of other organizations, processing welfare recipients, educating students, executing a war, bargaining collectively, or even, administering justice.

A fully-developed ideal bureaucracy is characterized by seven features: (1) division of labor, (2) hierarchy of authority, (3) impersonal treatment of individuals, (4) formal rules, (5) appointment of officials, (6) merit and/or seniority promotion, and (7) specialized administrative staff.

Division of labor in a bureaucracy involves far more than the traditional division of labor in factories. Each bureaucrat's official duties are delineated carefully in written documents. Then each official set of duties is grouped with geographically or functionally similar duties. Such groupings are the bureaus of which a bureaucracy is composed. Each bureaucrat within each bureau is then held strictly accountable for the performance of his/her specific duties. In this way a complex set of activities is broken down, specified, and assigned to the hundreds of different people in the organization. Each person is made to fit into a specialized niche within the organization and is held accountable to those immediately above.

Each niche within each grouping of niches (bureau) is subjected to the formal authority of a bureau head. Each bureau head is subjected to the formal authority of a higher official. The higher officials are grouped together and subjected to the authority of still higher officials and so on through several layers of authority. The only exception is the top official of the organization who is usually accountable to an outside political or economic power. The result is a hierarchy of authority, familiar to us all as the pyramid-shaped organization chart.

Within this hierarchy each bureaucrat is treated, not as a person with likes and dislikes or friends and family, but as the occupant of a particular bureaucratic niche with formal responsibilities and authorities. At least that is the ideal. In other words, the people in the organization are fitted into the organization's slots; the slots are not fitted to the people. The relations between bureaucrats and between bureaucrats and "outsiders" (clients, customers, suppliers, or whatever) are highly impersonal. In the ideal bureaucracy, relations are cold and precise, focused purely on utilitarian objectives. Clients are cases;

customers are accounts; suppliers are vouchers or contracts. Fellow bureaucrats are subordinates, superiors, or potential competitors for promotion.

The formal rules of a bureaucracy are the guide to proper behavior. Written rules, often very elaborate and detailed, specify the duties of each bureaucrat. Learning these rules and learning how to apply them to all cases are important technical skills which must be acquired on the job itself. Rules and rule applications become ends to each bureaucrat rather than means. Keeping track of the rules — filing, referencing, retrieving and distributing them — absorb a very significant portion of the bureaucracy's resources. In a bureaucracy run amuck, files and file clerks or computer tapes and operators become legion as the rules and records of their application multiply. Strangulation by "red tape" is the result. In an ideal bureaucracy, on the other hand, the formal rules ensure fair and equal treatment according to precise, universal standards within a reasonable period of time.

A bureaucracy is not a democracy. In fact, it is antidemocratic. Officials within the organization are appointed by higher authorities, not elected by peers or constituents. Appointment by superiors insures loyalty to the bureaucratic hierarchy itself. Original appointment usually requires formal training of some kind and university degrees or professional certifications. The formal training period can be quite lengthy and the certificates or degrees difficult to obtain. The result, if ideal, is the appointment of highly qualified specialists. If less than ideal, the result can be the appointment of "over-qualified," frustrated misfits, straitjacketed into boring dead-end jobs.

Once appointed, bureaucrats are promoted according to individual merit and/or seniority, at least in theory. Merit is often ascertained through formal examinations as in civil service systems or through the careful, formal evaluations of higher executives as in large American corporations. When the promotion system works well the result is a "meritocracy." Bureaucrats who perform their functions best are promoted up the hierarchy to levels of greater authority and responsibility. When it works poorly the result is a "mediocracy." Bureaucrats who never rock the boat and are timidly sycophantic are promoted for their rigidly conservative, obsequious, and mediocre performance.

Holding the bureaucratic organization together requires a large, specialized administrative staff. Not only must the rules and the records of how the rules have been applied be filed, retrieved, and distributed, but massive flows of information up from the ranks must be tabulated, directed, and interpreted. Also, reams of specific orders must be transmitted from the top down. Furthermore, the performance of each bureau and bureaucrat must be measured, recorded, reported, and evaluated against the rules and orders. In large bureaucracies the administrative staff can number in the thousands. Accountants, file clerks, computer specialists, typists, and platoons of various office personnel maintain the flow of information and implement the rules and orders.

The ultimate purpose of bureaucracy is the precise maintenance of organizational performance. The bureaucratic form is designed to make sure that organizations perform precisely as they were intended. Why then, are most of us so opposed to the extension of the bureaucratic form? Bureaucracy has both costs and benefits. On the benefit side, bureaucracy at its best is an efficient way of organizing and coordinating the work of a large group of people. On the cost side, the impersonality can be most alienating, particularly to clients dependent upon welfare bureaucracies. Individuals are unique. Each of us has our own special needs and each of us live under special circumstances. Yet bureaucracies make no allowance for special cases. When presented with a truly unique or novel case, a bureaucracy is stymied. The special case does not fit the rules, hence no *one* bureaucrat will take responsibility for deciding what to do. Consequently, nothing is done and the individual languishes, a casualty of bureaucratic buck-passing.

Another very real cost of bureaucracy is secrecy and the potential for conducting clandestine operations. In the post-Watergate era we are all aware of the organizational threats to individual liberty. But long before Watergate, Max Weber explained, "Bureaucratic administration always tends to be an administration of 'secret sessions:' in so far as it can, it hides its knowledge and action from criticism."[4]

Impersonality, inability to deal with special cases or new situations, secrecy and erosion of civil liberty are all real difficulties of our bureaucratized society. But these difficulties are not the sole cause of the general public outcry against bureaucracy. Since bureaucracy is a system of power and control, what one thinks about it often depends on whether one is in power and using it to exercise control over others or is out of power and is having bureaucracy used to control him. In power struggles between groups, bureaucratization is used as a weapon. For example, a bureaucracy can originate from below when unions attempt to use organized power to control the actions of management. But a bureaucracy can also originate from above when management tries to control the worker. Furthermore, a bureaucracy can originate in the public sector when the state organizes to control the clash of private interests or when the state attempts to pursue the public interest. Hence, nearly everyone has a bone to pick with bureaucracy. Workers see managerial bureaucracy as a threat; managers see union bureaucracy as a threat. Yet bureaucracy is merely a means of struggle and domination, not an independent cause. The causes run deeper. C. Wright Mills's cynical remark about the managerial response to "bureaucracy" probably applies to us all: "When the corporate official objects to 'bureaucracy' he means of course the programs of the Federal Government, and then only in so far as they seem to be against the interests of his own private business bureaucracy."[5]

Bureaucracies are composed of two parallel structures, a formal and an informal one. The formal structure is reflected in the organizational chart and the written rules and procedures. Not a trace of the informal structure will be found in the written documents, but it is as important as the formal structure. The informal structure is composed of a network of shifting personal friendships and alliances, of "extra-legal" or *sub rosa* ways of getting things done within the organization without going through formal channels. The formal structure is composed of a more rigid hierarchy of official authority and responsibility, of explicit and officially-proper ways of doing things through prescribed channels. Gossip and personal favors flow through the informal structure. Official orders and reports and official performance of duties flow through the formal structure.

The informal structure brings the personal touch into bureaucracy through the back door. Informal, personal relations between bureaucrats can be used to expedite action when the formal, "correct" procedures are too slow or cumbersome. In this way, special or critical cases can be handled effectively even though the formal rules do not apply. Hence, the informal structure often supplements the formal one by allowing the organization to adjust quickly to new circumstances and by allowing the rules to be bent, or humanized when needed. Yet the informal structure can also subvert the formal one. Friends in high places can help one avoid the rules and procedures entirely. Special favors can be granted or denied to clients, customers, or proteges. Friends can be rewarded; enemies punished. Personal loyalties and animosities can replace the formal rules as guides to action. In an advanced form, such organizational pathology can result in paralysis as the organization becomes factionalized by competing cliques and as the rules become things to fight with rather than work with. How these bureaucratic pathologies affect us, particularly those of us working in corporate bureaucracies, will be discussed below, but first the extent and trend of bureaucratization in general will be explored.

Extent and Trend of Bureaucratization

The current hue and cry against government bureaucracy has distorted public understanding of the bureaucratic phenomenon, even though the concern about bureaucracy in general may be well-founded. For example, the small businessman, that bastion of American values whose last refuge is in agriculture, services, and trade, is being ground to dust as giant corporate bureaucracies push against each other for larger shares of the trade and services markets, and as state and federal bureaucracies attempt to regulate the struggle. If not already squeezed into bankruptcy or merger, the small businessman fears being regulated out of existence. He often cannot pay the minimum wages, meet the safety standards, and afford the environmental safeguards that government bureaucrats impose on all businesses to protect the public from being victimized by the corporate behemoths in their struggle for supremacy. Crushed by both corporate and public bureaucracy, the small businessman cries out against the regulations of *public* bureaucracy. The public picks up the cry for help and confusion spreads.

So in this heated atmosphere, it is important to keep in mind just what a bureaucracy is. A bureaucracy is a formal way of organizing a large group of people telling them what to do; and making sure that they do it. This means that a *bureaucrat* is an organizational official or staff member who tells other people what to do and/or makes sure that they do it. This definition of a bureaucrat, a functionary who tells others what to do, and/or makes sure that they do it, will serve as a simple means of measuring the extent of bureaucratization in the American workplace. For if the number of people giving, enforcing and processing orders rises relative to the number carrying them out, then bureaucratization has increased. As we shall see, this is what has happened in most sectors of the economy, both public and private.

One of the first social scientists to measure the extent of bureaucratization in the United States was Seymour Melman in his 1951 study
of administrative overhead in manufacturing. Reinhard Bendix, in
Work and Authority in Industry also constructed some early estimates
of bureaucratization. This section can be considered an update and
extension of their earlier works.[6] My description will seek answers to
three basic questions: (1) How many of us are bureaucrats? (2) Where
do bureaucrats work? (3) Is the number of bureaucrats rising? Before
taking the plunge into detailed census data, a thumbnail sketch of the
changing U.S. occupational structure is in order. The U.S. Bureau of
Labor Statistics recently prepared a major study of the American occupational structure, with a base year of 1974 and a projection into
1985. Table 6.1 presents the highlights of that study.

Table 6.1 contains seven major occupational categories. Unfortunately, none of the categories can be classified as purely bureaucratic.
The first three categories come the closest. Yet is is not possible to
claim that all clerical workers, all professional, technical, and kindred

TABLE 6.1

U.S. Occupational Structure 1974, 1985

| | Millions of Workers | | Percent of Total | | Percent change |
Occupation	1974	1985	1974	1985	1974–1985
All occupations	85.9	103.4	100	100	20
Professional, technical and kindred workers	12.3	16.0	14	15	29
Managers, officials, and proprietors	8.9	10.9	10	11	22
Clerical workers	15.0	20.1	17	19	34
Sales and service workers	16.8	20.9	19	20	25
Crafts and kindred workers	11.5	13.8	13	13	20
Operatives and nonfarmer laborers*	18.3	20.0	21	19	9
Farmers and farmworkers	3.0	1.9	4	2	–39

*Largely unskilled and semiskilled industrial and transportation workers

Source: Max L. Carey, "Revised Occupational Projections to 1985," Bureau
of Labor Statistics, *Monthly Labor Review*, 99 (November, 1976), Table 2.

workers, or all managers, officials, and proprietors are bureaucrats, because not all of them are involved in telling other people what to do and/or making sure that they do it. At the other extreme, the last three categories of Table 6.1 contain very few bureaucrats. Farmers and farmworkers, crafts and kindred workers, operatives and nonfarm laborers generally do not tell others what to do. Instead, they end up doing it themselves. They are production rather than nonproduction workers.

Employment in each of the first three occupational categories is expected to grow faster than total employment. But employment in the last three occupational categories of Table 6.1 is expected to grow at a rate equal to total employment in one case, grow at a rate less than total employment in the second case, and actually decline in the third. Excluding the highly mixed category of sales and service workers leaves the following rather weak conclusion: Employment in occupations with very few bureaucrats is expected to grow at rates equal to or less than total employment, while employment in occupations with large numbers of bureaucrats is expected to grow at rates faster than total employment. In short, it appears that a kind of "bureaucratization hypothesis" can be supported. That is, the number of bureaucrats working in America appears to be rising relative to the size of the work force.

Let us now turn to detailed census data for some fleshing out of the "bureaucratization hypothesis." The Bureau of the Census has published reliable and fairly comparable censuses of most of the major industrial classifications for as far back as 1947. The census establishment data on employment gives the total number of employees and the number of production or nonsupervisory workers for each of the major industrial classifications. Subtracting the latter from the former yields the number of employees not engaged directly in producing a good or a service. By a kind of process of elimination, the number of these "nonproductive" workers can be taken as a proxy for the number of bureaucrats in the work force: Most workers not engaged directly in producing a good or a service can be assumed to be telling other workers what and how to produce or can be assumed to be making sure that other workers do as they are told. That is, most workers not engaged in doing it themselves can be called bureaucrats – those that tell others what to do and/or make sure that they do it. Therefore, the number of nonproduction or supervisory employees, derived by subtracting the number of production or nonsupervisory workers from the total number of employees in different industries, will be used as a proxy for the number of bureaucrats in the different industries. This counts as bureaucrats the clerical staff, cleaning staff, and all others not directly producing a good or a service.

Furthermore, the ratio of production workers to bureaucrats (as defined operationally above) can serve as a simple measurement or index of the degree of bureaucratization in an economy or in an industry. The ratio can be interpreted as the number of production workers "supporting" each nonproduction worker (bureaucrat). This means that a fall in the ratio indicates a rise in the degree of bureaucratization and a rise in the ratio indicates a fall in bureaucratization. Diagram 6.1 shows the ratio for the nonagricultural private sector of the United States for 1947-1981. The striking decline in the ratio lends additional

DIAGRAM 6.1

Number of Production or Nonsupervisory Workers
per Nonproduction Employee
in the Private Sector (Excluding Agriculture)
1947–1981

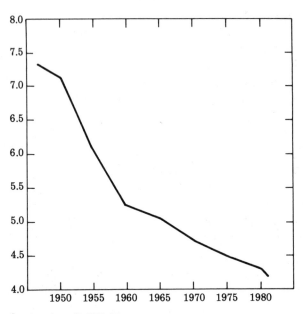

Source: Appendix Table 1A

support to the "bureaucratization hypothesis," at least for the aggregated, nonagricultural private sector. But does aggregation obscure diverging trends in different parts of the private sector? Diagrams 6.2, 6.3, and 6.4 show the ratio or "bureaucratization index" for each of the major industrial classifications. A strikingly uniform pattern emerges. The ratio falls in all industries, indicating widespread bureaucratization in the post-war U.S. economy. No divergence from the direction of the trend exists.

Although in all industries the trend is toward increased bureaucratization, the extent of the changes in the different industry ratios varies widely. In the aggregate, the ratio fell from roughly seven production workers for one bureaucrat to roughly four production workers for one bureaucrat. (See Table 1A in the Appendix at the end of this book for the precise numbers and ratios.) This represents a fall of about 40 percent over the period 1947-1981 for the aggregate ratio. In the manu-

DIAGRAM 6.2

Number of Production Workers
per Nonproduction Employee in Manufacturing
1947-1981

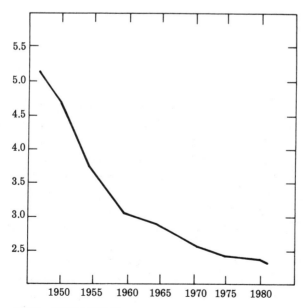

Source: Appendix Table 2A

DIAGRAM 6.3

Number of Production or Nonsupervisory Workers
per Nonproduction Employee in Mining,
Construction, and Transportation and Public Utilities
1947-1981

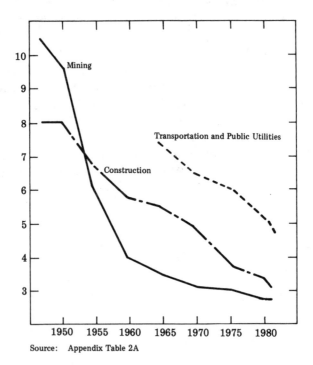

Source: Appendix Table 2A

facturing core of the economy the ratio fell roughly from five to a little over two production workers per bureaucrat, a decline of about 50 percent. The largest decline in the ratio – 70 percent – occurred in mining where production workers per bureaucrat plunged from ten to three over the period 1947 to 1981. The second largest decline was 60 percent in the construction industry where construction workers per bureaucrat fell from eight to a little over three. In wholesale and retail trade – one of the last refuges of the independent proprietor – the ratio fell about the same as the overall economy, by 40 percent. So not even in trade is the trend toward increased bureaucratization being resisted effectively. Disaggregated data exist only back to 1965 for two major industrial classifications – Services and Transportation and Public Utilities. In Services, the ratio fell by about 30 percent, over

DIAGRAM 6.4

Number of Production or Nonsupervisory Workers
per Nonproduction Employee in Trade, Finance,
Insurance, and Real estate, and Services
1947-1981

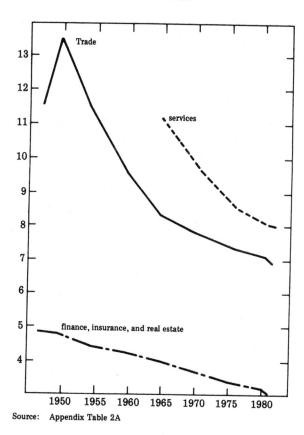

Source: Appendix Table 2A

this shorter period, from roughly eleven to eight; while the ratio fell
by only about 10 percent in Transportation and Public Utilities, a decline from about seven to about 6 production workers per bureaucrat.

Both the decline in the aggregate ratio and the declines in all of the
disaggregated ratios support the "bureaucratization hypothesis." The
needed data does not exist for agriculture so the only possible major
exception to the trend in the private sector appears to be agriculture.
Since the bastions of the independent producer and of the nonbureaucratic mode of work have long been agriculture plus trade and services,

and since neither trade nor services are going against the bureaucratization trend, agriculture is probably the last holdout. With that exception, rapid and extensive bureaucratization of the private sector has taken place in the U.S. economy since the Second World War. Fewer and fewer production workers are supporting more and more nonproduction workers.

Table 6.2 gives a brief picture of the result, in 1980, of the bureaucratization of the private sector by showing the number of bureaucrats now occupied in each industrial classification.

Unfortunately for this investigation and description, the Census Bureau does not classify government employees with respect to production versus nonproduction workers. Rather, government employees are classified according to broad function – such as defense, justice, education, or according to the level of government at which they are employed – federal, state, and local; or by branch – executive, legislative, or judicial. These classifications do not allow us to separate production from nonproduction personnel. Hence, a detailed description/investigation as was done for the private sector cannot be done at this time for the public sector.

Nevertheless, from a broad, perhaps simplistic view of the basic function of government in the United States private enterprise economy, one can support the assumption that virtually all civilian government employees are "bureaucrats." That is, since government is not sup-

TABLE 6.2

Private-Sector Bureaucrats* by Industry 1980 (in thousands)

Industry division	Number of bureaucrats
Mining	256
Construction	937
Manufacturing	6,066
Transportation and Public Utilities	847
Trade	2,489
Finance, Insurance and Real Estate	1,241
Services	1,929
Total Private-Sector Bureaucrats	13,765

*Nonproduction and/or supervisory personnel.

Source: Appendix Table 2A

posed to engage in production of private goods in a private enterprise economy, one can assume that government employees do not produce goods or services themselves; instead, they tell others how to do so and/or make sure that instructions are followed. The major exception to this reasoning is defense. But following my line of reasoning, one can conclude that virtually all civilian government employees are "bureaucrats." I do not believe it, but am willing to grant the conclusion for the sake of discussion and continued inquiry.

Table 6.3 presents the number of civilian "bureaucrats" in federal and in state and local government, the number of private-sector bureaucrats, the total number of bureaucrats, and the total number of non-farm civilian employees for the period 1947-1981. Some interesting trends have developed. First, very rapid growth has occurred in the number of state and local employees. The number of people in this category of bureaucrats increased from about three and a half million to about thirteen and a half million, an increase of 280 percent. Second, relatively slow growth has taken place in the number of federal civilian employees, whose ranks rose from slightly less than two million to about two and three-quarter million, an increase of 47 percent. The number of private-sector bureaucrats, as defined above, rose dramatically from about four and a half million to over fourteen million, an increase of 204 percent. Total public-sector bureaucrats increased from about five and a half to about sixteen and a half million. This represents an increase of 200 percent; almost identical to the percentage increase in the number of private-sector bureaucrats. Because of the rapid growth of state and local employees, the growth in public bureaucrats has kept pace with the growth of private bureaucrats, even though federal bureaucrats have been falling behind.

The number of bureaucrats in the work force, as defined here, has grown faster than the work force itself. The work force is being bureaucratized, including that portion of the work force occupied in the private sector. But bureaucracy as a social phenomenon has another dimension. Not only is the extent of bureaucratization indicated by the number of bureaucrats, but also by the size of the organizations in which they work, for bureaucracy is a phenomenon of large-scale organizations. Interestingly enough, in the civilian public sector, the fastest growth in employment has been at the state and local government level rather than at the gargantuan federal level. That is, smaller-scale state and local government organizations have grown faster than the larger-scale federal government organizations. (See Table 6.3)

TABLE 6.3

Total Private and Public Civilian "Bureaucrats" 1947-1981 (in thousands)

Year	Public employees			Private non-production employees	Total "bureau-crats"	Total nonfarm Civilian employees
	Federal	State and Local	Total			
1947	1,892	3,582	5,474	4,635	10,109	43,857
1950	1,928	4,098	6,026	4,821	10,847	45,197
1955	2,187	4,727	6,914	6,227	13,141	50,641
1960	2,270	6,083	8,353	7,320	15,673	54,189
1965	2,378	7,696	10,074	8,411	18,485	60,765
1970	2,731	9,823	12,554	10,169	22,723	70,880
1975	2,748	11,937	14,685	11,268	25,953	76,945
1980	2,869	13,576	16,445	13,765	30,210	90,316
1981	2,772	13,630	16,402	14,126	30,528	90,828

Sources: Public employees, 1947-1975, from *Employment and Earnings, United States, 1909-78*, Bulletin 1312, BLS, 1979; for 1980 and 1981, March data of each year from *Employment and Earnings*, BLS (May, 1981). Private employees from Appendix Table 1A.

The reverse has been the case in the private sector where economic concentration has long been the trend. That is, the larger-scale organizations have tended to grow faster than the smaller-scale ones in the private sector. The extent to which gigantism has come to predominate in the private sector is quite striking. For example, in 1976 corporations with over $249.9 million in assets represented only one-tenth of one percent of all active corporations but they held two-thirds of all corporate assets! This share of all assets was up from less than half in 1960.[7] Hence, in the private sector at least, the continued trend is toward larger-sized bureaucratic organizations. Like it or not, even those of us in the private sector are being drawn increasingly into bureaucracy; corporate bureaucracy, true, but bureaucracy nonetheless. Fewer and fewer of us are doing the work while more and more of us are telling the others how to do it.

THE BUREAUCRATIC LABOR MARKET

Introduction

The labor market, in our increasingly bureaucratic economy, has been altered fundamentally. It no longer resembles the free market where supply and demand are stabilized through a price adjustment process. The old price adjustment mechanism used to work as follows: If an excess supply of workers existed in an occupation, wages or salaries (the relevant price) fell. This encouraged some workers to go elsewhere in search of higher earnings and it encouraged employers to hire a few more workers at the lower wage or salary. Supply eventually equaled demand again because of the price adjustment. If an excess demand for workers existed, the price (a wage or salary) rose. The higher price attracted more workers into the occupation and induced employers to economize on the more expensive workers. Again, supply and demand were brought into "equilibrium" by the price adjustment. But in our bureaucratic economy, an administrative adjustment rather than a price adjustment is made to bring supply and demand back into "equilibrium." Of course, premiums are still paid in many occupations where workers are scarce and low wages are earned in many occupations where workers are overabundant. But increasingly, this price adjustment process is being replaced by an administrative adjustment process. The replacement is not complete, but it is widespread already.

The administrative adjustment process is used in bureaucratic occupations and it ideally works roughly like this: If an excess supply of workers exists in a particular occupation, salaries do not fall. Instead, the formal qualifications for the job are raised so that fewer workers meet the higher qualifications. The excess supply is "filtered-out" of the occupation by the higher qualifications. If an excess demand for workers in a particular occupation exists, salaries do not rise. Instead, the formal qualifications for the job are lowered so that more workers meet the lower standards. More workers are allowed into the occupation by opening up the qualifications "filter" which formerly excluded them.

Furthermore, our bureaucratic labor markets have evolved in two directions. On one hand, the recruitment of new employees has evolved into an external labor market. On the other hand, the promotion of existing employees has evolved into an internal labor market. The result of both evolutionary branches resembles less and less the old market where supply and demand are adjusted by price. Different means have evolved for administering the two labor markets. While the external market is administered through filtering, the internal market is administered through sponsorship. The end served in administering the external market is a simple one, that of institutional recruitment and selection. Corporations need a reliable supply of new recruits to fill vacancies as they occur. Administering the internal market, on the other hand, serves a more complex end, that of institutional reproduction. The top corporate roles must be filled by individuals who can be counted on to perform as their roles require. To ensure corporate survival, these roles and the individuals who perform them usually are reproduced rather than recruited. The process of institutional reproduction is no longer a market process at all. That is, the play of supply and demand have little to do with the process or with the result. The internal labor "market" is clearly a misnomer. This nonmarket process of institutional reproduction must be discussed at length below, but an introductory word about the process of institutional recruitment and selection is in order.

The external labor market is still a market, but one which now clears through a process of filtering rather than through price adjustment. If an excess supply of potential workers exists for a particular occupational vacancy, the educational credentials, test scores, moral character, etc., required to enter that occupation are raised to filter out of the occupation the excess supply. At the lower levels of the labor market a labor union usually does the filtering and the results are often accompanied by great public outcries. At the higher levels, filtering usually is done by corporate personnel managers in cooperation with educators and public officials. Then the results are called upgrading the workforce and investing in human capital. Leaving to one side the legitimacy of labor unions versus personnel experts, in neither case of filtering does the external labor market adjust through the price mechanism. Filtering is a new kind of market adjustment process, no matter who administers it.

The traditional workings of supply and demand in the labor market have all but disappeared in the bureaucratic, planned core of the private sector. They have been replaced (if they ever existed) by institutional recruitment, which sorts young people into or out of various occupational slots or ports of entry and by institutional role reproduction, which determines the differential ascents of the "sortees" up the various occupational hierarchies into which the lucky ones have been sorted. Both processes are highly selective. The first selects those who show promise of a facile adjustment to institutionalized corporate norms of behavior. The second selects those who show actual adjustment and even virtuosity.

These are strong claims, both of which run counter to the orthodox view. Yet empirical evidence of two sorts supports them. First, in a traditional, free labor market the earnings of individual workers would depend closely upon the various attributes (years of schooling, grades, cognitive skills, etc.) each brings to market. What they get should be determined by what they have to sell. But when we observe the actual earnings of different individuals, we see that such is only very loosely the case. This first sort of evidence implies that the price mechanism does not clear the market. For if it did, workers with similar characteristics would receive similar pay. But, as we will see below in more detail, they do not. The available evidence suggests there are two quite different mechanisms at work. One (institutional recruitment and selection) determines where in the corporate hierarchy the worker enters. Then, given his occupational entrance, the other mechanism (institutional role reproduction) determines the worker's actual earnings.

Needless to say, the empirical evidence relied upon here does not come from orthodox economists. Instead, it comes from sociologist Christopher Jencks and his co-workers. Jencks et al. studied numerous surveys of American males, generally aged 25 to 64, in order to determine the effects of the workers' characteristics (years of schooling, cognitive skills, personality traits, and family background) on their occupation and on their earnings. Findings on racism and sexism will not be discussed here so as not to belabor the obvious. Jencks et al. found that 55 to 60 percent of the variance in occupational status could be explained by worker characteristics, but only 24 to 28 percent of the variance in annual earnings could be so explained.[8] The link between worker characteristics and earnings is substantially different from the link between worker characteristics and occupation. The link between characteristics and earnings is governed by institutional role reproduction; the link between characteristics and occupation is governed by institutional recruitment and selection.

In other words, a worker's cognitive skills, education, and so forth do not really determine his earnings. Workers with similar individual characteristics do not earn similar incomes, but these characteristics do influence the beginning occupational slot into which workers are fitted. This evidence is not consistent with orthodox labor market theory which stresses individual characteristics and the price mechanism. But it is consistent with an "institutional labor market theory" which stresses institutional selection and role reproduction, the processes here hypothesized to have replaced the price mechanism in the labor market.

Institutional Selection and Recruitment

The external labor market in the United States is not really composed of homogeneous labor suppliers and homogeneous labor demanders. Instead, on the supply-side is a set of heterogeneous workers, possessed of different family and class backgrounds, cognitive skills, years of schooling, and so on. Each worker is not just looking for a job but for an entrance into an occupational hierarchy. On the demand side is a hierarchical structure of entry-level positions, many of which are very low in the occupational hierarchy and lead nowhere, a few of which are higher and lead all the way to the top (chief executive of a large multinational corporation). The two sides are brought together through institutional selection, an administrative adjustment process as opposed to a price adjustment process. Since an institution is both an organization (a going concern made up of people performing their assigned roles according to working rules) and a habit of thought (a set of roles people must perform to keep the concern going), the selection of people to fit into the various organizational roles is of paramount importance. Institutions, more precisely, corporate bureaucracies, must select or recruit the most likely candidates to perform the needed roles from the set of potential candidates. The roles being filled are organized into a status ranking. Janitors, mailboys, keypunch operators, secretaries, managerial trainees, junior and senior executives, are organized into a status ranking. In an open and equal status scramble everyone would try to become the chief executive, but most would fail and become bitterly disillusioned. Hence, fitting the set of aspiring job applicants to the set of status-ranked jobs or roles, without embittering the workforce, is very difficult. Yet this is the function of what is here referred to as filtering.

The filtering process is performed largely in school. From the first grade through graduate or professional school, people are sorted into their proper roles and taught to like them. The "best" people squeeze through each successive educational filter on their way to the corporate executive suite. The others cannot squeeze through and are channeled out of the educational sequence at their "appropriate" levels. The bureaucratic corporation has succeeded in getting educational institutions to serve as the means of filtering. Educational officials, in their rush to maintain enrollment and financial support, try ever harder to meet the needs of the labor market (the set of corporate demanded jobs or roles). The labor market needs a means of filtering people into the vector of status-ranked corporate jobs. And educational institutions are trying to deliver. What they deliver is educational certification. Educational certificates serve as job tickets, at least they do so in good times when these jobs are available. But if too many job applicants are trying to squeeze through desirable ports of entry into the higher levels of corporate jobs, great cries of alarm are sounded throughout the business establishment about the lack of educational standards. Too many people are being given too many degree certificates. Every certificate holder knows that he is qualified but the others are not. "They" snuck through because of low standards, so standards must go up after "he" graduates.

Before standards can be pushed up, a considerable amount of discontent is caused among disappointed job seekers. After all, each one knows that he is qualified to enter the higher levels. He has the certificate to prove it. But then so does everyone else. It is in these times, when filtering is failing, that the real function of education in bureaucratic America becomes clear. But as soon as standards are pushed up, the number of "qualified," that is, certified, job applicants is brought into line with the limited number of jobs that lead into the higher circles. Then the "qualified" pass through the desirable ports of entry and the others look elsewhere. But the others no longer feel cheated because they know they are not qualified. They lack the required degree or educational certificate and they have no one to blame but themselves for not doing better or staying longer in school, or so they have been taught to think by the filtering process.

While educational officials are coordinating standards with the needs of the labor market, corporate officials are raising the qualifications needed for entry into the higher levels. The unqualified are filtered out with a cool indifference which appears to be legitimate because it is based on "scientific" testing and "objective" grading. Higher degrees are required by corporate personnel managers while at the same time those degrees are made harder to get by university officials. An unintended result is a kind of educational speed up of our youth. The significant result is a more effective filtering of "unqualified" candidates out of the higher circles. And most of the filtered people see the process as legitimate, whether they are filtered in or out of the higher circles. So the very difficult process of matching a set of aspiring job applicants to a hierarchy of status-ranked jobs is performed by a coordination of educational and corporate action, the former in our culture being now subordinated to the latter. This process of institutional selection occurs in the external labor market but it does not occur through the price mechanism.

Lest the reader infer that the filtering process creates a meritocracy, one more of the empirical findings of Jencks et al. should be mentioned. Specifically, they discovered that schooling contributes little to a man's economic success through improving his general skills or through providing him with job-related skills. Jencks and his co-workers found that very little statistical relation exists between academic achievement and subsequent worker performance in specific occupations.[9] Rather, schooling contributes to worker's success through providing the certification needed to pass through the higher ports of entry into the corporate status ranking.

From a slightly different perspective, Lester Thurow explains filtering as a market process in which "job competition" has replaced price competition. In his view, workers compete for "training slots."[10] These training slots are actually ports of entry into the internal labor market. Once candidates for jobs in the higher corporate circles have been recruited and selected, they pass through the ports of entry located at roughly the middle white collar level. Engineering, sales, accounting, law, and general management are where most executives begin their careers.[11] But they have merely gained access to a career ladder by passing through these particular ports of entry. They have a long and precarious climb ahead of them before a tiny fraction of the status seekers actually reach the top.

Role Reproduction (Cloning in the Executive Suite)

Once the appropriate applicants have been selected for candidacy in the higher circles, the function of filtering, performed in the external labor market, is complete. Now a second mechanism's function becomes paramount. Corporate leadership roles must be reproduced in the new generation of executives. In general, the higher roles are both learned and filled through what is here referred to in the large as homosocial reproduction.[12] That is, the next generation of corporate leaders is either drawn from the same social origins as the original generation or is habituated to the habits of thought of that social milieu. In the first mode of homosocial reproduction, sons easily follow their fathers into the higher circles, but not necessarily in the same organization. In the second mode, sons of non-elite fathers have to struggle into the higher circles, but not "on their own," as will be explained below. Regardless of which mode is used, the result is similar to the cloning of plants with the exception that these clones are human.

Empirical evidence of the first mode (father-to-son) of homosocial reproduction is abundant. In a classic study, W. Lloyd Warner and James C. Abegglen surveyed over 7,000 executives of the largest U.S. firms in 1952.[13] Table 6.4 presents their relevant findings. Clearly, young men whose fathers were business leaders have a much higher probability of becoming business leaders themselves than young men whose fathers were in other occupations. For example, the table indicates that 31 percent of surveyed executives had fathers who were also executives. This contrasts with only 4 percent of the adult male population who were executives. Dividing 31 percent by 4 percent yields

TABLE 6.4

Father and Son Occupations

1	2	3	4
	Percentage of fathers of 1952 business	Percentage of total male adult	Degree of over or under
Occupation	leaders	population in 1920	representation*
Executive or owner of large business	31	4	7.75
Owner of small business	18	5	3.60
Professional	14	4	3.50
Other occupation	2	1	2.00
Foreman	3	2	1.33
Clerk or salesman	8	10	0.88
Skilled laborer	10	16	0.63
Farmer	9	20	0.45
Unskilled or semi-skilled laborer	5	31	0.16
Farm laborer	0	7	0.00

*Column 4 = column 2 divided by column 3. If the result is greater than one, the father's occupation is over-represented; if less than one, the father's occupation is under-represented.

Source: Warner and Abegglen, *Occupational Mobility in American Business and Industry*, pp. 40–41, Tables 2 and 3.

the ratio of 7.75 which indicates the degree of over representation of executive's sons in the population of executives.

The first mode of homosocial reproduction is an important one. It is also the easiest and surest way for the corporate elders to clone themselves, that is, reproduce the habits of thought essential for successful performance of the higher roles because such habits of thought are inculcated in youths beginning in their earliest years, not just at school and later at work. Nevertheless, this mode of homosocial reproduction is falling out of use. Inherited status is now frowned upon in the bureaucratic corporation. The second mode of homosocial reproduction (sponsor-to-protege) may be gradually replacing the first as the higher corporate circles are opening up to people of nonelite social origins. Perhaps this change represents progress or perhaps it represents more effective and widespread habituation to the uses and wonts of corporate capitalism.

Homosocial reproduction, particularly of the increasingly more frequent second mode, is facilitated by an important personal relationship between two corporate managers. One manager, higher up the corporate hierarchy than the second manager, adopts the second as his protege. The relation between a protege and his sponsor is crucial now, and has been crucial for some time, in the world of business, even though its significance is consistently denigrated and obscured by the American ideology of individualism and the mythology of the self-made man. Sponsorship in business has been with us for a long time and its meaning is indicated by the following cynical bit of underground folk wisdom: "It is not *what* you know, but *whom* you know that counts."

The sponsorship relation is a personal link to corporate power for it allies a man on the make in the corporate bureaucracy (the protege) to one who already has it made (the sponsor). The sponsor protects and aids his protege in the protege's struggle to the top. The sponsor will eventually expect something in return, however. So as his protege rises up the hierarchy, the sponsor's stake in his protege's continued success gets larger and larger. This is cloning or "investment in human capital." Successful investments pay off handsomely, for proteges are expected to return favors in kind when the opportunity presents itself. Clones (proteges) are usually loyal to their progenitors, for both blood and institutional bonds are thicker than water. In this way, those who possess a vested interest in the corporate status quo ensure that their replacements are beholden to them, and through them, to the corporate bureaucracy itself. Viewed cynically at the personal or individual level, the sponsorship relation may appear to be little more than sycophancy. But viewed clinically at the institutional level, this relation can be understood for what it is — a major mode of institutional role reproduction. Sociologists would call it a means of norm internalization; Thorstein Veblen would call it habituation to corporate use and wont.

Once again, claims that run strongly counter to the conventional wisdom have been made. Supporting empirical evidence is called for. Even during the nineteenth century, the era of entrepreneurial capitalism and the self-made man, sponsorship played an important role in the reproduction of business leaders in America. Relying on biographies and company histories (not always the most candid of sources), Bernard Sarachek investigated sponsor-protege relations in the careers of 187 nineteenth- and early twentieth-century entrepreneurs. He found that at least 64 and perhaps up to 76 percent of them were sponsored by either their fathers (the first mode of homosocial reproduction) or by other established businessmen (the second mode of homosocial reproduction).[14] The self-made business leader was a rarity, even in the nineteenth century. The majority rose, even then, through sponsorship of one form or another.

Corporate sponsors are not only career boosters, but "significant others" for their proteges. A significant other is one whose behavior is used as a role model and whose norms are internalized. Significant others are very important to the construction of a person's character or personality. Hans Gerth and C. Wright Mills state, "A person is composed of an internalization of organized social roles . . . "[15] And the roles internalized are those of significant others, sponsors in this case. In a dated but interesting organizational case study of supervisors and their subordinates, Ronald Corwin, Marvin J. Taves, and J. Eugene Haas conclude, "Showing friendship toward selected subordinates (proteges?) is a way in which superiors endorse the implicit values underlying the basic structure of the organization."[16] Here we have the crucial link between the norms and values — habits of thought — of new institutional members and the institution itself. Sponsorship and the "significant other" provide the causal connection between institutions and personal values and behaviors. These concepts also explain who rises to the top of the corporate hierarchy — the protege with the most powerful sponsor and with a personality which is the most amenable to corporate use and wont, as demonstrated by the sponsor's role modeling.

So institutions, the corporate bureaucracy in particular, reproduce their top roles and the people to fill them through, primarily, the sponsorship relation in the internal labor market. Of course, where new blood is not so easily habituated or co-opted, hereditary reproduction can still fill the void. If sons with fathers who were outside the higher corporate circles are resistant to habituation to the corporate way of life, sons born and reared in the higher corporate milieu can still fill the void. Little has been said about daughters because, frankly, they generally are excluded from business leadership. And the corporation selects new employees, in the external labor market, through filtering. By either raising or lowering entry-level qualifications, just the right number of qualified applicants are allowed into the bureaucratic hierarchy. To conclude, in neither the external nor the internal labor markets does the traditional price mechanism have a significant role to play in adjusting supply to demand. That role is now played, predominantly, by filtering and homosocial reproduction.

THE PERSONAL IMPACT OF CORPORATE BUREAUCRACY

Now we can explore more directly the impact of bureaucracy on the American character. The narrow, red-tape-restricted world of the government bureaucrat, particularly those in the growing ranks of state and local government, is constantly before us in the newspapers. But the more important world of the corporate bureaucrat is unfamiliar to many of us. We now turn to that world, and to its personal effects on its inhabitants. What kind of people will we find there?

Peering within the bureaucratic structures of the modern corporation, investigators have found, at the top, few of the rational, specialized experts envisioned by Max Weber. The trained experts are there, but at lower levels, efficiently turning out The Memo and The Proposal. The higher levels of corporate bureaucracy are inhabited by other types, and their world is not one of cool calculation, efficiency, and impersonal rationality. Instead, it is a world of frenzied and fearful scrambling for personal position, a world of emulation and predation, a world which Mills described as "The Status Panic."[17]

Striving is so intense at the higher levels because results are so uncertain. In a status system in which all know their place and that of others, very little striving occurs. But when some people can rise quickly (Kanter calls them "fast-trackers," Maccoby calls them "games-men," and their associates have even more colorful names for them), so that status becomes uncertain, the striving intensifies, and status considerations begin permeating all activities. Following the work of Kanter, we can see how the intense status striving within corporate bureaucracies manifests itself in ways very different from the behavior expected in Weber's ideal type bureaucracy. Status striving results in intensely personal or particularistic human relations rather than in rationally impersonal or universalistic ones. It also results in inequality of treatment. Company policy either is applied more equally to some than to others, or is different for different employees.

Contemporary investigators have found that when uncertain status is combined with the general uncertainties and pecuniary animus of the business world, the human results are quite striking. Human relations within the corporate bureaucracy are not rationally impersonal and universalistic. The specialized expert does not necessarily rise to higher levels of decision making where his knowledge can be brought to bear effectively. Instead, the socially acceptable candidate for promotion often takes his place. With the outcomes of managerial work always so uncertain, social acceptance rather than technical performance is the way people are judged. This leads to a very restrictive and conformist type of bureaucratic environment where tight little inner circles of friendship and alliance become very important to personal success. Kanter coined the phrase for this bureaucratic phenomenon: " 'homosocial reproduction' – selection of incumbents on the basis of social similarity."[18] Another observer of the corporation goes even farther; Wilbert Moore states: "The corporation seems to seek an arrangement which is surely an anomaly in human society, that of homosexual reproduction."[19] He refers to a system in which men in leadership positions reproduce themselves in the next crop of leaders. The result is best described as the cloning of male bureaucrats.

Homosocial reproduction results in a dramatic restriction of opportunity. Those whose social origins differ significantly from those of the existing bureaucratic elite do not have an equal opportunity to rise to levels of authority. Their human potential is wasted. Clearly, this is not efficient. Clearly, this is not equality, despite orthodox claims to the contrary. Talcott Parsons makes such a claim in his introduction to *Max Weber:* Bureaucracy "has a leveling influence, in that it treats social class by birth and other privileged statuses as to a large degree irrelevant to status in the system of authority."[20]

For men in the bureaucracy this orthodox image is wearing thin, and for women it was always a mirage. Homosexual reproduction has excluded women from full participation in corporate activities for as long as the corporation has existed. The combined effects of homo-social and homosexual reproduction amount to a monstrous waste of human potential, among both males and females. This waste is neither efficient nor rational, Max Weber's ideal type notwithstanding. The more investigators such as Kanter discover the workings of corporate bureaucracy, the more the orthodox image shaped by Max Weber's ideal type looks like a mirage. Weber's bureaucracy bears little resemblance to the reality of corporate capitalism. Not only is opportunity severely restricted, but also the demands of the corporation on the bureaucrat's personal life are extensive and intensive.

The demands are not limited to the individual. The long arm of the corporation reaches out to control one's spouse, family, and choice of friends. Even though most people want to marry, corporations demand it. Single men do not rise in the corporate world. Once a wife is supplied, she must become a corporate wife, personally devoted to her husband's career, sensitized to the demands of corporate bureaucracy. She must be a good hostess, a moderate drinker, a good sport, intelligent but not argumentative, be willing to move frequently and, above all, be a cheerful corporate widow because her husband, to rise to the top, must put career above family. The wife of a successful bureaucrat is not her own person; she is an extension of her husband's occupation. She is *incorporated*.

A bureaucrat's family life and home are subject to extensive corporate influence, albeit in an indirect fashion. Not even corporate bureaucrats welcome direct control of their family relations. Nevertheless, corporate bureaucrats on the make, according to Kanter, view their family lives and homes as "a springboard for success." Other ideals regarding home and family have been replaced, with social ramifications as yet unassessed.

Corporate employees must exercise considerable discretion in acquiring and discarding friends. They must add to, but never subtract from, the bureaucrat's status and chances for promotion. Unsuccessful friends from school days are to be avoided. Former colleagues who have risen too slowly in the corporate hierarchy should be replaced with more promising allies. If at all possible, a personal friend, a sponsor, in the bureaucracy should be obtained. In short, all personal relations must be turned to account. Bureaucrats do not simply deal with one another as impersonal officials; instead, they use personal alliances, personal favors, and personal obligations in their struggle for status. No quarter is asked and none is given.

The sponsorship phenomenon is representative of the highly personal nature of human relations within the corporate bureaucracy. Influential friends must be acquired to sponsor the aspiring bureaucrat in his rise. There are so many hopefuls in the lower ranks that an ambitious young executive in a large corporation needs a personal connection with the top. The sponsor provides that connection. Sponsors perform four personal services for their protege. (1) They make introductions to the proper people and give informal social training in the art of ladder-climbing. (2) They support and promote their protege, mentioning his name (the protege needs a booster) and fighting for him in controversies, if necessary, and if not too costly. (3) They help bypass the formal hierarchy, getting needed information and avoiding formal procedures. (4) They lend a halo effect of power and prestige to the protege, turning him into a fast-tracker, one who moves rapidly up the corporate hierarchy. In return, the protege must be grateful as he rises, he must reciprocate. An unfaithful protege is in danger not only of losing his sponsor, but also of retaliation from a sponsor scorned.

Sponsors are investors, for their personal accounts, in future allies. They are speculators in the personality market. Proteges are chosen according to the principles of homosocial and homosexual reproduction. That is, a sponsor usually chooses a protege with a similar social background. Also, virtually all proteges are male. In short, social characteristics and sex are more important for candidacy, and therefore for success, than is technical knowledge. Furthermore, proteges are commodities, not persons. A successful speculator cannot afford to let his investment portfolio be filled with real friends. It must contain winners, commodities that will pay off.

While Weber believed that bureaucracy as an ideal type made power impersonal and nonarbitrary, the corporate bureaucracy actually works quite differently. The sponsorship relation is only one indication of the often arbitrary and highly personal nature of its operation.

What kinds of people choose corporate work, and what does it do to them? Psychoanalyst and corporate investigator Michael Maccoby has given some indication in *The Gamesman*. He emphasizes the psychological impact of the corporate institution: "Corporations like BDC and RI (fictitious names for real firms) organize more human energy of higher intellectual quality than any other institutions in America. Each year, they hire and eventually shape the character of a large percentage of the most talented college graduates, reinforcing certain human potentials and not others."[21]

The corporate bureaucracy not only selects and then reinforces certain character traits, but also creates them, even in individuals outside the corporate world. Maccoby found that the basic orientation of the bureaucratic character is toward a career, that is, toward rising above the occupational status of one's friends. Careerism, reflected in the bureaucrat's desire for successful children, has penetrated very deeply into the American character. The bureaucrat's expectations for his family are turning that fundamental institution into a new kind of "satellite industry" to supply the human support needed in the struggle for bureaucratic success. A similar process is reshaping the schools, which are expected to prepare the bureaucrat's children (the males, at least, and increasingly also the females) for success in their bureaucratic careers.

In the psyche of the careerist, the main desire is for a rise in status and the main emotion is fear. In careful psychological probings of individual corporate bureaucrats, Maccoby found that a generalized feeling of fear is a common character trait of managers. The reason is obvious: "He is afraid that external events beyond his control or his inability to control himself will damage or destroy his career."[22] J.R.R. Tolkein's Gollum and his "precious" are excellent literary representations of the careerist's obsession.

To be successful, to rise to the highest levels of the corporate bureaucracy, one must become a gamesman. To cope with the fear and frustration, one must treat the climb up the bureaucratic ladder as a game. The gamesman, in playing the game of managerial career, must design himself for success and protect himself from the fear of failure. Through constant adaptation to the changing requirements for success and through constant insulation from the fear of failure, the gamesman loses, or perhaps never has a chance to develop, the internalized norms of moral conduct. In Maccoby's words, he has an "underdeveloped heart." That is, he is readily adaptable to different external rules of the game because he has suppressed his internal directions – his conscience. Maccoby summarizes: "The gamesman will pollute the environment, unless the law is such that each corporation must clean up its mess....He will produce and advertise anything he can sell unless food and drug laws or other legislation stop him....Even when he believes that the Government spends too much on weapons, he will make them."[23]

The gamesman's lack of personal direction (conscience) is a direct result of the institutional milieu in which he is embedded. Veblen remarked: "Freedom from scruple, from sympathy, honesty and regard for life, may, within fairly wide limits, be said to further the success of the individual in the pecuniary culture."[24] To succeed, life must be seen as a career game, and the careerist is driven by emulation. Veblen called it "the stimulus of an invidious comparison which prompts us to outdo those with whom we are in the habit of classing ourselves."[25] Under this relentless emulative pressure, personal relations with wife, child, friend, and colleague are turned to account; and poisoned in the bargain.

Even the most fundamental human potentials are distorted. Emulation is the force which drives the bureaucrat in his game, not a desire to serve or to be useful, not a desire to live a full life. The game he plays is pervaded by invidious distinctions or status panic, not perfect competition or performance of duty. Furthermore, the game includes not only the gamesman, but also his wife, child, friend, and colleague – and the fundamental institutions of our economy. His game is played at great cost not only to himself, but also to society at large. Some pretend that the entrepreneur is still led by an invisible hand. Others pretend that the bureaucrat faithfully performs his duty, guided by professional codes of conduct. A few entrepreneurs and bureaucrats do, and they are so rare that they make the front page of the newspaper. But the entrepreneur is actually an endangered species, and most bureaucrats use the corporate bureaucracy for their own personal advancement over their peers.

To some extent, Weber's ideal type is empirically valid: A bureaucracy is a system of authority, with potential for rational planning and impersonal direction. But a large corporate bureaucracy embedded in a pecuniary culture is also an "organized" and very personal scramble for status. The latter features now dominate the former.

Galbraith, whose insight is usually quite sound, argues that the large corporation has become a technostructure.[26] Technocrats, through group decisions, rationally plan how to achieve maximum growth and technological virtuosity. Galbraith sees the technocrats, with their rationality and expert knowledge, as the new breed of bureaucrat. Is he correct? Is the mature corporation a technocratic rather than emulative bureaucracy; a technostructure instead of a status structure? Or has Galbraith been led astray by his optimistic managerial colleagues at the Harvard Business School? A more realistic assessment of the new corporate bureaucrat cannot avoid the conclusion that gamemanship has replaced workmanship in corporate hierarchies. Bureaucratic career is far more important than technical craft. And since a career is such a socially tenuous thing, the corporate careerist is a devout conformist, always on guard against appearing not quite right, not quite with it, not on top. Such a life is a far cry from the rugged individualism of the American frontier. Perhaps that is why we cling to our frontier fantasies so tenaciously.

CONCLUSION

Bureaucracy has spread into almost all of the private sector. The number of production workers per nonproduction employee has fallen everywhere we have measured it. Agriculture is the last holdout to the bureaucratic trend. As part of this trend, our bureaucratic economy has developed new forms of labor markets where the old price mechanism has been replaced by the bureaucratic processes of filtering and homosocial reproduction. Except for dead-end jobs and for production work, new employees for corporate bureaucracies are not selected on the basis of their desire to work for low pay. Instead, they are selected on the basis of their academic credentials. Those with high (expensive) credentials are hired, those without them are not. This is filtering. It works as a barrier against the poor and minorities. Filtering based on sex, race, age, religion, and ethnic origin is now illegal but still practiced either by corporate bureaucracies or by academic institutions. After filtering out the undesired, homosocial reproduction ensures that corporate leaders will be replaced by people just like them. Filtering and homosocial reproduction seal off the corporate elite from the lower classes, allowing the elite to rigidify. The result is not only a growing frustration among the excluded but also a growing lack of new people and new ideas in the higher circles of corporate bureaucracies. Dynamism is being lost and productivity gains slowing down as our corporate elites begin their slide into self-righteous

senility, all the while condemning government bureaucracy while for-
tifying their own bureaucracy.

At the same time, a profound change is occurring in the American
character. The old American character was molded on the frontier.
Frontier individualism was real, then. Now, the American character is
being remolded in the corporate bureaucracy. Frontier individualism
is being replaced with corporate careerism. The careerist is engaged in
a fierce scramble for status. Since his status depends upon the fleeting
opinions of others, the careerist is in a perpetual status panic. Anxiety
is his constant companion, probably the only constant companion he
will have in his life. Fear and greed are the new American character
traits.

Now, what should we do about all of this? Cut the federal government back to nineteenth century size and return to laissez-faire? That
will not open up opportunities for the excluded. That will not change
corporate filtering and homosocial reproduction. That will not revive
economic productivity because it will not push new people and new
ideas into the higher corporate circles. That will not free us from the
character-distorting effects of corporate careerism. Instead, cutting
the federal government back and returning to laissez-faire will leave
the field open to more of the same: more restriction of opportunity,
more filtering, more homosocial reproduction, more lagging productivity, and more unrestrained corporate careerism.

7 REVITALIZATION

INTRODUCTION

As explained in an earlier chapter, economic progress is a result of two propelling forces. The first force is the push from below, from the excluded, for full participation. This, of course, is the egalitarian drive which has been an integral part of western culture since at least the time of Christ. The second force is the march of science and technology which began at least two million years ago when man's evolutionary ancestors began using tools. These are incredibly strong historical forces. Though often sidetracked, resisted, and stalled, equality has resumed the general advance and so has science and technology, up till now at least.

Today, the corporate bureaucracy has become a major hindrance to these two forces, particularly to the advance of equality. A few decades ago, the corporation was a major vehicle for implementing mass-production technology and for employing millions of immigrants in modern U.S. industry. The corporation is still the major vehicle for the planning of production and capital accumulation on the massive scales required by modern technology. However, the corporation has become bureaucratized and the bureaucratic processes of filtering and homosocial reproduction are choking off corporate dynamism. The flow into the corporation and then up through the corporate hierarchy of new people with new ideas is a trickle. True, more people go to work for corporations everyday. But they are not new people to the corporation. Instead, they are just more of the same kind of people who are already there. Reform has become essential.

Yet we lack the nerve to face reality and to change it for the better. Instead, we retrench. Assuming that we finally can face ourselves and assuming that we resolve to do something positive about what we see, the following is offered as a way to begin. I offer, not a utopian blueprint nor a call for revolution, but a few concrete, practical reforms.

What we need to do is improve our existing institutions, not start all over again. In particular, we should leave corporations intact but alter some of the ways they work and make a few additions to their formal structures. In this chapter the alteration of corporate recruitment (filtering) and promotion (homosocial reproduction) will be discussed. Further specific reforms of the corporation are discussed in the remaining chapters of Part 2. In Part 3, attention will shift to the need for making public policy more effective.

REFORMING CORPORATE RECRUITMENT

Preliminaries

Corporate bureaucracies hire most new employees at entry level positions. These positions are either technical production jobs, clerical or blue collar dead ends, or portals to the corporate ladder leading up the bureaucratic hierarchy. Whatever the nature of the position, it is increasingly filled by a filtering process rather than a market process. Furthermore, no matter how nostalgic we become, the market process cannot be brought back to reform corporate recruitment procedures. Filling positions through the market process requires that wages and salaries be flexible. In particular, if more qualified people exist than positions, the market solves the problem by lowering the salaries or wages offered with those positions. In most occupations experienced workers earn more than inexperienced ones, but only slightly more. For the market process to work, experienced workers would have to accept a decline in their wages or salaries for an oversupply of qualified applicants to be absorbed into their occupation. But wage and salary cuts are demoralizing to such an extent that they threaten organization survival. Hence, they are not cut, outside of a real emergency.[1] So instead of an oversupply of qualified applicants driving salaries down, the oversupply drives qualifications up. New workers end up being overqualified, but old ones do not have their salaries cut.

The general overqualification of new workers makes my reform proposal viable. First, the way in which qualifications (educational certificates) are earned can be changed without threatening the technical viability of corporate organizations. After all, most new workers are overqualified anyway. Second, the actual selection process conducted by personnel staffs can be changed, also without threatening technical viability.

Education: The First Stage of Filtering

Since filtering really begins in educational institutions, reform must begin with them. My modest proposal is that schools actually educate students for full and intelligent participation in a democratic society. To do so, however, they must stop functioning as extensions of the corporate personnel offices and begin performing their historical mission, which is to reinforce the egalitarian push from below, to prepare all young people for the intellectual and moral challenges of the democratic way of life, not just to provide them with vocational training. Schools are not playing their historical role in our democracy. U.S. educational institutions, particularly universities and colleges, have been criticized by Marxists, Institutionalists, and even by Libertarians for failing to educate students for full participation in a democratic society. The critics from virtually all points of the philosophical spectrum believe that the U.S. educational system constitutes little more than an elaborate mechanism for providing the labor "market" with a painstakingly graded supply of labor. Libertarian Joel H. Spring calls the educational system a "Sorting Machine."[2]

The role of education in a democratic society, where the push from below is encouraged, is to prepare young people for their democratic roles, for the pursuit of freedom through full participation in all areas of life. John Dewey laid the philosophical foundations of democratic education in the United States. He argued that democratic schools must "...send out young men and women who will stand actively and aggressively for the cause of free intelligence in meeting social problems and attaining the goal of freedom..."[3] The purpose of democratic education is *free inquiry*, unfettered by vested interest and unhindered by shortsighted interest. Democratic education imparts an ability to participate in a process. It does not just impart a vocation or a set of facts. Dewey was no ivory tower theorist, but a social activist committed to putting theory into practice. He knew that democratic education was possible, for he had practiced it in his own teaching.

But two limits to democratic education are immediately encountered. First, many walks of life do not allow all individuals in them to participate fully. The corporate world in particular is bureaucratic rather than democratic. Managerial hierarchies tell others what to do and make sure that it is done. Government bureaucracies often do the same. Nevertheless, Dewey saw the major resistance to the full participation of all coming from industry. Despite the efforts of a few democratic educators, Dewey lamented "...the whole existing industrial system tends to nullify in large measure the effects of these efforts even when they are made."[4] The second limit to democratic education is related to the first. Not only does bureaucratic hierarchy in the corporation, military, and government limit the democratic process in the world outside the school, it also limits the process inside the school. For the U.S. educational system itself is not autonomous. Instead, the educational system is highly dependent upon other institutions or individuals for support. Only a very few universities are financially independent. In fact, Hans Gerth and C. Wright Mills pessimistically declared, "Only under quite special conditions do professional educators emancipate themselves from the control of superordinate institutional orders."[5] This institutional dependence has far-reaching consequences for democratic education.

Dependence upon the nation-state often means that education is expected to inculcate patriotism and a respect for the national honor rather than humanism and free inquiry. Dewey stated:

> Patriotism, National Honor, National Interests and National Sovereignty are the four foundation stones upon which the structure of the National State is erected. It is no wonder that the windows of such a building are closed to the light of heaven; that its inmates are fear, jealousy, suspicion, and that War issues regularly from its portals.[6]

When war or the threat of war exists, as it has throughout much of this century, education for democracy is crowded out by education for war. Dependence upon the garrison state is costly for educational institutions.

But so is dependence upon the private sector. The state demands patriotism, the private sector free enterprise. Both demands limit the free play of intellect inside the school so essential to preparing young people for a democratic way of life outside the school. The lack of educational autonomy — the dependence of educational institutions upon other institutions — is a severe limit to democratic education, even more severe than the public demand for practical rather than theoretical education. At all educational levels the cry for practical relevance is constantly heard from those seeking vocational – professional training. The cry is loudest during times of mass unemployment — a frequent occurrence in the twentieth century, for a diploma is often mistaken for a job permit. But given real educational autonomy — a possibility at least for a great university — the conflict between the public's cry for practical relevance and the free intellect's need for theory can be reconciled by applying theory to existing problems. This can only be done in education when educators are not intimidated by direct or indirect pressure from vested interests or shortsighted interests. To realize their potential, democratic educational institutions must be autonomous from the demands of other institutions and involved in the great social and scientific issues of the day. They must unite freewheeling theory with practical problems. If the young are to be prepared for full participation in the democratic process nothing less will do.

This democratic educational ideal is far from being met, not only because our society outside the school is not thoroughly democratic but also because educational institutions themselves are stunted by their dependence upon the state and the corporation. How this dependence evolved is important. Since the public school — the lower learning — is abjectly dependent, the following discussion will be of the evolution of American colleges and universities — the higher learning, which shows at least a semblance of autonomy.

The ancestor of the American university is the medieval European univeristy, which reached its zenith in the thirteenth century. Far from being smothered by scholasticism and rigid theological dogma, the thirteenth century European university was a vital intellectual center and university faculty were esteemed members of society. This was no golden age of science, of course, but it was not as dark an age as often depicted. The following description by Richard Hofstadter is worth quoting in full:

> At the time of their greatest independence the universities lived in the interstices of medieval society, taking advantage of its decentralization and the balance of its conflicting powers to further their own corporate interests. The absence of a monolithic structure of power, the existence of a real plurality and diversity of interests within the frameworks of both the ecclesiastical and secular powers, put the uni-

versities in a postion in which they were not easily over-
whelmed.[7]

A long medieval tradition of guild self-government had freed university scholars to a significant degree from the close supervision of
both secular and ecclesiastical authorities. In addition, in the thirteenth
century university scholars possessed an ultimate weapon. If thoroughly aroused by local interference, the community of scholars could
and did migrate en masse to another, more congenial locality. In those
days, universities were not tied to massive libraries, laboratories, and
classroom facilities. In their poverty, they were free, after a fashion.
Nevertheless, in the late fourteenth and into the fifteenth century,
university autonomy waned in Europe. For one thing, migrations
resulted in a general "overbuilding" of universities, rendering migra-
tion more difficult. Hofstader emphasizes, "But it had been, above all,
the pluralism (?) of medieval life that provided these powerful [uni-
versity] corporations with the source of their autonomy...."[8] The
rise of the nation state changed all that. The medieval university's
autonomy faded.

The higher learning in the English colonies started out quite differently from that in Europe. Both were heavily influenced by eccle-
siastics, but American colleges were sponsored by private denominations of religious dissenters, who were devoted enough to their cause
to migrate to a new world. Also, while European universities were clustered into great centers of learning with close connections between
professional and advanced faculties, American colleges were geographically diffused and were not great centers of learning and advanced
study. The weak, infant American colleges evolved under a system of
academic government headed by people other than faculty members.
Unlike their European ancestors, American colleges were directed by
nonacademics. From the very start, American institutions of higher
learning were dependent institutions.

The nonacademic government and complete lack of autonomy of
early American colleges grew out of three unique characteristics of the
American case. First, the early American milieu was Protestant and
hence isolated from the medieval Catholic university tradition of wide
autonomy within commonly accepted, ecclesiastical limits. The
American college was also isolated from the guild tradition of self-
government. Second, the higher learning in America was a forced

growth which did not evolve out of established traditions and communities of scholars, but was created almost de nouveau, requiring a long period of support and guidance from nonacademic circles. Third, European universities emerged after there already existed a body of men that could be called a teaching profession. But American colleges were created before an indigenous teaching profession had emerged. This meant that early American college teachers were rank amateurs as opposed to the mature professionals of Europe. In short, the higher learning in America was not only an "infant industry" for an extended period of time but it was an infant growing up in an environment which separated it from its European parentage and made it dependent upon distinctly nonacademic foster parents — strongly dissenting Protestant sects. The free play of intellect essential to democratic education was not one of the strong points of early American colleges.

By the 1830s, plutocratic Federalism was waning, the nation had become established, and Jacksonian Democracy was in flower. But another characteristic of evolving American higher learning manifested itself: a very real tension existed between popular democracy and higher learning, for the early American colleges were usually aristocratic institutions. And yet the people were not necessarily hostile to higher learning, only to its apparent aristocratic traditions. In fact, from the turn of the century to the Civil War, a tremendous number of new colleges were founded all over the country. The people supported colleges, particularly new ones, but not necessarily good ones and not always for good reasons. Popular support for new colleges was more often due to local pride and real estate boosterism or competitive denominational sponsorship than to a desire for higher learning. The result, Hofstadter concludes, "...was to fill the country with precarious little institutions, denomination-ridden, poverty-stricken, keeping dubious educational standards, and offering little to teachers in freedom or financial reward."[9] The Morrill Act of 1862 meant even more expansion and overbuilding as Federal aid was channeled to agricultural and mechanical colleges.

Yet, in spite of the overbuilding, the university movement began in earnest after the Civil War. Soon the German university became the ideal toward which most American colleges were striving. The Johns Hopkins University opened in 1876, modeled after the German university with emphasis on graduate study and free intellectual inquiry.

Until then, no graduate-level institution had existed in the U.S. Other institutions quickly followed suit. The flowering of free inquiry meant that Darwinism clashed with sectarianism in the 1870s. In the end, secular natural science and free inquiry carried the day in the universities against the sectarians. Free inquiry soon spread into the social sciences as many American scholars returned from their graduate studies in Germany and continued their inquiries in the states. However, by the 1890s free social inquiry was clashing with a truly formidable opponent — corporate capitalism. In the social sciences, particularly economics, the clash continues to this day. But at least free inquiry has picked up a staunch supporter. The AAUP (American Association of University Professors) was founded in 1915. Interestingly enough, many of the founders were economists of Institutionalist or Marxist persuasions. Marxists, Institutionalist, and the AAUP have weathered the Red Scare of the 1920s, the McCarthyism of the 1950s, and the Vietnam War of the '60s and '70s. Now we all face the reactionary '80s.

And through it all the curious twist given to the higher learning in America still survives, a cultural lag of serious import to democratic education. American universities, with only a few exceptions, are still dependent institutions long after the cultural conditions which caused the dependence in the first place have passed from the scene. In particular, American universities are still governed by nonacademic boards. This, in spite of the facts that strong traditions of academic freedom have been established for some time, that a mature profession of university teachers has evolved, and that narrow-minded denominational colleges largely have faded from the scene. The American university is still treated like an infant institution even though it is now a mature one. It is still very dependent even though capable of performing its role on its own. Even though most American universities are capable of managing their own affairs and are teaching young people how to engage in free inquiry and to fully participate in the democratic process, most American universities are still treated as if they were not capable. They are still governed by nonacademic boards. In the best private universities, the power in purely academic areas of governing boards has been curtailed or has fallen into disuse. Not so with many state universities and weaker private ones; certainly not so with most public schools below the college level. The membership of these nonacademic boards has changed from predominantly sectarian leaders to predominantly corporate leaders. But the nonacademic boards retain their power. Now the power is exercised by corporados instead of clerics.

This cultural lag must be remedied. For in every case in which free inquiry has been restricted, the restrictions have come either through the nonacademic board or through its agents. Far too frequently, the board has been a conduit through which vested or shortsighted interest has restrained free inquiry, particularly in the social sciences.[10] Not until the majority of American institutions are independent centers of higher learning, free from outside pressure, will democratic education become a reality for the majority of American youth. Democratic education means free inquiry, but free inquiry is not a traditional academic subject that can be learned like the calculus. It is a way of life into which one must be socialized. And this most universities are not strong enough, not independent enough, to do. Teaching calculus is value-free; socialization into a life of free inquiry is not and that is why only the strongest, most independent universities dare to try. Unfortunately, only a minority of our youth are able to go to these rare institutions which do offer a democratic education.

That most of these rare, independent institutions are from an aristocratic heritage is no coincidence. Only universities with many years of endowment support from the wealthy are now independent enough to rise above the immediate demands of their supporters, most of whom, long since deceased, can no longer demand anything of the board. When demands are made, of course, they are made by or through the nonacademic board. This cultural artifact has long outlived its usefulness. It has become a hindrance.

American universities must throw off the historical fetters which bind them. As a first step, the power of nonacademic governing boards must be severely restrained. Hofstadter states, "Nowhere outside the United States and Canada are modern universities governed by boards of laymen."[11] This has been the most important channel through which vested and shortsighted interests have made demands upon the independence of the universities. Most importantly, nonacademic boards have hampered the independence required for, not *teaching* free inquiry because it cannot be taught, but for *doing* free inquiry. Academia is no longer an infant institution in America. Now it must assert its independence from its nonacademic parents. Free inquiry will remain stifled until this paternalistic cultural lag has been removed. For, particularly in the social sciences, free inquirers are bound to run up against resistance from the corporate interest represented by the nonacademic boards.

If the university is freed from nonacademic dominance, the public schools eventually will follow. Teachers educated at independent universities will insist on applying their education to their own young charges. Free inquiry, in this way, will begin to spread into the public schools, if Reaganomics does not close them all first. Then, rather than filtering students into various occupational slots, education will socialize them into a democratic life of free inquiry and full participation. This requries, of course, that vocational education be eliminated from all but the professional schools. This will free the student time and faculty resources needed for real education. It will also transfer the financial burden of specific job-training to where it belongs—the employer.

Personnel Selection: The Second Step of Filtering

No longer able to get schools to do part of their job for them, personnel managers will become very busy corporate officials faced with selecting new employees who have not been presorted by schools. Two additional changes in the filtering process need to be made if the push from below through the democratic school is to be continued into the corporate bureaucracy. First, the Equal Employment Opportunity Commission needs drastic strengthening. Second, the adoption of standard affirmative action plans by major corporations should be encouraged.

The EEOC was established to enforce Title VII of the 1964 Civil Rights Act which outlawed employment discrimination on the basis of race, color, religion, sex, or national origin. Age discrimination was added by amendment. Since the EEOC is a function-specific rather than an industry-specific regulator, it has remained free of industry co-optation. Nevertheless, its effectiveness has been less than hoped for. It faces a large number of legal and institutional problems in its role of facilitating the push from below into better jobs.

Principal among the legal problems is the requirement that its advocacy of employment opportunities for minorities not result in discrimination against majorities (white males). Case law is still being made on this front and the EEOC is desperately in need of more legal talent to push for more favorable court decisions and to formulate new, creative affirmative action plans. So the first thing that must be done is to drastically increase the staff of the EEOC.

The EEOC now works primarily like this: Before it takes any action, an employee or potential employee must file charges with one of its 49 field offices within 180 days of the alleged discrimination. Then the EEOC investigates the charge and, if warranted, attempts to work out a settlement between employer and employee. If no voluntary settlement is reached, the EEOC continues to investigate the charge and attempts to conciliate the matter. If no conciliation results and if the EEOC finds "cause," it can take the case to Federal court. If it decides not to litigate, the employee is then free to do so. But it will cost the employee about $30,000 to pursue a complaint (in Chicago, 1981). About 94,000 actionable charges were filed with the EEOC in 1980. It has nowhere near the staff needed to pursue all of these cases with the vigor they warrant.

More staff is essential to remove all vestiges of discrimination against minorities in the "filters" used by employers to select new employees. Cleaning up the employment "filters" through legal action by the EEOC is painstakingly slow and, because of the kind of cases that can be won in court, only the worst abuses will be removed. Most employers are not blatantly racist, or sexist, even though their selection process often results in unintentional discrimination.

A second step must be taken also. Uniform affirmative action programs need to be designed by the EEOC in conjuction with model employers. Then the programs need to be adopted by most employers, with free technical and legal consultation provided by a new EEOC division, the "affirmative action consultant division." The new division should be created by legislation and funded adequately.

A uniform affirmative action plan needs to be designed for each of several broad occupational categories because traditions and conditions in the different occupations call for slightly different approaches. In the professions of law, medicine, and accounting (CPA), where state-administered examinations of one kind or another filter out "unqualified" candidates, special kinds of affirmative action plans need to be developed which do not discriminate against majorities. In the organized skilled trades, specialized plans need to be worked out to dovetail with collective bargaining, seniority, and apprenticeship. Clerical occupations require plans that build career ladders out of clerical dead ends. Managerial occupations need plans that bring more minorities into higher corporate circles.

The use of quotas in these EEOC plans is essential. A quota is a quantified objective, a benchmark against which actual performance can be measured. A quota is not a straitjacket for restraining action but a guide for encouraging new action and a stimulus for changing old patterns. Quotas for selecting new employees and guiding promotion policies not only will clean up existing filters, but will also provide new human material to make the assault on homosocial reproduction.

By strengthening the EEOC and building a democratic educational system, filtering will no longer thwart the push from below. New blood will begin to flow into corporate bureaucracies. The process, unavoidably, will be very threatening to the old guard entrenched in the corporate hierarchies. But it will also invigorate the corporation with new people and new ideas. Invigoration is long overdue. The longer we wait, the more painful it will be. In spite of all the cries of alarm about hiring "unqualified" employees, we must push ahead with affirmative action. Most new employees are overqualified as it is. Boredom is already a very real problem among both blue and white collar workers. Besides, why should corporate employers expect prospective employees to already be trained in the specific skills of a job? Should schools and, ultimately, taxpayers pay for vocational training that could be provided by the corporate employer on the job? From this angle, the self-serving nature of the outcry about hiring "unqualified" people becomes all too clear.

REFORM OF CORPORATE PROMOTION AND CORPORATE STRUCTURE

Homosocial reproduction is the process whereby the corporate elite reproduces itself. Two modes of reproduction occur. In the first mode, sons of the corporate elite simply follow in their fathers' footsteps, but generally not in the same corporation. In the second mode, which may overlap the first, members of the corporate elite sponsor young men as their proteges. In each mode, the norms, values, and ideas of the old corporate elite are reproduced in the new. The clones quickly rise up the corporate ladder, passing those with less pliable characters on the way. In the process, new people and new ideas are usually lost to the higher circles of the corporate bureaucracy. This must change. Aided by the following reforms of the corporate promotion process, the new blood admitted to the lower levels of the corporate bureaucracy, through reform of the filtering process, will flow into the higher circles.

The suffocating effects of homosocial reproduction will not be cured by cosmetic changes or managerial fads. Nor will other improvements come from minor "tinkering." Radical surgery is called for. In particular, four major changes need to be made in the corporate bureaucracy: (1) Replace promotion by selection with promotion by election. (2) Place Advisory Councils and Ombudsmen in each major corporate division. (3) Include a corporate bureaucrat's bill of rights in the corporate charter. (4) Restructure the Board of Directors by including both public and worker directors.

Bureaucrats are selected for promotion by their superiors. This makes the promotee beholden to the existing hierarchy and makes homosocial reproduction work. It also makes the fate of potential promotees dependent upon winning the fancy of members of the hierarchy and dependent upon staying in their good graces. Max Weber thought that selection by superiors ensured that bureaucratic duty was performed according to the rules handed down from on high. He was correct, but selection by superiors also ensures that their personal norms, values, and ideas continue unchallenged, it ensures that they are homosocially reproduced in the next generation of bureaucrats, and it ensures that those who do not share those personal norms, values, and ideas are excluded from rising up the hierarchy. In short, promotion by superior selection shuts out new people with new ideas. The very people who could invigorate the bureaucracy are routinely passed over by it, to everyone's harm, everyone except those entrenched in the higher levels.

This bureaucratic selection process should be replaced by a democratic process. At every level of the corporate bureaucracy, from the foreman to the president, officials should be elected in formal, secret balloting by the people they will supervise. We all should have the right to elect our own boss from among our fellow workers or from outside applicants. A foreman should be elected by the group of workers he supervises. And a corporate president should be elected by the vice-presidents. The same should apply to everyone in-between. In this way, bosses will be replaced by leaders. A boss rules through authority. A leader guides through consent. The difference between the two is fundamental. People submit to authority because they must; they respond to leadership because they wish. Furthermore, elected leaders represent those who elect them, thereby opening up the organization to the vital push from below.

But an organization will be torn apart if duties are not performed and rules not followed. Undermining all authority at this juncture of corporate evolution might very well destroy the corporation. Lest we kill the goose that laid the golden eggs, authority must be preserved in reduced form. To do so, elected corporate leaders at all levels must remain subject to demotion by their immediate supervisor if they fail to perform adequately. The work group being supervised will elect the supervisor, but the supervisor can be removed by higher authority for lack of performance. Then a new election must be held.

Many problems and frictions will be encountered by replacing selection with election, but given time to develop, the new promotion process will prove itself superior to "bossism" in the corporation just as democracy has proven itself superior to dictatorship in the body politic. Democracy in both the corporation and the body politic harnesses the energies and ideas of us all, particularly those of us who were formerly excluded from full participation.

In addition to election, Advisory Councils and Ombudsmen should become inherent parts of the invigorated corporation. Each corporate division should have an elected Advisory Council. The Council will then hire one or more Council Ombudsmen to investigate all employee complaints within the particular division. The Ombudsman can be called in by anyone to investigate a complaint or a conflict. The Ombudsman then reports his findings to the Council which, in turn, formulates its advice to the aggrieved parties. This "advice" is to be immediately implemented unless written appeal is made directly to the Division Head. Upon receipt of a written appeal, the Division Head will investigate the matter and determine what action to take. That action can be appealed only by the Council directly to the Board of Directors for review and reconsideration. Having exhausted all internal means of redress, the Council can then sue in Federal Court if dissatisfied. Of course, if the matter falls within its jurisdiction, the aggrieved party can file charges with the EEOC at any time.

Contested elections and claims of illegal discrimination will be major problem areas dealt with by the Advisory Councils and Ombudsmen. But another set of complaints and conflicts will be encountered when, in addition to the election, Advisory Council and Ombudsman, an employee's bill of rights is added to the corporation. This bill of rights should do for the corporate employee what the first ten amendments to the Constitution does for the U.S. citizen — guarantee that certain individual rights are inviolate. The Constitutions's Bill of Rights primarily protects the citizen from the state. And, outside of war hysteria (both hot and cold variety) and periodic Red terrors, the Bill of Rights has served even the new and the dissident citizen well in his role as citizen. But, in the role of employee we have not fared so well.

This lack of formal employee protection has very clear historical roots. In the age of the market — the eighteenth and nineteenth centuries — the employee was protected by the free labor market. (This, of course, did not apply to the slave.) If an employee were abused in some way, he could usually find another job in the free market. Changing jobs generally did not involve major career disruptions. Besides, opportunities for going into business for oneself were plentiful, particularly in farming. Protected by access to the free market and by plentiful opportunities as an independent businessman, workers needed little formal protection from their employers. And they were already protected from the state by the constitutional Bill of Rights.

But times have changed — a repeated refrain of this book. Opportunities for independent businessmen have shrunk, the free labor market is largely a memory, and job changes often mean a major disruption of one's career. In short, the options which used to protect employees from potential abuse are closed or closing. Furthermore, the typical employer of the eighteenth and nineteenth centuries was a small businessman of some sort, a far cry from the huge conglomerates of today. Early employers (outside of slaveowners) were not powerful enough to dish out much abuse to employees, on purpose or by accident. But the corporation of today can easily violate the civil liberties of whole groups of employees. Now we need, in addition to the constitutional Bill of Rights, a corporate bill of rights.

With the old, informal protections gone, the twentieth century employee needs formal protection and that protection should apply to actual employees, prospective employees and retirees as well. The following set of rights, enforceable by Advisory Councils or Federal Courts, should become a written part of all corporate charters.

1. The corporation shall take no action respecting an establishment of religion, or prohibiting the free exercise thereof; or abridging the freedom of speech, or of the press; or the right of the employee peaceably to assemble, and to petition the corporation for a redress of grievances.

2. The right of the employees to be secure in their persons, houses, papers, and effects, against unreasonable searches and seizures, shall not be violated by the corporation.

3. In all dismissal proceedings, the employee shall enjoy the right to a speedy and public hearing by his Advisory Council, and to be informed of the reason for the dismissal; to be confronted with witnesses against him; to have compulsory process for obtaining witnesses in his favor, and to have the assistance of his Ombudsman in his defense. Final decision will be made by secret jury vote, six members chosen by the Ombudsman and six by the employee's supervisor. A temporary layoff is not a dismissal.

These rights have been adapted, almost word for word, from the Bill of Rights in the U.S. Constitution. Some of the provisions are not applicable to the employee-employer relation so they were dropped.

Individuals in the twentieth century need protection from "Big Brother" whether he is the mammoth state or the mammoth corporation, for both have become truly awesome organizations. The power of the individual has dwindled as the power of the organization has expanded. The result is a serious imbalance between the virtually powerless individual and the very powerful organization. The imbalance has become acute for unorganized workers, particularly for those joining the swelling ranks of the white collar corporate occupations. The imbalance needs to be righted by an employee bill of rights.

The fourth change proposed for the new corporation is a restructuring of the Board of Directors. Today, the Board has become a moribund organ of the corporation. Originally intended as the body through which shareholders could exercise their collective control over corporate affairs, the Board's actual activities have atrophied as the separation of shareholder ownership from managerial control has continued to widen. In proxy battles and in rare emergencies the Board might spring back to life. Nevertheless, outside of those rare occurrences, the Board lies dormant. Its meetings are largely ceremonial, its membership mostly tired old men with a token black or woman thrown in for the public relations effect. Real power generally is exercised at the Presidential and Vice-presidential levels. In most operating decisions, the Board is informed of the decision, after the fact; rarely does it participate in the actual decision.

But not for long, if we choose to revitalize it by creating a new Board. The new Board should contain eleven members: Five elected in the usual way by the shareholders, three elected by corporate employees, and three appointed by the Federal Corporation Administration, a new function-specific regulator required to oversee the reforms proposed in this chapter and the next one. The three worker directors would receive the same salary as they received as workers plus any director fees paid to the shareholder directors. They would serve the same term as shareholder directors. Each worker director would represent a particular employee group. One would come from the union-represented employees or from the nonsupervisory operatives if no union exists. Another would come from the clerical and technical staff; the third from line supervisors. No changes have to be made in the selection of the five shareholder directors, but cumulative voting privileges should exist so that minority or renegade shareholders have a better chance of electing at least one director.

The worker director is not really an innovation, more like a borrowing, because worker directors have been used for some time now in Europe. The best known example is Germany's codetermination. Borrowing this practice from Germany would help ensure that employees' rights and voices would be represented at the very top of the corporation. The new Chrysler Corporation had to accept a worker director from the UAW to get labor to accept lower wages and benefits.

Although the practice is unfamiliar to most of us, the worker director is not without precedent in the U.S. and Europe. As with most reforms, the worker director has not completely solved the problem to which it was directed. In particular, it has not increased worker participation in corporate decision making to the extent hoped for by its backers. Yet improvement has taken place and, when instituted in conjunction with the other reforms suggested here, some very real progress should occur.

Opponents of the worker director emphasize two potential problems with the new practice. First, how can the worker director be made effective without conflicting with some aspects of union organization and collective bargaining? Without assurance on this score, labor often is opposed to the worker director. But, as demonstrated by the Chrysler case, that problem does not arise if the worker director comes from the union itself. Second, will worker directors gain access to inside information which might be leaked to competitors or used to undue advantage against the corporation? The corporation takes a very similar kind of risk when it uses outside directors and since outside directors are widely used, the risk must not be too great. Furthermore, directors are personally liable to shareholders if inside information is used for personal gain to the harm of the corporation. This liability should act as sufficient deterrent to malfeasance.

In addition to the new worker director, the revitalized board should contain the new public director. The three public directors, unlike the three worker and five shareholder directors, will not be elected by a particular corporate constituency. Instead, the public director will be appointed by the, also new, Federal Corporation Administration. The proposed FCA will be discussed at length in the next chapter. The public director, as well as the worker director, would have a vote in all matters before the board, and sit on all board committees in the same proportion as on the board itself. The public director, however, would not be employed or paid by the corporation but by the FCA. Public directors would be civil service employees of the highest rank and would be salaried accordingly. Each public director would also have a competent civil service staff officed in the corporation but not of the corporation. The public director's term of office on a particular corporate board would be four years. Rotation from corporate board to corporate board every, say, eight years would be mandatory. Rotation would reinforce personal loyalty to the FCA and weaken ties to any given corporation.

Also, after a trial period of acceptable public service, acceptable to the FCA, public directors would be vested with tenure to age 70. All pension rights and benefits would be forfeited immediately if a corporate position or corporate remuneration of any kind were accepted by an active or retired public director. For an active director, immediate dismissal would be mandatory. Furthermore, all corporate remuneration received at any time during FCA employment or for five years after dismissal or resignation would be seized as illegal contraband. Acceptance or offering of such remuneration would be bribery, a felonious offense. The revolving door that *now* leads from public employment to lucrative private employment would keep revolving right into the federal penitentary for those who use the public trust for private gain.

Other appropriate positive and negative sanctions would be built into this new role. In broad outline, every attempt would be made to create a new profession of highly-respected and highly-paid public officials. The profession of public director would have its own standards of technical performance, professional responsibility, and code of ethics. The status and salary reward structure of the profession would be divorced from the corporation. Peer acceptance and approval or disapproval would come from the profession, not the corporation.

The primary responsibilities of the public director as opposed to the worker director would be implementation of public policy within the corporation and verification of performance. The public director would also keep senior executives abreast of all new developments in public policy, acting as ambassador from EPA, OSHA, EEOC, and other relevant agencies. Precedence for the public directorship as a new institution and a new profession can be found easily. English factory inspectors in the nineteenth century played similar roles in implementing new public policy. Furthermore, no less a figure than Supreme Court Justice William O. Douglas had proposed the institutionalization of a new profession, similar to the one proposed here, but with less public authority. As early as 1940 he argued, "...salaried, professional experts would bring a new responsibility and authority to directorates and a new safety to stockholders."[12]

The public directorship could form the bridge connecting public purpose and corporate interest. It could result in much closer cooperation between government and the corporation. If public directors were highly paid and highly respected professionals with competent staffs, it is quite likely that their reception in corporate circles would be different than the current reception of government regulators, many of whom are viewed either as incompetent meddlers or as easily-co-opted pawns. But the new public and the new worker directors would be neither.

CONCLUSION

Democratic schools, promotion by election, Advisory Councils and Ombudsmen, the bureaucrat's bill of rights, and the new corporate board may all seem like hopelessly utopian schemes, far removed from American reality. But thinking about the tremendous level of popular discontent with jobs and the economy in general, it is clear that something will be done. People voted for Ronald Reagan in 1980 for the same reason they voted for Jimmy Carter in 1976. They want change—now. The same demands that swept Reagan's radicalism into Washington swept socialism into Paris and Athens and Thatcherism into London. But the radicals of the right are historically bankrupt. The conditions which would have made a return to rugged individualism actually work, have passed into historical memory. Only severe repression and suppression can recreate them today. The radical right in the United Kingdom and in the United States are drawing checks on an account that closed nearly a hundred years ago. When those checks bounce, and Thatcher's may have already begun to do so in the United Kingdom, the time will be ripe for either reform of basic institutions or real repression of those pushing up from below.

If we choose reform, it must build on what we already have. In the United States we have corporate capitalism. We must build on it. In the United Kingdom and Europe, a long tradition of democratic socialism and labor party politics exists. The Europeans must build on them. Seen from the perspective of history, and from the reality of our contemporary condition, the reforms proposed here take on a less utopian tone. In the United States, they just might work. In the United States, what are the alternatives? Full-blooded socialism died out after the first war. Fascism is still to be tried. So is corporate reform.

The corporate reforms we choose do not have to be the ones here. But real reforms must change corporate recruitment practices. Corporate filters must be cleaned up. Since we lead the world in college enrollment, we could easily start there. Instead of education producing finely gradated material for corporate filters, it could produce citizens and employees capable of full participation as both members of a polity and members of a work organization. Since equality of opportunity is an American tradition and since a viable Equal Employment Opportunity Commission is functioning already, both the tradition and the Commission could be used to continue the reform of filtering and then homosocial reproduction. Since most Americans consider the Bill of Rights in our Constitution as almost sacred, is it really utopian to extend the rights to cover corporate employees? Since democratic elections are used to choose the most important official of the world — the President of the United States — is it really preposterous to elect our own supervisors? And if we accept that these American principles be extended into the corporate world, then should we not accept the need for Advisory Councils, Ombudsmen, and a new board of directors to ensure the implementation of these principles?

But how do we get the corporate higher circles to agree?

8 THE FEDERAL CORPORATE CHARTER

INTRODUCTION

It is asking a lot of those with a vested interest in the corporate status quo to accept an employee's bill of rights, Advisory Councils, Ombudsmen, selection of officials by election, and a new Board of Directors. Vested interests have rarely given up their entrenched power when asked, or challenged. In general, such is the stuff of revolution. Yet vested interests occasionally have relinquished some of their power, if there was something in it for them. A quid pro quo can turn the trick, sometimes. Possibly, in the near future, when Reagan's retrenchment has been thoroughly tried and failed, will be such a time. Within the next few years (a decade at most?) the social and economic shortcomings of our conservative distemper should be apparent to most people. Of course, the true believers will find some reason to cling to their beliefs. But, by then, most people will be ready for a real change. Perhaps a few corporate statesmen also will see the need for reform, as long as there is something in it for them. More about that later.

Although it has been delayed, corporate reform is still on the national agenda. When it comes up again, one of the contradictions of grassroots reform movements must be recognized lest the resulting reforms misfire. The push for reform comes from below, from the grassroots level. But in our federalist political system, corporate reform can only be enforced at the national level. This is the contradiction: The reform push comes from below, but reform must be enforced from above. That is, to be effective, reform must be wedded to a political power which is large enough to enforce the reform provisions. State and local governments are too small and too weak. They can easily be played off against each other and become neutralized. They are no

match for corporate conglomerates. Only the federal government car-
ries such clout. Distant from the grassroots level and centralized though
it may be, civil liberty advocates, civil rights activists, and leaders of
the women's movement have learned the hard way that it takes action
at the federal level to enforce reforms.

Competition in laxity is the ultimate result of relying on state and
local government for protecting the public interest against corporate
abuses. Three examples immediately come to mind. First is the widespread erosion of local tax bases caused by reliance on the property tax
for funding local services. Corporate facilities (outside of mines and oil
wells) can be moved to different tax jurisdictions. As a result, corporate investment planners can play localities off against each other,
offering juicy payrolls to local boosters in exchange for tax breaks.
Renters and homeowners take up the slack, or launch tax revolts and
thereby push the burden further down the line onto the really poor
who are dependent upon the services funded by local tax revenues.
Second is the erosion of union strength after the states were allowed
to adopt so-called "right-to-work" laws. Major facilities have been
moving away from high wage union states to low wage nonunion states
ever since. Some corporations have gone even farther, leaving the U.S.
entirely for countries like South Korea, where labor is kept in its
"proper" place. Third, and most important for the structure of the corporation, the fact that the individual states can charter corporations
that operate all over the U.S. and the world has meant that corporate
charters place no effective constraints on corporate behavior. The
states of New Jersey, Delaware, and Maryland have competed against
each other throughout this century, each trying to outdo the others
in writing the most lax incorporation laws possible. Their competition
in laxity has eroded the effectiveness of virtually all major provisions
contained in corporate charters.[1]

The only way to stop such erosion is to rely on a level of government powerful enough to resist it. Nostalgia about townhall meetings
and grassroots democracy must be replaced with an understanding of
the new realities of corporate power and political weakness. Reliance
on state and local government authority will not lead to solutions for
the problems facing us today. We must turn to where the power is, the
federal government, for the reforms of the future. The scope of the
problems to be dealt with is simply too broad for state and local gov-

ernments. The lower-level governments lack the ability to respond effectively to the push from below against racism and sexism, against inflation and unemployment, even against community deterioration. If city hall only hired minorities, racism and sexism would continue. If city hall wanted to attack the inflation-unemployment dilemma, it would have nothing to use. If city hall attacks community deterioration, it must raise tax rates for the funds and this scares off new industry. The problems are too big; the government units too small; and that reality will not go away. Earlier reforms, which relied on state and local government, are inadequate.

But previous federal level reforms often have been disappointing as well. The failure of industry-specific regulators was discussed above. Trust busting as a reform is seriously limited by the fact that breaking up huge corporations not only reduces their power to push up prices and close plants but it also eliminates the economies of scale and the ability to plan enjoyed by the megacorps being broken up. Antitrust action against specific corporate abuses that restrain competition should be taken only as a last resort. The side effects of antitrust are simply too costly in terms of economies of scale and ability to plan.

Besides, with the introduction of the new function-specific regulator such as EPA, OSHA, and EEOC, better ways of controlling corporate abuses are evolving. A difficulty encountered by the new function-specific regulator must be overcome, however. The old industry-specific regulator had very close ties with the industry it regulated so the regulator had access to internal information and could exert pressure on the internal workings of the industry being regulated. Unfortunately, this closeness led to co-optation by the industry. The new function-specific regulator is not co-opted easily because it is not closely tied to any one industry. Nevertheless, the lack of close ties means a lack of access to internal information and an inability to exert pressure on the internal workings of the corporations being regulated. To compensate for this lack of access to internal information and to internal control structures, the new regulators try to overregulate. That is, they issue mountains of very detailed regulations to deal with every possible contingency and send out blizzards of forms seeking detailed information.

OSHA, in particular, has become infamous for such actions. Lacking close personal ties with the myriad of industries regulated, OSHA regulations are often too formal and too specific. In the regulatory game, if the regulator has close personal access to the internal workings of the regulated, general guidelines can be used because close informal contact ensures that exceptions to the general rules will be handled by the regulated in accordance with the spirit of the rules. But the regulator without these contacts, though free from co-optation, cannot be assured that the spirit of general rules will be followed in the numerous exceptional cases. The regulator responds to this uncertainty with over-regulation, with very elaborate formal rules designed to deal with all possible cases and with blizzards of questionnaires about compliance. To minimize the overregulation tendency of the new function-specific regulator, access to the internal workings of the regulated corporations must be provided. The access, however, must be of a kind that does not provide an avenue for co-optation. The public director on corporate boards can provide such non-co-opting access, if we design the public director's role properly.

One last introductory remark is in order. If the reforms proposed here are to work, the Sellers Inflation now endemic to our economy must be brought under control. A society reeling from inflation cannot be reformed because all groups within it are fighting mightily to protect, if not enlarge, their share of real income. The struggle, in addition to distorting the economy, makes all groups fearful of reform and compromise. If a group accepts a new way of doing things, in an inflationary world, the cost might be immense. So we all hang onto what we have and refuse to try something new lest we come out the loser. Continued inflation has made us all fear that ours is a zero sum economy. If I compromise and accept a reform of my bailiwick, I lose because the public wins — or so we have all begun to think. As our thinking has become ever more fearful, the resistance to reform has hardened. To overcome the fear and resistance, inflation must be controlled permanently.

The historical record on controlling inflation is spotty at best. Fighting inflation through restricting spending is extraordinarily costly in terms of unemployment. Whether spending is cut back through a tight federal budget or through a tight monetary policy the result is the same — an unacceptably high unemployment rate. The only other tested anti-inflation policy with real teeth is wage-price control, to be discussed at length in a later chapter. Wage-price controls have been effective when applied equitably and with resolve. To be equitable, however, controls must allow for flexibility in the face of real cost increases and wage-salary inequities. In the 1980s a wage-price controller could be effective as a function-specific rather than industry-specific regulator, if it had access to reliable information on costs, wages, salaries, and profits. As in the case of other function-specific regulators, the wage-price authority needs the public director to provide the right kind of access to the internal workings of powerful corporations.

To sum up these introductory remarks, corporate reform can be made acceptable to corporate vested interests if based on a quid pro quo. Once accepted, corporate reform must be enforced by a level of government powerful enough to enforce it; this means the federal level. Furthermore, non-co-opting access to the corporate inner circles must be provided for the new function-specific regulators. I believe that these practical requirements can be met in the following way.

THE FEDERAL CHARTER

The Practical Details

Tax cut mania is sweeping the land, so why should reformers let supply-siders get all the credit? As a first step in the corporate reform movement of the 1980s we should propose abolishing entirely the corporate income tax as a quid pro quo for federal chartering. Eliminate the corporate tax — corporations probably paid little of it anyway — but only if corporations are required to take out a federal charter in place of their existing state charter. Also, treat all personal income derived from corporate activities the same way. Since individuals who provide labor to the corporation must pay income tax on it, the same should apply to individuals who provide the corporation with capital. In other words, stockholders should pay taxes on their financial capital earnings at the same rate that workers pay taxes on their human capital earnings. Of course, this proposal would tax stockholder earnings whether or not those earnings were paid out as dividends or kept as retained earnings. Otherwise, some earnings (retained earnings on financial capital) would not be taxed at the appropriate rate — the rate applicable to earned income.

Lester Thurow, who favors eliminating the corporate tax because it will improve both horizontal and vertical tax equity, calculated that the radical tax reform proposed here, instead of the Reagan cuts, would cost the U.S. treasury far less than what one would think. The treasury would suffer a net loss of between 4 and 10 billion dollars a year.[2] The reason the loss would be so small is that the increased personal tax liabilities of wealthy stockholders would offset most of the loss in revenues from the elimination of the corporate income tax.

Corporations would get an approximate doubling of their profits (profits would exactly double if the effective tax rate were exactly 50 percent and if none of the tax reduction were passed on to other groups). But to get it, they would have to operate under the provisions of a federal charter. Those provisions would include, in the corporate charter itself, the employee's bill of rights, the Advisory Councils, Ombudsmen, new Board of Directors, and selection of officials (bosses) by election.

Corporations would then be under the supervision of the Federal Corporation Administration through its professional corps of public directors. The tax incentive and the growing public demand for real change could be enough to tip the scale toward acceptance of the federal corporate charter, even though it would mean drastic changes in the corporate world. Let me flesh out in more detail the nature of those changes.

First, a new federal regulator would be created. The Federal Corporation Administration should be run by six commissioners, three of them elected by the FCA's corps of public directors and three appointed by the President. Having three of the commissioners elected would apply the new election of superiors principle to the FCA itself, protecting the professional integrity and technical competence of the corps of public directors against inappropriate Presidential appointees to the commission. More than one federal regulatory agency has been rendered ineffective or worse by unfortunate political appointments. The FCA must be protected from suffering the same fate. For that matter, the other federal regulatory agencies and departments would benefit if they too followed the election of superiors principle. Imagine the difference it would make if a James Watt were replaced by six commissioners, three of whom were elected by competent government environmental professionals. Yet, in the case of government bureaucracies, the election of superiors principle can only go so far lest elected professional government employees completely replace political appointees, who are supposed to be agents of democratically elected Presidents.

The FCA would be a function-specific regulator charged with appointing competent public directors to all federally-chartered corporations and charged with seeing that those public directors discharge their duties in the public interest. Public directors would serve two purposes. On the one hand, they would serve as reliable sources of information for other regulatory bodies. EPA, OSHA, EEOC, and other government agencies would use the public directors as their access to needed information. Corporate employees would not be used to make up (sometimes, literally) the various reports required by federal agencies. Instead, the public director and support staff (all FCA employees) would be responsible. All the paper work that supply-siders make such noise about, would be taken off the corporate back. On the other hand, public directors would serve a second purpose. They would be representatives of the public interest in the actual decision-making processes which take place at the highest corporate level. Along with the worker director, the public director could breathe new vigor into the board of directors. The practice of putting token minorities and worn-out executives on boards would change quickly when shareholder directors faced aggressive worker and public directors.

Two administrative details of the FCA also need to be discussed. First, the internal organization of the FCA itself must not be along industrial lines. That is, divisions of the FCA, if needed, should not be industry specific. The FCA should never have, say, a steel or auto industry division because if such a division were formed, it could become a perfect conduit for co-optation from the specific industry. Co-optation must be guarded against at all costs. Second, the FCA should be given the authority to classify corporations according to their importance to public policy. Very small family-held corporations do not need public directors on their boards. The public interest is too small to justify the expense. Furthermore, paper corporations owned by conglomerates do not need public directors either. The FCA may find that the public directors on the conglomerate's board can handle the job for the organization as a whole. In intermediate cases of large family-held corporations or of independent subsidiaries, the FCA may find that the public directors could handle several such board positions at once. But in large corporations — all the Fortune 500 — the public directors would devote all their time to one corporation. They would not serve on several boards simultaneously as is the current custom of many shareholder directors.

The second major change in the corporate world, in addition to the supervision of the FCA, would be mandated by standardized provisions in the federal corporate charter. In addition to the public director the charter would provide for the worker director, supervisor election, Advisory Councils, Ombudsmen, and the employee's bill of rights. All parties affected by these provisions, not just the corporate share-holders, could bring suit to enforce the provisions in federal court. This could make the provisions effective and bring about a peaceful revolution within the corporation itself.

The New Corporate World

Contemporary observers of the American corporation are becoming convinced that fundamental reforms are needed to improve productivity and revitalize the corporate world in general.[3] Michael Maccoby calls for new corporate leaders, more open to participative decision-making and more committed to democracy in the workplace. The old patriarchs and gamesmen are no longer able to give the kind of leadership corporations need if they are to keep up with the productivity revolution occurring in Europe and Japan. Not only is a change in leadership called for, but a change in corporate culture is also on the agenda. Driven to the wall by more productive Japanese organizations, corporations as entrenched as GMC are responding with innovative organizational forms and processes. Other American corporations, founded by humanistic entrepreneurs and scientists, also have developed new organizational forms. From their very beginning, new corporations like Hewlett-Packard have used more trusting, intimate, and subtle processes and structures for managing people than those used by traditional bureaucratic corporations. Ouchi has found that these new corporations, and old ones able to respond positively to the productivity revolution abroad, use a new theory of management. This new theory is called "Theory Z" by Ouchi, who argues that Theory Z must replace the hierarchical and bureaucratic managerial theories used by most American corporations. Otherwise, productivity gains will continue to be abysmal when compared with those in better managed corporations. Taking a look at psychological rather than organizational factors, Maccoby concludes that "the leader" must replace "the gamesman" before the top individuals in American corporations will be able to respond positively to the organizational crisis they face.

Theory Z corporations, Ouchi argues, are similar to Japanese corporations in several respects. First, decision-making processes in Theory Z companies are consensual and participative rather than hierarchical and authoritative. Unlike Japanese organizations, however, the final responsibility for a specific decision rests with one person. Election of supervisors would promote consensus and participation. But, in keeping with the profound individualism of American culture, supervisors must retain personal responsibility for decisions reached by their work groups. The right to demote them must remain with their superior. Second, Theory Z companies are wholistic organizations where people deal with each other in more informal and personal ways with professional specialization and organizational rank de-emphasized. Third, Theory Z organizations are more egalitarian than the traditional bureaucratic corporations. "Egalitarianism," Ouchi observes, "is a central feature of Type Z organizations."[4] Fourth, egalitarianism is supported by trust, the trust that others share basic values and are personally well-meaning, helpful, and never harmful. An employee bill of rights, Advisory Councils, Ombudsmen, and a new Board of Directors, as suggested here, could go a long way toward establishing more wholistic personal relations, egalitarianism, and trust in American corporations, most of which are far from becoming Type Z organizations on their own. If Theory Z is to spread in the U.S., it will need a push. Waiting for participative management of Type Z to spread on its own merits to most established, unthreatened U.S. corporations, will take decades. In corporations dominated by an entrenched elite, which reproduces itself in succeeding generations of managers, the change will never come unless the issue is forced by public policy. The federal charter proposed here will force it.

Participative, egalitarian, wholistic, trusting organizations also need a new model of leadership. Maccoby provides it in his latest book, *The Leader*. The dominant psychological type of corporate executive in the U.S. is now the gamesman. Described by Maccoby in his earlier book, *The Gamesman*, such an executive is driven by a personal need to win, again and again, in career games leading to chief executive officer of a major corporation. Such career game-playing often generates negative personality traits in the players. The gamesman easily becomes rash, manipulative, and unprincipled, according to Maccoby. Corporate leaders with these negative traits are generally unable to forego their unprincipled manipulation of subordinates in order to establish trusting, wholistic, egalitarian forms of participative decision-making. A new breed of corporate executive is required to bring the American corporation out of its self-induced stupor.

This new breed of executive, the leader, must be able to transform the values engendered by corporate bureaucracy into values consistent with social democracy. For the push from below, described by Maccoby as "the challenge to paternal authority,"[5] is inconsistent with the homosocial reproduction from above which characterizes corporate bureaucracy in America. One or the other must give, eventually. Either the drives against racism, sexism, and paternalism will move into the corporate bureaucracy proper and democratize it or the homosocial reproduction of the corporate bureaucracy will move into the rest of society and "bureaucratize" it. The two social hemispheres are mutually exclusive because the values engendered by each are contradictory. As described earlier in this book, corporate values have the upper hand in the early 1980s. But in a value crisis, such as confronts the U.S. today, change occurs suddenly and dramatically — remember the 1960s.

Guiding this hoped-for change, according to Maccoby, requires leaders who care deeply about others and have the flexibility to accept and encourage participative decision-making. The leader in the 1980s must be able to bring out the best democratic values in people. Maccoby identified six leaders from several different organizations who had these traits. He studied what they did and how they did it. As they tried to introduce their new managerial style two things generally happened. On one hand, organizational efficiency and effectiveness often rose as participation from below rejuvenated the spirits of many workers.[6] On the other hand, institutional resistance from above also rose as managerial prerogatives were threatened by the increased participation. Maccoby found that the values represented by his six new leaders, the new managerial style they had tried so hard to implement, usually began to fade under the impetus of continued institutional resistance when the leaders left.

New leadership is not enough. Major institutional change is required. In particular, to create permanent participative management within a trusting, egalitarian organization, the organization itself must be restructured. Full-fledged participation means that those being led should be protected formally (a bill of rights in the corporate charter) and that formal structures should be created to enforce those rights (Advisory Councils and Ombudsmen). To ensure that resistance to these reforms from above is overcome, the very top of the corporation must become actively supportive of them (a new Board of Directors). Then democratic reform will not be dependent upon the haphazard emergence of Maccoby's leader. Given fundamental organizational reform, strong leadership is not needed. Maccoby's leader can retire.

Also, in Ouchi's Theory Z type organization it is very likely that personalistic rather than universalistic human relations will allow racism, sexism, and paternalism to re-emerge. Ouchi observes that Japanese corporations, after which Theory Z is modeled, are extraordinarily paternalistic. Furthermore, Ouchi emphasizes, "Probably no form of organization is more sexist or racist than the Japanese corporation."[7] This force toward excluding outsiders, found in organizations based on wholistic or all-embracing personal relations, must be offset by an equally strong force that maintains an open door to new people. A strengthened EEOC would provide such a counterbalancing force.

Corporate bureaucracies will not reform themselves. Instead, the fundamental changes suggested by Maccoby and Ouchi must be supported by public policy coming from the highest level of government. The real tragedy of the Reagan administration is that in a time when the need for change is great, change is being implemented; but the change is taking us backward into the era of frontier individualism rather than forward into an era of the mature corporation.

HISTORICAL PERSPECTIVE

Historical Precedents and Logic

Federal chartering of corporations actually began in those good old days of frontier individualism.[8] Both the First and Second National

Banks of the United States operated with federal charters. Even though short-lived, they set a precedent which would be followed in the years to come, albeit very sparingly. During the Civil War, the north established a national banking system based upon federal chartering of banks. After the war, however, the proliferation of banks with state charters resulted in a dual banking system in the United States. Also, during the era of Jacksonian democracy, general incorporation procedures adopted by the states made it relatively easy to obtain state charters for any legitimate purpose. No such general incorporation legislation was adopted at the federal level, although nothing precluded it. And, more to the point, nothing precludes it now. Yet even today, federal chartering of corporations extends just to national banks, federal savings and loan associations, credit unions, and a few special purpose, quasi-public organizations created by special legislation. Here is a powerful tool of public policy which has remained virtually unused for two centuries! It is time we used it.

Others have agreed. Three Presidents have suggested it to Congress (Teddy Roosevelt, Taft, and Wilson). U.S. Senator Joseph O'Mahoney, a populist from Wyoming, also supported it. In O'Mahoney's closing statement to the famous TNEC he argued in 1941,

> It is idle to think that huge collective institutions which carry on our modern business can continue to operate without more definite responsibility toward all the people of the nation than they now have. To do this it will be necessary, in my judgment, to have a national charter system ... [9]

Ralph Nader also supports federal over state chartering of corporations, as does progressive labor. But more important than personal endorsements is the historical logic of it. When most economic activity was of a small-scale, local nature, state and local governments were the natural levels to use for conducting public economic policy. They were closest to the problems and were powerful enough to deal with them. It was only natural in the age of Jacksonian democracy for reformers to rely on state charters for corporations. Repulsed by the aristocratic federalists, the people had elected one of their own — Andrew Jackson. The Jacksonian Democrats opened up the statehouses and state legislatures to the man on the make and turned their back on the central government in Washington (except when native Americans become restive), for Washington was perceived as the stronghold of the man who already had it made. After Jackson defeated the Second National Bank, symbol of aristocratic privilege, little thought was given to granting federal charters of incorporation. The state chartered bank, canal company, turnpike company, and later, railroad company were used to settle the moving frontier (after federal troops had cleared the field of native Americans). And it worked, as long as economic activity remained on a small scale.[10]

Today most economic activity is of a large-scale, national, and even international nature.[11] Business has outgrown state and local government. But the charters of national and international businesses are still issued by individual states. The practice has become an anachronism, a hold-over from an earlier age which limits our capacities for dealing with contemporary problems. The idea that one of the fifty states can issue a charter to a multinational megacorp and the belief that the charter is adequate for the problems encountered by and created by that megacorp have become ludicrous. But old ideas die hard, particularly when supported by powerful vested interests.

The Long Sweep of History

History is often interpreted as the rise and fall of great empires, great civilizations, and great men. Yet history should be the story of the little people. For our blood built the great empires, our minds carried forward the values of the great civilizations, and our support made the great men. What does history, properly perceived, tell us about the little people? Although often deceived, misled, tortured, and murdered, throughout the ages the little people have struggled to be free — not just free from constraints, but free to participate fully in the life processes of their societies. The struggle has been for the freedom *to*, not just the freedom *from*. Freedom has always meant the ability to act for oneself, not merely the defense against others' actions. It means human liberation. And history, properly perceived, is the story of human liberation, of the push from below. The push from below for human liberation has continued from at least the time of Jesus of Nazareth through the time of Martin Luther King, Jr. But in the United States at the close of the twentieth century, we stand at a crossroads. Perhaps we want to go back to an earlier time when people knew their place: when women were wives and good cooks, when blacks were negros and good hands, when children were seen but not heard, and when employees were obedient and good servants.

This temporary flirtation with authoritarian romanticism must pass quickly lest the pent-up demands burst out in senseless violence. The push from below will not go away. Nor will it be satisfied easily. In the United States the civil rights and women's movements will continue to push for liberation from sexism and racism but that will not be enough because corporate "bureaucratism," even in the absence of the others, will still be an effective barrier to the full participation of all in the workplace. As sexism and racism fade, the push from below will take a different form, is already taking a different form. Rather than struggling against status differences based on race and sex, the struggle is moving against status differences based on economic position, bureaucratic position in particular. The Solidarity movement in Poland is a manifestation of the new push from below. Solidarity is nationalistic, but more importantly, it is a push for worker control, for participative management. Full participation in the workplace has been a major aim of Solidarity from the beginning. The sit-down strikes (illegal in the U.S.), protests, and general agitation have been centered around workplace issues. In addition to the traditional religious and political freedoms, the Polish push from below has been for economic freedoms. The freedom to participate in decision-making at work, not just the freedom to buy and sell has driven Solidarity. It also will drive the American worker.

Perhaps American corporations will respond differently to that drive than the Polish authorities. The reforms suggested here, if adopted, will provide positive avenues of development. In place of authoritarian romanticism and repression, we could try equality in the workplace. Industrial democracy is just as important to free people as political democracy. As Chris Argyris explains, "there is a lack of congruence between the needs of healthy individuals and the demands of the formal [bureaucratic] organization."[12]

CHAPTER SUMMARY

The reform proposals discussed here are not utopian blueprints for the future. Rather, they are concrete proposals that can be implemented without major disruption of the economy. Furthermore, they are proposals that come from deeply held American values. The respect we have for equality and participation is central to our democratic way of life. These are very dear to the American tradition; they are not merely borrowed from other societies; they are not utopian. They have guided the American dream and will do so again. Ours is not a fearful society. We will not retreat forever into authoritarian romanticism. Neither our consciences nor our minorities will let us.

When the pendulum of public opinion swings back to reform, the institution that will receive the most attention will be the corporation. When that happens, reform must be enforced by the federal government. State and local governments are too weak, compared with the institution being reformed. Given a major tax break as a quid pro quo, corporate leaders could be induced to accept more egalitarian and participative ways of doing business. Some corporations, founded by humanistic entrepreneurs, have done so already. Other corporations, forced to the wall by foreign competition like GMC, have done the same. Type Z organizations, as Ouchi calls them, have demonstrated their productivity. Theory Z works. So does the new leadership style described by Maccoby. But a strong public policy push and concrete reform proposals are needed for the new practices to spread and for them to take permanent root.

The new organizations are there, though few in number. Federal chartering of corporations has been practiced for 200 years, though very sparingly. Equality and participation are strong American values. The push from below will continue, though its form is changing. New, function-specific regulators have shown that they can work. And a quid pro quo for corporate cooperation would not be too costly. The time will come when we put it all together, and the corporation will become a more vital, egalitarian, and participative place to work. At least, to keep going, we must keep the faith.

9 PLANNING AND CORPORATE ADMINISTRATION

INTRODUCTION

In addition to reforming the American corporation's internal relations, its external relations are also in need of reform. Not only do the internal decision-making processes need to be humanized and democratized, but the external workings of the corporation need to be coordinated with the requirements of a humane, democratic society. In many respects, the corporation serves our economy very well. Corporate administration of the production and distribution processes of our technologically advanced economy has made large-scale, low cost mass production possible. The small, independent businessman of pre-Civil War days could not amass the capital required and could not administer the far-flung organization needed for the task. Corporate bureaucracy can, and we must preserve that capability. On the other hand, the small, independent businessman could not exercise much power over his workers, suppliers, competitors, consumers, or government officials. The corporate bureaucracy can. This power must be curtailed and turned to public account.

But first we must understand how corporate power evolved. In a nutshell, it evolved through internal growth, merger, diversification, and, above all, through improvements in corporate administration. Through an evolutionary process, corporate administration came to replace the old price mechanism of the free market.

Before the Civil War, the American economy was composed, almost exclusively, of single-unit firms. These firms owned only one factory, farm, or mine and they were run by the owner-manager with no managerial hierarchy. As commodities moved from raw material to the finished product stage, they changed hands many times in a network of intermediate product markets. Before raw materials were finally sold as finished products, they were bought and sold in numerous transactions between independent businessmen. In each transaction, price was set by the free ebb and flow of supply and demand and by the bargaining skill and business acumen of the buyers and sellers. This market price system guided the flow of products at each stage of production. Today, however, the evolution of the corporate institution has changed all that. The flow of production is now guided by an administrative accounting system rather than a market price system. To understand our corporate economy and to reform it, we must first understand how corporate administration has replaced the price system.

THE ADMINISTRATIVE SYSTEM REPLACES THE PRICE SYSTEM

The Merger Waves

The transition from a price system to an administrative system began in earnest after the Civil War. By 1890, the public outrage against the use of trusts to monopolize markets resulted in the passage of the Sherman Antitrust Act. The act outlawed combinations and conspiracies in restraint of trade. It also outlawed monopolization of a market. Yet the Sherman Act was followed by the first major merger wave to sweep across the American economy. The wave crested in 1897–1903, leaving behind it about 200 merged corporations. Most of these were horizontal mergers, combinations of former competitors.[1] Many of these horizontal combinations were unstable and later broke up. Administering them was a monumental task, often beyond the abilities of their financial backers. Nevertheless, many of the most powerful corporations in the world were created by the first merger wave to sweep across the American economy, notable among them being the United States Steel Corporation.

The second merger wave occurred in the 1920s. By 1929, this wave had etched the major oligopolistic outline of American industry. That out-line has remained intact through the Second World War and beyond. The merger of the 1920s resulted primarily in a vertically integrated oligopoly. This remained the major form of corporate combination until the 1960s, for the vertically integrated oligopoly had far more staying power than the looser horizontal combinations formed in the first merger wave at the turn of the century. From the late 1920s through the 1950s, little change occurred in the market structure of the American economy. The vertically integrated oligopoly became and remained the dominant market participant in U.S. enterprise. Most industrial markets became oligopolistic in the 1920s and have stayed that way ever since. Orthodox economists point out, correctly, that markets have not become markedly more anticompetitive in over 50 years. From this observation they then conclude, incorrectly, that since it has not declined, competition must still thrive in the U.S. economy. But competition has not declined recently, because it was already moribund in 1930. The lack of further decline is not evidence of thriving competiton. Rather, it is evidence of the low level to which competition had already fallen over fifty years ago.

The third merger wave crested in the 1960s but shows strong evidence of revival in the 1980s. This third wave has ushered in a new form of corporate enterprise — the conglomerate. The conglomerate merger differs from the horizontal and vertical mergers in that the conglomerate acquires corporations producing goods or services which are unrelated to the line sold by the acquiring corporation. Conglomerate acquisitions are not attempts to buy out competitors or to acquire material suppliers or retailers. Instead, conglomerate acquisitions are moves into new markets. Product diversification rather than technical integration or market consolidation is the object. The best known conglomerates emerging in the 1960s were International Telephone and Telegraph, Litton Industries, Gulf and Western Industries, and Ling-Temco-Vought.[2] Many others were formed and though not as well known as IT&T or LTV, the other conglomerates became just as important.[3] The conglomerate form of corporate enterprise freed the corporation from the constraint of selling just one product line which, up until the 1960s, had restrained corporate pricing power. Lifting that old constraint was a major triumph for the corporation, but a disaster for the economy. With that market constraint gone, the age of stagflation could begin. Conglomerates began aggressively pushing up prices in their newly acquired markets, sure in the knowledge that when one market dried up, another could be tapped.

The Administrative Waves

Before the conglomerate form of corporation could become dominant, corporate administrative structures and procedures developed to manage huge business empires. As early as the first merger wave at the turn of the century, severe administrative problems were encountered in managing the large organizations resulting from the mergers. So in addition to the merger waves that marked the evolution of the American corporation, waves of new administrative structures and procedures also shaped the evolving corporate institution. As it grew in size and complexity, the corporation began taking on a more bureaucratic form.

Alfred D. Chandler, Jr., describes two distinctive stages through which successful corporate organizations have passed: (1) The horizontal consolidations of the first merger wave were eventually reorganized into centrally controlled enterprises complete with managerial hierarchies, cadres of salaried managers, and functionally departmentalized organizational structures. (2) The vertically-integrated oligopolies of the second merger wave grew so large that they eventually had to be decentralized into multidivisional structures composed of autonomous divisions, each division responsible for all the functions required to serve a particular market or product line, and all divisions reporting to a general office or holding company headquarters.[4] This multidivisional form developed the administrative structures and techniques required by the conglomerates of the third merger wave. With minor adaptation the multidivisional organization, first developed by the growing vertically integrated oligopolies, was easily borrowed by the conglomerates of the 1960s.

In addition to the merger waves and, partially as a result of them, two waves of administrative change swept over the American corporation in the twentieth century. Each administrative wave was a response to the particular set of administrative problems encountered at that stage of organizational evolution. Of course, like the three merger waves, the two administrative waves did not reach all parts of the economy. Laggard industries and firms, even within progressive industries, are still in evidence. But like "missing links," they remain behind as clear indications of the evolutionary path through which most of Corporate America has passed in the twentieth century.

At the beginning of the century, the first merger wave left behind unstable horizontal combinations, tenuously maintaining their near-monopolies against new competitors. Most of them could not last. Nearly all of them lost their monopoly-like grip. They encountered two major problems in administering their far-flung, hodge-podge combinations. First was the problem of coordinating the product flow through the organization. Excessive inventory in some areas and production delays in others were costly inefficiencies. Second was the problem of accounting for and controlling product cost. The successful structural response to these problems was vertical integration and centralization into functionally-specialized departments. Continued horizontal combination generally was unsuccessful because, with the horizontal combine suffering from high-cost, inefficient production processes, new competition seemed to pop up as fast as it could be bought out by the over-extended combine.

Vertical integration and centralization, however, gave a functionally-specialized management the power to cut costs and to control the flow of materials through the production and distribution processes. The resulting internal efficiency created a very effective barrier to new entry. New competitors simply could not match the low costs of the vertically-integrated, centrally-managed oligopolies. The managerial control over production and distribution, according to Chandler, "...permitted the visible hand of administrative coordination to make more intensive use of the resources invested in these processes of production and distribution than could the invisible hand of market coordination."[5] The central planning of the functionally-specialized managers working for vertically integrated oligopolies was more efficient than the earlier market system's coordination of the flow of product from the old independent raw material supplier through the raw material market to the old independent manufacturer, then through the market again to an independent wholesaler then back through the market to a retailer, and finally through the market one more time to the ultimate consumer. All those time-consuming and costly market interruptions in the flow of product were replaced by the centrally-planned, vertically-integrated oligopoly. And, since the result was increased efficiency, the huge oligopolies survived and prospered. By World War I, the first wave of administrative change had begun, and by the end of the 1920s it had transformed most of the progressive combines in American industry.

Yet the centralized, functionally-departmentalized organization left in place by the first wave of administrative change began to develop new kinds of problems. Continued internal growth and the merger wave of the 1920s created serious strains in the centralized corporate organizations. The prosperous oligopolies began developing more elaborate product lines. As they did, fluctuations in product demand caused more serious adjustment problems for the functionally-specialized and centralized managerial hierarchies. Two major problems emerged in the larger, more elaborate corporate bureaucracies.

First, it became very difficult for the centralized bureaucracies to calibrate the flow of production to fluctuations in demand. Before the "visible hand of management" had replaced the "invisible hand of the market," fluctuations in demand resulted in fluctuations in product price. Particulary when demand fell, product price also fell to clear the market of excess production at discount prices. But huge oligopolies learned to avoid price discounting to move excess production because cutting prices easily led to disastrous price wars. Nevertheless, by avoiding price cutting, the oligopoly created the problem of excessive inventory build-up when demand fell. Furthermore, the centralized organizational structure adopted by oligopolies had removed the functionally-specialized managers from close contact with actual market conditions. Being out of touch with the markets for its full product line, the corporate bureaucracy responded too slowly to changes in demand, particulary to declines in demand. Expensive inventory build-up resulted. The problem of calibrating production to demand became severe, particularly during the declining demand period of the Great Depression. The corporate bureaucracy needed a way of keeping very close tabs on demand so that a fall in demand was met immediately with production cut-backs before unsold inventory would become excessive.

To calibrate production to demand, a new organizational structure was required. Partial decentralization was the solution provided by the second wave of administrative change to sweep over the American corporation. Autonomous divisions replaced centralized, functionally-specialized departments. Each autonomous division became responsible for all of the functions required to service a particular part of the product line or to service a particular geographical market area. The activities of the autonomous divisions were then coordinated by a central general office. But decisions regarding the flow of production for each product market or geographical market were made by the autonomous divisions, so that output could be calibrated to demand by managers who were intimately familiar with the market being served.[6]

In addition to the problem of calibrating production to demand, the decentralizing corporate bureaucracies encountered a second problem. It became difficult for the central office to evaluate and control the performance of the managers in charge of the autonomous divisions. The quantification of general criteria for evaluating managerial performance became essential. The head of each autonomous division encountered different market conditions and different organization and production problems. How could the effectiveness of their different responses to different challenges be compared? A comparable indication of success or failure, of course, was the rate of profit earned by each division. The bottom line naturally became the rate of profit on investment earned by each division head. Elaborate accounting methods evolved to determine division profits and yearly bonuses came to depend increasingly on yearly profit rates. The evaluation practice spread and even subordinate departments of the autonomous divisions were treated as distinct "profit centers." Managerial rewards became closely tied to profits — too closely tied, as we shall see below.

By the end of the Great Depression, the decentralized organization composed of autonomous divisions had proven itself, but that organizational form did not become the dominant form of corporate enterprise until after the Second World War. Chandler emphasizes, "Indeed, the years after World War II mark the triumph of modern business enterprise."[7] In the 1950s most large, progressive corporations had adopted the new decentralized organizational structure.

From that organizational base, completed in the 1950s, it was an easy step into the conglomerate mergers of the 1960s. For once an organization composed of autonomous divisions was developed, it was natural to use the organizational structure to manage even larger corporate empires. The autonomous divisions were ideal ways to manage acquired corporations, even if the formerly independent corporations serviced totally unrelated markets. The decentralized divisions reporting to a central general office were, and still are, very adaptable. Furthermore, with a uniform criterion for evaluating divisional performance (the rate of return on assets), it made no difference to the central office what the divisions made or how they made it. The only important thing became, and remains, the rate of profit on assets. In short, the conglomerate corporation is a natural outcome of the autonomous divisions; but so too is the obsession with the bottom line. The 1960s saw both a conglomerate merger wave and a wave of profit obsession sweep over the American economy.

After the "go go years," we would never be the same. Two changes are of particular importance. First, the modern conglomerate is able to calibrate production for numerous markets very closely to changes in demand for those products. Second, the manager of each market-oriented division or subsidiary is responsible for a specific profit center, with bonus and promotion prospects determined by the short-run profit generated by the center. The first change has made the paradox of thrift a grim reality in the American economy. The second change has increased the inflationary tendency of the American economy. Because the rate of production in many of our markets is so closely calibrated to demand in those markets, an increase in consumer saving causes an immediate and pronounced rise in unemployment for the economy as a whole (the paradox of thrift). When consumers save more, they spend less. The fall in consumer spending is a fall in demand in consumer markets. With production tightly calibrated to demand, a fall in demand results in immediate production halts and layoffs. So consumer saving causes immediate unemployment. Also, because of the managerial obsession with the short-run profits of their profit centers, a marked trend toward higher prices has emerged. A higher price in a specific market generates higher short-run profits before consumers adjust their purchases downward. By the time the downward adjustment is made, the long-run losses will affect someone else's salary and promotion. The price-gouger will have received a bonus and promotion before the losses start.

The Narrowed Scope of the Market System

Three merger waves and two waves of administrative change have profoundly altered our market system. In general, what has occurred is a dramatic narrowing of the scope of the market system. Our economy can no longer be characterized as "market capitalism." It is now "corporate capitalism," because corporate management has replaced the free play of market supply and demand in much of our economy. True, consumer demand is still the determining force in the product market. Consumers are free to choose what they buy or, more precisely, consumers are *free to be sold* what corporations have to sell.

But the full-blown market system was composed of four interrelated markets, not just one: (1) In the *final product market*, bargaining between retailer and consumer determined what was purchased and at what price. Consumer demand still determines what is purchased, but it has increasingly less effect on price. Furthermore, consumer demand is increasingly the artificial result of the American status panic and the barrage of advertising aimed at the anxiety-prone consumer. (2) In the *intermediate product market*, production began with the farmer, miner, or fisherman working with their own individual holdings to produce raw materials for sale to various independent processors, who then sold to various independent wholesalers, who sold to various retailers. Each time, the sale occurred in the elaborate network of markets, collectively referred to as the intermediate product market. That network of markets has been replaced in large areas of our economy by vertically integrated corporations. Managerial planning is now found where the intermediate product market used to be. (3) In the *labor market*, workers and employers bargained about jobs and wages. Now we find the filtering and homosocial reproduction of corporate bureaucracy. (4) In the *capital market* investors bid for the money and savings of American households, with banks, stockbrokers, and other financial intermediaries serving as middlemen between the two. Increasingly the top general managers of conglomerate corporations are acquiring huge volumes of corporate cash flow from subsidiaries and reallocating it to other subsidiaries or using it for additional corporate acquistions. The central office of the conglomerate has become a kind of mini-capital market, acquiring financial capital from one subsidiary and reallocating it to another. American households never even see the money, except when they pay the high prices of corporate conglomerates, thus making the consumer's contribution to corporate prosperity. Conglomerate managers never have to borrow in the open capital market to finance corporate expansion, unless an unexpected shortfall in cash flow occurs. Then red-faced corporations can be seen in the boardrooms of major banks, but they will not have to wait in line in the lobby with the struggling small businessman or hopeful homebuyer.

We still have a market system, of sorts. Just enough remains to comfort those of us who still have an ardent faith in the market. But the scope of the market mechanism has been drastically reduced in all four of the basic markets. It is better to face up to the new realities of corporate capitalism than to cling to the old myths of the market system, for only by facing reality will we be able to transcend it.

Markets and Transactions

Institutional economics, that hearty breed of weed growing on the fringes of the academic turf, was the first school of thought to recognize the passing of the market. Early institutionalists even applauded its demise (contemporary institutionalists still do) because they also recognized the advantages of administrative planning over market bargaining. Two American economists, John R. Commons and Thorstein Veblen, were the co-founders of institutional economics. Both Veblen and Commons emphasized the differences between administrative and market coordination of economic activities, and both realized that the former was replacing the latter. At the turn of this century, when they did their major work, the demise of the market was clear to them. Now at the close of the century, their recognition is slowly spreading among other economists. A few otherwise orthodox economists even refer to themselves as "new institutionalists" and they dig into the work of the "old institutionalists," particularly the work of Commons. Veblen, apparently, was too radical for them. Oliver E. Williamson is the most prominent of the "new institutionalists" who refers back to Commons for insight.[8] And a great deal of insight is in Commons for the taking.[9]

Commons approached the study of economics by observing the transactions engaged in by workers, consumers, managers, and financiers. He found that these economic transactions were of three types: (1) bargaining, (2) managing, and (3) rationing. Only bargaining transactions took place in the market. Also, all three transactions were more complex than allowed for by formal economic theory. Each transaction involved more than just two different parties; a bargaining transaction actually requires five. Transactions never take place in isolation. A social system with traditions, working rules, and laws provides a framework for transactions. This social system is continually evolving as traditions, working rules, and laws change. This introduces a wide scope for conflict of interest when interpreting, performing, and enforcing the contracts agreed to in the transactions. Conflict of interest, Commons insisted, is a paramount element of transactions. But so too is harmony of interests, for if the transactors fail to agree, they all lose. Agreement or a *created* harmony of interests is a requirement for successful transactions even though conflict of interest is always present.[10]

Bargaining transactions take place in the market. They are the substance of the "law of supply and demand" myth. The objective of bargaining transactions is the acquisition of wealth in its myriad of forms. Bargaining transactions require five legal parties: a buyer, a seller, a potential buyer, a potential seller, and a court or sovereign power of some sort. The need for a buyer and a seller is obvious. But a potential buyer and a potential seller are also required to keep the transaction from changing into a managing or a rationing transaction. The potential buyer gives the seller the ability to bargain. The seller can always sell elsewhere if a particular buyer tries to dominate the transaction. In the absence of an alternative buyer, the seller has less chance, less bargaining power. He must submit to the will of the single buyer, push the buyer into submission, or not transact at all. Then the transaction has changed into a different type all together or has vanished. On the other hand, the potential seller gives the buyer the ability to bargain. Remove the potential seller and the buyer no longer bargains. He dominates, is dominated, or does not transact. The fifth party required to keep a bargaining transaction from deteriorating is a court which stands ready to settle disputes when they arise. And they will arise because of the pervasiveness of conflicting interests. If some kind of court for dispute resolution is not available, the bargainers will create one or stop bargaining. Needless to say, bargaining transactions are exciting, treacherous, full of surprises, and often *very* expensive when legal action must be taken.

Managing transactions are not conducted in the market. The objective of a managing transaction is the creation of wealth rather than the acquisition of wealth. A managing transaction is between a legal inferior and a legal superior. The simplest managing transaction involves a worker receiving instructions from his boss and carrying out those instructions under supervision. An increasingly frequent managing transaction involves the general corporate office of a conglomerate giving instructions to its subsidiaries regarding profit objectives. As in bargaining transactions, both conflict of interest and harmony of interest exist simultaneously in managing transactions. The superior party in the transaction wants maximum production from the inferior party while the inferior party often desires to hold back or to pursue other objectives. But if the transaction breaks down, both parties lose. The worker is laid off and production is lost, or the subsidiary is sold off and profit is lost.

• Managing transactions, like bargaining ones, also involve a court or some form of sovereign power to settle the disputes that constantly arise. Organized workers and their bosses rely on elaborate grievance procedures. Unorganized workers and their bosses rely on the formal courts or break off the transaction. Conglomerates and their subsidiaries or potential subsidiaries wage battle in the courts as well, or they too break off the transaction.

Disputes over managing transactions are usually settled because both the manager and the managed have too much to lose if the transaction breaks down. Disputes over bargaining transactions frequently have the result of transforming the nature of the transaction from bargaining to managing. Such a transformation was the major dynamic behind the growth of huge, vertically-integrated oligopolies. Bargaining transactions in the intermediate product market were transformed into managing transactions within the vertically-integrated oligopoly as the open conflict of interest between buyer and seller was internalized, transformed into a literally more manageable form of conflict, the conflict between manager and managed. In this way, administrative control was substituted for the expensive and uncertain haggling and hassling of market bargaining. The dramatic reduction in the costs of coordinating the flow of product through the production process has been demonstrated theoretically by Oliver E. Williamson. The cost reduction is proven historically by the fact that a large portion of the intermediate product market has disappeared. Now, in terms of sheer volume, managing transactions have surpassed bargaining ones. And, the rise of managing transactions has given far broader scope to rationing transactions.

We must turn to Thorstein Veblen, the radical co-founder of institutional economics, for an understanding of the broad implications of managing and rationing transactions. Veblen, because of his detached, yet critical view, was the most astute of all U.S. observers of business enterprise. In fact, he is our only national claim to fame in economic science, for he is the only purely-original American economist to rise to international prominence. His *Theory of Business Enterprise* is unique in its grasp of the fundamentals of the corporate world. Veblen realized that merger wheeling and dealing – the "pecuniary element," he called it – have, as one objective, the elimination of the expense and the uncertainty of bargaining transactions. Bargaining is full of surprises. Fraud and chicane are not uncommon, nor unprofitable for the perpetrator. Veblen referred to fraud and chicane also as the "pecuniary element" because they are constant financial dangers encountered in the open markets, the "interstices of the system." To avoid such pitfalls corporate mergers took place. Mergers replace costly bargaining transactions between businessmen with less costly and more predictable managing and rationing transactions between bureaucrats. Corporate consolidation was, Veblen explained, "a casting out of business men by the chief of business men."[11] In this way, business bargaining was internalized into bureaucratic planning. That is, mergers replaced the business bargain with the business bureaucracy, fraud and puffery with memo and balance sheet, surprise and legal expense with certainty and controlled cash flow, market adjustment with administrative planning.

UNFINISHED BUSINESS

But the replacement is incomplete. Two major steps remain to be taken to complete the system. First, three major merger waves have swept across the economy leaving giant corporate bureaucracies in their wake, but only two waves of administrative change have been completed. Second, rationing transactions have become very important, particularly for the new form of conglomerate rationing, however, a new form of court or sovereign power has not emerged to settle disputes. Following the evolutionary logic of corporate development, a crying need exists for a new form of corporate administration to make huge conglomerate bureaucracies at least tolerable to work for, and a crying need exists for a new form of sovereign power to deal with the stagflation arising from conglomerate rationing. The administrative ways and means of humanizing and democratizing corporate bureaucracy have been discussed in earlier chapters. Now attention must be turned to the ways and means of reducing stagflation. Nothing less than a revolution in public administration will do the job, for the private administration of corporate conglomerates is the source of stagflation. The conglomerate has adapted the administrative structure used to manage the huge vertically-integrated oligopoly. But the structure is not used to create wealth, rather, to ration it out. The ability to closely calibrate output to demand and the ability to closely calculate the profit earned by each part of the conglomerate empire have given rise to "conglomerate rationing." Originally used by vertically-integrated oligopolies to decentralize managerial decision making, the administrative procedures developed by the autonomous division organizations are being used by the conglomerates to ration wealth rather than create it.

Now a conglomerate can move from market to market, and it can reward or punish its managers according to the short-run rate of profit each manager can milk out of his particular market. It should come as no surprise that management circles have placed increasing emphasis on maximizing profits. Nor should it come as a surprise that inflation and unemployment have been on the rise. In the United States, the managerial vision has become myopic. The immediate profit rate is all that is seen. The longer view is seldom taken. Let philosophers and sociologists worry about the long run. In the long run we retire. In the short run we make profits and receive bonuses.

But the long run we began to ignore in the 1960s and 1970s now haunts the 1980s in the form of stagflation. And the 1980s are haunted by another specter: Unable to understand the real source of our economic problems, we turn to the verities of the past. We try to return to the simple days when laissez-faire economics worked. Furthermore, when we discover that the verities of the past are not working in the present, the temptation to try harsher remedies will grow. I feel very strongly that fascism is a real possibility for our immediate future. The thought is frightening. Fascism worked, for a while. It replaced conflict with order. It would work again, for a while. But at what cost!

Better to try another way: Complete the evolutionary logic of the corporate system with democratic public planning. Use the federal government as the sovereign power required to resolve the conflict caused by conglomerate rationing and democratize the corporation through the reforms suggested earlier. We need to turn the incredible administrative apparatus of the huge corporation to public account by supplementing it with federal planning in areas that corporate planning cannot handle. And, in that area where corporate planning results in public damage – "conglomerate rationing" – we need to substitute federal planning for corporate planning. In short, the next step in corporate evolution, in a democratic society, is public planning.

Public Planning: The Needs

Before proceeding further, two points should be emphasized. First of all, we do not need "the plan." That is, our economy cannot be forced to fit someone's blueprint. Instead of "the plan," we need a planning process. We need to discuss, through the democratic political process, what we need. Then we have to discuss, again through the democratic political process, the ways and means of meeting our needs. Next, we have to implement our program. Last, we have to evaluate our progress in the democratic political arena and correct our mistakes so that we can try again. The planning process is a never-ending sequence of political discussions, mistake corrections, and new implementations. Planning is the series of new beginnings we make as we correct our mistakes; each new beginning building on our experience. Planning is a process, not a blueprint.

Second, the differences between types of planning need to be emphasized. Three types of planning exist: (1) The Soviet style central planning of state officials in pursuit of state interest, (2) The administrative planning of corporate managers in pursuit of private interest, and (3) The democratic planning of elected politicians in pursuit of public interest.

The central planning of a Soviet-type command economy must be avoided because commands from above retard the flow upward of new ideas and new people, depriving the economy of its dynamism. Furthermore centralized command planning conducted by the state easily leads to political tyranny. When a part of the central plan fails, the political response often is to control oppressively that offending part of the economy, and to repress those elements of society that complain about the plan's failure. Individual freedom and central command planning seem incompatible. For a severely impoverished society, that price may be acceptable. But for the affluent U.S., it is and has always been out of the question.

The administrative planning of corporate managers is effective, as far as it goes. But severe problems have arisen.[12] It is no mere coincidence that stagflation became a problem at the same time that the conglomerate merger wave swept across the economy. The 1960s saw both conglomeration and stagflation spread across the economy. Stagflation, the simultaneous rise of the price level and the unemployment rate, is a direct result of the conglomerate's ability to push up prices and close plants in one market, reap the profits, and move on to another market. The stagflation problem is so severe that a whole chapter will be devoted to it. In addition to the stagflation side effect of conglomerate planning, a number of public needs simply cannot be met by corporate planning. The remainder of this chapter will be devoted to those public needs that remain unmet by corporate planning. This is an area that cries out for the third type of planning.

The third type of planning is the democratic planning of elected officials in pursuit of public interest. This planning is now done in very haphazard, ad hoc ways. Public protest mounts about a particular problem and Congress responds with special, ad hoc legislation. But the resulting programs and agencies are under-funded, uncoordinated, and run by underpaid civil servants or opportunists from affected businesses. No real planning takes place. Instead, the harried civil servants spend most of their time "putting out fires" or correcting errors made by the opportunists, rather than formulating the longer view, coordinating programs, and implementing new approaches in the light of experience and in response to democratic dialogue. And the revolving door between public agencies and affected businesses whirls around faster and faster.

Democratic planning takes place, but it is so uncoordinated, under-funded, and distorted by the opportunism of the revolving door, that public needs generally are unmet. Those needs are legion: *Environmental planning* is the formulation, implementation, and correction through experience of programs to regulate waste generation and disposal, and to expand the national park system. These fall woefully short of realizing the public's often repeated desires for clean air, clean water, decent recreational facilities, and wilderness areas. In numerous public opinion polls, year after year, these needs are emphasized by the public. Corporate planning clearly cannot deliver. It is time that democratic public planning did.

Affirmative action planning is called for by every document Americans hold sacred. The Constitution and The Declaration of Independence are unambiguous on this point. Racism and sexism have no place in the fulfillment of the American Dream. Yet the Equal Employment Opportunity Commission is so underfunded and riddled with opportunism that is has become a shadow of the dream that once stirred a nation. Corporate planning of employee recruitment and promotion give us filtering and homosocial reproduction. Corporate planning clearly will not deliver equality in the workplace. It is time that democratic planning did.

Small business planning is nonexistent even though the small businessman still manages to survive, innovate, and provide jobs. Room still exists for the small businessman, in spite of the tremendous growth of the huge corporation. But no planning takes place to preserve or enlarge the role played by the small businessman. Instead, small business is either grist for the conglomerate mill or is largely ignored. Considerable public dialogue must take place about the desired role of the small businessman in our corporate capitalism before public planning can begin to either enlarge the role of the small businessman or ease his absorption into the corporate system. Corporate planning will do neither in the headlong rush to expand. It is time that the small businessman's fate seriously be discussed within the democratic planning process. Subsidizing a modest flow of credit into small businesses through the Small Business Administration is a mere palliative, a holding action.

Growth planning is also a basic public need largely unmet by corporate planners. True, corporate growth is a major objective of corporate planning. But the overall growth of the economy (macroeconomic growth) is not planned. It just happens or fails to happen. Furthermore, the rate of macroeconomic growth may or may not coincide with public employment goals, environmental goals, or small business goals. Nor, in the absence of public planning, will macroeconomic growth be balanced. Energy-intensive production and consumption sectors may grow faster than capital goods supplying sectors. Within each sector, the planning of integrated corporations has smoothed out and balanced the intra-sector flow of production. But between sectors, the only mechanism for balancing the inter-sector flow of production is the costly and uncertain bargaining transaction of the market. The visible hand of management has replaced the invisible hand of the market for intra-sector coordination. It is time that democratic planning provide for inter-sector coordination to avoid costly bottlenecks and imbalances. We now turn to the vehicles of public planning.

Public Planning: The Vehicles

Planning requires a set of planning vehicles, a means of getting us from here to there, a medium for expressing and pursuing goals.[13] The vehicles of public planning include planning bodies, planning documents, and implementation tools. Each of the three planning vehicles will be discussed in turn. Planning bodies are the organizations that formulate the goals and programs of planning. Planning documents are the formal statements of the goals and programs formulated by the planning bodies. Implementation tools are the means by which planning objects are met. In democratic planning, the planning bodies are composed either of a representative group of citizens or of political officials. In democratic planning, all aspects of the planning documents are open to public discussion and criticism. In democratic planning, implementation tools are inducements, never commands.

Three major federal planning bodies already exist and can easily be improved by a few modifications. Then by creating two new planning bodies, one at the state level and one at the federal level, a solid foundation can be laid for the democratic formulation of goals and programs. The three existing federal planning bodies are the Council of Economic Advisers, the Office of Management and Budget, and the Congressional Budget Office. Other powerful forces also exist at the federal level, particulary the House Appropriations Committee, but the CEA, OMB, and CBO contain the greatest potential for developing democratic planning. The new planning body needed at the federal level is a National Economic Council composed of citizen representatives from all major parts of the economy and from all major interest groups. The new planning body needed at the state level is a State Economic Council, composed of representatives from all major interests within the state.

The President's Council of Economic Advisers has deteriorated to the point that the Advisers are little more than salesmen for the President's pet programs. But the Council could regain its former influence if the three Advisers were selected differently. One Adviser should be selected by Congress from its own economic staff in the Congressional Budget Office, another should be selected by the National Economic Council, and the third should be selected by the President. The three Advisers would then designate one of themselves as the Chairperson of the Council. Each adviser would serve a four-year term and could be removed only by the body that selected the Adviser. In this way, only one of the Advisers would be "the President's man." The others would represent other groups, giving balance and independence to the CEA, and reestablishing its credibility.

The Office of Management and Budget, though weakened by a series of first incompetent, then incredible, and now opportunistic Directors, still does its job reasonably well. The Presidential budgets have reflected the overall goals of the Administration. And that is what the President's budget is supposed to do. No structural change in OMB is essential at this time. Nevertheless, the public deserves more consideration in the selection of Directors than has been shown in the past. Demonstrated honesty and intelligence, at least, should become prerequisites for future Directors.

The Congressional Budget Office, along with a House and a Senate Budget Committee, were established by the Congressional Budget and Impoundment Act of 1974. The CBO reports to Congress on general fiscal policy and each Budget Committee works toward a concurrent resolution setting revenue and expenditure goals for the coming fiscal year. Although weakened by Congressional timidity in the face of recent Presidential temerity, the CBO has the potential for exercising useful guidance to the budget-making process. When the potential is realized, the CBO will do for Congress what the OMB does for the President – reflect in the budget the overall goals of the Congress.

The new planning body suggested here for the federal level is already used, in one form or another, by most nations in Western Europe. In one variant or another, most advanced capitalist countries use a National Economic Council to help formulate goals and programs. The members of our Council should be selected, half by the Congress and half by the President, in such a way that the Council represents the broadest spectrum of American economic life. The NEC should be boisterous, quarrelsome, and very active in holding public forums across the nation where goals and programs can be openly and widely discussed. All views would be heard. No one could be shut out. The Council would be advisory, but its advice would carry weight because it would come from the grassroots.

To complete the needed planning bodies would require beefing up the capacities of the state level gubernatorial budget agencies. The tremendous growth of state expenditures (they have grown much faster than federal expenditures) has forced improvement in state budgeting. But further improvement is necessary, particularly in politically backward states. (Texas with its biennial budget is a prime example.) Then, most importantly, we need a new organization which can formulate and discuss goals and projects at the state level. In particular, each state needs the equivalent of a National Economic Council to ensure that the boisterous and quarrelsome citizen input into decision-making, which is the essence of democracy, takes place. Such input is needed at both the state and the federal levels, even though democratic planning is most powerful at the federal level.

With these planning bodies either created or improved, we need to move on to the planning documents. At the federal level, two kinds of planning documents would become major vehicles for democratic planning, American style.[14] Short-term goals would be expressed in an annual, national economic budget. The long-term goals would be expressed in a five-year national economic budget. These economic budgets would not be merely the budget of the federal government, although the federal budget would be a significant part of the national economic budget. Instead, the national economic budgets would include goals for the whole economy, sector by sector and in the aggregate. Balanced growth of the sectors would have to be built into the aggregate goals to avoid bottlenecks on one hand and to avoid the construction of idle plant capacities on the other hand. Furthermore, both the long and the short-term budgets would include goals for equal employment attainment, goals for environmental quality, and for the role of small business. Of course, some goals would have to be modified in order to satisfy others. The formally stated national economic budget would make these trade-offs public knowledge, inviting criticism and the formulation of alternatives. Each sector's use of resources, both in the annual economic budget and in the five-year budget would be public knowledge. The often abused "national security cloak" would not be available for hiding any major trade-off. Nor would the argument that giving up one goal in the short run is necessary for achieving some other goal in the long run be so easy to use in the support of dubious strategies.[15] The five-year national economic budget would show clearly how annual, short-term goals are connected to long-term goals. The old trickle-down myth of economic progress would be exposed for all to see.

These two planning documents, the annual and the five-year national economic budgets, must be realistic. That is, the goals they contain must be achievable. To achieve the goals requires the last of the three planning vehicles – implementation tools. In democratic planning, as opposed to command planning, goals are attained through inducement rather than command. The inducements used must be specially designed to fit the particular goal being sought. To be specific, at least five kinds of goals would be sought in the democratic planning process for the U.S.: (1) aggregate goals for the economy as a whole, (2) sector-by-sector goals for balanced growth, (3) equal employment goals for minority participation in the workplace, (4) environmental goals for clean air, for clean water, and for recreation, and (5) small business goals either for easing the transition of the small businessman into the corporate system or for enlarging his role in the system. Each of these five goals will require specially designed inducements.

To achieve aggregate goals for the economy as a whole will require coordinating the macroeconomic tools of both fiscal and monetary policy. In fiscal policy, the tax structure and the set of expenditure programs must be formulated by Congress and the President with an eye toward providing the aggregate demand needed to fulfill the aggregate goals. Then monetary policy cannot be allowed to thwart the achievement of democratically chosen goals, as has often been the case in the past. Bankers and central bankers always want high interest rates. It is a part of their nature. They cannot help it any more than the sellers of anything can help their obsession with higher prices. But the banker's greed can easily be sold as a public virtue. The general producer's greed cannot. Tight money is supposed to be good for us all, not just for bankers whose business is lending us money. Tight money is always good for bankers because it keeps interest rates up. But it also keeps spending down and that is good for the rest of us only when our economy is growing faster than the goals we have set for it. Only then does the public interest coincide with the banking interest. This simple truth must become a part of the democratic planning process: A monetary policy of high interest rates is in the public interest only when the economy is growing at an excessive rate. For our aggregate goals to be reached, Congress and the President must set monetary policy so that it reinforces, rather than negates, fiscal policy. Then tax rates, expenditure programs, and interest rates will all serve as inducements for meeting our aggregate goals.

Meeting sector-by-sector goals for balanced growth requires two different kinds of inducements. First, for corporate planners to build the new capacity needed in their industry, they must be sure that it is needed. Excess capacity is very costly. From the aggregate goals for the economy as a whole, public planners must derive specific sub-goals for each sector of the economy. These sub-goals must then be explained to the affected sectors so the private planners in those sectors know how much new capacity will be needed. Information, then, is the first kind of inducement. But before some private planners will take the risk of adding new capacity, some assurances may be required. Assurance that new capacity will not be an idle burden is the second kind of inducement. Public planners can extend that assurance in two ways. The new capacity can be purchased by the federal government and then leased to the private firm on a short-term basis. If the new capacity is idle, the lease is terminated automatically. Or, the private firm can purchase the new capacity with an agreement that automatically requires the federal government to pick up the carrying costs of the new capacity if it remains idle. Carrying costs would be stipulated in advance. They would include only the costs of physically maintaining the facility and the full borrowing costs of financing it. The planning documents would provide an inducement in the form of information, thus reducing uncertainty. Then the assurance that idle capacity would not be an overhead burden would be a second inducement, thus reducing risk. Risk and uncertainty, impossible for private firms to plan against, *can* be reduced by public planning which begins with a set of planned aggregate goals that can be used to derive sector-by-sector goals. Private planning lacks that crucial aggregate planning capacity.

Meeting equal employment goals through the democratic planning process poses a difficult moral dilemma. Democratic planning must rely on inducement only, never command. But this means that employers whose practices result in racist and sexist outcomes cannot be commanded to change their practices. They must be induced to do so. Or must they? On one hand, if a practice is illegal, justice requires that the lawbreaker be commanded to stop. But on the other hand, if a practice is socially detrimental, expedience requires that the practitioner be helped to change his ways. Democratic planning, in my opinion, must opt for expedience in this case. Although justice requires that individuals harmed by discrimination have effective access to legal redress, democratic planning must rely on economic inducement. Affirmative action plans, specially designed by the EEOC, should be a basic part of public planning. The inducement for adoption of affirmative action plans is the abolition of the corporate income tax. But individuals must remain free to bring legal action to the courts.

Environmental quality goals for clean air and clean water have already been set by the Environmental Protection Agency. However, under the Reagan Administration the EPA has been seriously weakened by budget cut-backs and by uncontrolled opportunism at the highest level of the agency. Once we return to sanity, the opportunism can be removed and the budget restored. But the EPA also needs more effective inducements. By and large, the EPA works like this: various technical, medical or general health considerations are used to formulate emission standards for different industries. Lengthy hearings ensue and the standards are modified. Then the industry involved is told to meet the standards at a specified date in the future. The industry often claims that the standards cannot be met by that date, and, finally, the date is pushed back. Eventually standards *are* met, but usually after much delay, expense, and exasperation on all sides. The standard-setting and standard-meeting procedure actually followed is highly variable, but the essentials are as stated.

Inducements, with a few exceptions, are not offered by the EPA. This is unfortunate for the simple reason that inducements work. Several simple inducement and standard-setting plans have been widely discussed, pity that they have not been widely used. An example is called for. Emissions from coal-fired generating plants make us sick, kill our lakes, eat up our houses, cars, bridges, buildings, and wreak untold havoc upon our ecosystem. From all of these different standpoints, how should we set *the* emission standard? To save our lakes would call for one emission standard; to save our cars would call for another; to save our bridges, another; to save us, another; and so on. The simple-minded say that we should spend more money on emission reduction up to the point where the extra money spent just balances with the extra money saved because of the cleaner air. But measuring the "money saved" from cleaner air is impossible because many of the benefits gained from cleaner air are not money values at all, and, because many of the harms done by dirty air are not known, how can we measure precisely the benefits of clean air? Instead of setting standards in such a fashion, we should first observe the actual rate of emission for all the coal-fired generators in use. Some will be very dirty, others very clean, most about average. Find the cleanest existing generator and find out how that utility does it. Now we have something concrete, a low rate of emission and a proven way of attaining it. We have found our emission standard – the best existing practice. Next, it is simple to induce others to meet the standard. Pay the best firm to teach them. Buy the firm's patents, if patents apply, and arrange with the firm's engineers to conduct on-sight inspection and instruction tours, paying generous consulting fees to the firm and providing all patents and tours to the other firms free. As this is being done, determine the time it takes to adopt the new practice and use that time to set the date for the standard to take effect.

By building our standards and inducements around the best existing practice, emissions can be cut quickly, not to zero, but to the lowest practical level. And it can be done without many of the delays, entanglements, and obfuscations of other methods. The air and water will not be pristine, but they will be as clean as practical.

What should be done for the small businessman depends upon the role we desire him to play in our economy and upon the price we are willing to pay to help him play it. Frankly, the thrust of economic history is against him. His role has shrunk as the scope of the market has shrunk. With the exception of agriculture, some services, and some retail trades, he is being pushed out of existence by the more efficient huge corporation. If, through the democratic planning process, it is decided to expand the role of small business, then small businesses will need substantial inducements in the form of subsidized credit, technical advice, and reduced risk and uncertainty. Small business could be "reserved" a place in different expanding sectors of the economy by earmarking the new capacity required in those sectors by the aggregate economic goals. By the way, that is the strong point of the argument for economic growth – it makes more room for more participation from those who have been excluded. Yet, for the small businessman, I remain pessimistic. In the absence of democratic public planning, his role will continue to shrink. With it, the question remains, how much will the public pay to preserve small businesses?

But for achieving aggregate economic goals, for achieving sector-by-sector balanced growth, for enlarging the employment opportunities of minorities, and for cleaning up our air and water, I confess to optimism. If we can avoid the repression that frustration breeds, democratic public planning will have an important role to play in our future. Nevertheless, the immediate outlook is bleak. Reaganomics will fail and frustration will rise. This, we can count on.

Reaganomics runs against the grain of history. It is true that man makes his own history, but not as he chooses. We can choose "free enterprise" but we will get economic retrenchment. Free enterprise flourished in the conditions created by an earlier time. Those conditions are gone forever, replaced by the expansion of the huge, efficient corporation. Three merger waves have concentrated economic power in the hands of a few thousand corporate managers. Two waves of organizational change have forged the corporation into a truly incredible organization, a planning mechanism capable of planning the flow of product through all the stages of modern large-scale production, capable of calibrating output very closely to demand in many markets, capable of calculating the rate of profit earned by numerous diverse profit centers, capable of reproducing (cloning) its upper echelons from lower-level managerial material, capable of milking numerous markets and moving on to others, but also incapable of planning how to provide jobs for all the workforce, incapable of bringing inflation to a stop, incapable of rooting out racism and sexism, incapable of providing a clean environment, and incapable of assuring the survival of the small businessman. A third wave of organizational change is needed to supplement the planning of the mature corporation in some areas and to curtail it in others. Supplementation is required to meet needs that corporate planning cannot meet. Curtailment is needed in those areas where corporate planning causes social harm. The third wave of organizational change called for by our current stage of economic evolution is democratic public planning, for only it can meet the needs not met by corporate planning and only it can effectively curtail the harm done by corporate planning while preserving the benefits of corporate planning.

How It Could Work

The process of democratic public planning could work in a number of different ways. My proposals are merely suggestive. Others might work far better. Only through experience can the processes best suited to American needs evolve. Nevertheless, one thing is certain, the democratic planning process has become a historical imperative for the U.S.[16] Either we begin planning to meet the material needs of a democratic society, or we cease being a democratic society. The push from below will continue. It can be met positively, through democratic planning. It can also be met negatively, through militarism, repression, and ultimately, through fascism. It can happen here. It will happen here. It is happening here. But it can be reversed.

Suppose we adopt democratic planning. How might it work? Given the adoption of the planning vehicles suggested above, the planning process could begin with the Council of Economic Advisers. With one adviser representing the Congress, one representing the President, and one representing the National Economic Council, the CEA is the logical place to set the macroeconomic goals which would provide the foundation for the planning process. First, a goal or goals would be set, after wide-open public discussion, for five years into the future. Then, annual goals or an annual goal would be set for each of the five years. For our underemployed economy, an employment growth goal would be of the highest priority.

Next, the CEA, the Congressional Budget Office, and the Office of Management and Budget would work out the coordinated fiscal and monetary policies required to assure that the aggregate demand required by the employment growth goal would be forthcoming. During the formulation of the required fiscal and monetary policies, the NEC would be an active conduit for public input into the process. Furthermore, the appropriate House and Senate Committees would hold hearings and modify goals if need be. The Federal Reserve System, on the other hand, would participate in the formulation of monetary policy only to the extent that policy formulation required input regarding how policy could be implemented. The Fed should carry out policy, not make it. In the past, in good times or bad, the Fed's policy preoccupation has been with the need for tight money and high interest rates.

After the broad outlines of monetary and fiscal policies have been drawn, and after the macroeconomic goal(s) have been modified, the sector-by-sector goals must be determined. These goals must be compatible with the macroeconomic goal(s) for employment growth. The sectoral goals could be formulated in the same way as the overall macro-economic goal(s). That is, after ample consultation and public discussion, the CEA would set the sectoral goals, consistent with the macro-economic goal(s), as modified by Congressional input, and consistent with publicly discussed goals for small business, environmental quality, and minority participation.

Once again, these goals would require that the CEA, CBO, and OMB work out the policies (inducements) necessary to achieve them. During this second policy formulation stage, the NEC would again serve as an open conduit for public input into the process. The appropriate House and Senate Committees would also hold hearings, modifying goals and adopting new policies as needed. In sector-by-sector planning, particular attention must be paid to the problems of bottleneck sectors. Such bottlenecks can be dealt with in a number of ways. Existing firms can be offered inducements to expand their capacities. Inducements can be given for the formation of new minority firms in the bottleneck sector. Or trade agreements for expanding imports, preferably from the poor nations, can be made to offset limited domestic supplies. Above all, a bottleneck in one sector of the economy should not be allowed to drag down the rest of the economy, as usually happens in the absence of public planning. Too many alternative ways to expand the bottleneck are opened through the public planning process to allow bottlenecks to stymie us. If all else fails, a new publicly-owned firm can be created either to obtain the needed commodity abroad or to produce it at home.

At each step of the democratic planning process, the Environmental Protection Agency should provide detailed environmental statements clarifying the environmental implications of goals and policies. The Equal Employment Opportunity Commission should prepare similar impact statements for minority employment and for the formation of new minority firms. The same applies to the Small Business Administration and the small business sector. Needless to say, the EPA, EEOC, and SBA cannot do the work unless they are adequately funded and freed from the opportunism plaguing them.

During the early years of democratic public planning, many mistakes undoubtedly will be made and many shortcomings will be discovered. But democratic planning is an ongoing process, not a finished blueprint. Mistakes can be corrected and shortcomings remedied in an ongoing process. Undoubtedly, the proposals made here also contain mistakes and shortcomings. But the need for democratic public planning, of some kind, is not affected by my personal faults. The need is clear and unavoidable. A democratic alternative to economic retrenchment, the inevitable outcry against it, and the real temptation to repress those who will cry out, must be tried. Short of outright fascism, we have tried everything else. Even so, democratic public planning is not a grasping at straws. It is a historical imperative, forced upon us by the growth of private corporate planning. It is the next step in the evolution of our democratic society, if we are to keep it democratic.[17]

PART 3

Reforming Economic Policies

I have a dream.

MARTIN LUTHER KING, JR.

10 WAGE-PRICE CONTROLS

INTRODUCTION

Even after we revitalize the corporation and adopt a democratic economic planning process that turns the corporation toward the public purpose, our task will not be complete until we also reform the conduct of traditional economic stabilization policies. First, in our attempt to stabilize the price level, we must stop creating a depression-level unemployment rate. We have to squeeze so hard to stop inflation in this way that the cure has become worse than the disease. Second, the central bankers' dominance of our Federal Reserve System must be replaced with a democratic guidance that emphasizes regulating the cost and the flow of credit in the public interest. Third, we have to conduct fiscal policy with the long view in mind so that the tax structure and spending programs are fair and are directed toward buliding up our human potential.

To achieve our first objective, that of stopping inflation without causing depression-level unemployment, we must realize that our current inflation is a new kind. It is Sellers Inflation; it is caused by the use of concentrated economic power on the part of sellers, not by an excessive rate of spending on the part of buyers. Reining in this kind of inflation requries wage-price controls. Chapter 10 contains a discussion of such control programs, the kinds of inflation, and what we could do in our current situation.

To achieve our second objective, that of reconstructing our monetary policy, we must give up our futile attempt to apply Milton Friedman's quantity theory of money to our modern financial system. The theory is simply not relevant to the reality. Instead, we must begin regulating the cost of credit to encourage new investment and ensure adequate flows of credit to socially useful sectors as well as to privately profitable sectors. The first half of Chapter 11 deals with the needed monetary reconstruction.

To achieve our second objective, that of a fair fiscal policy emphasizing the human side of public spending, requires first that we bring the arms race to a halt. Spiraling military spending has been the chief destabilizing element of government spending. Once the race toward oblivion has been stopped, the billions of wasted public monies can be redirected toward gradually realizing the human potential of all Americans, particularly of those pushing up from below. In realizing that potential, we will learn that a deficit in the federal budget is far less damaging than a deficit in human capabilities. Tax reform must also be on the public agenda, but reform that closes loopholes instead of opens them, that treats all incomes equally, and that establishes, once and for all, a simple and fair tax system. These issues are addressed in the second half of Chapter 11.

My conclusion is in Chapter 12. Economic revitalization will put America back on track as a democratic, dynamic society that encourages the push from below. Continued economic retrenchment will push us further down the track of an authoritarian, rigid society that represses the push from below.

CONTROLS IN PERSPECTIVE

Introduction

Wage-price controls are like sins: we denounce them heartily but return to them frequently, and how righteously we denounce them is directly related to how frequently we return to them. Since the Great Depression we have imposed wage-price controls a number of times, often denouncing them even as we imposed them. (Recall President Nixon's promise not to use them and his subsequent imposition, not only of controls, but of a wage-price freeze?) Our aversion to controls is so strong that we are willing to use them only after extreme suffering. Usually, wage-price controls have been imposed only in desperate inflationary situations. Then, as soon as the inflation abated, we dropped the controls. Furthermore, when inflation resumes after the controls are lifted, rather than reimpose the controls to stop the inflation, we usually take the resumption of inflation as evidence that the controls did not work. If diabetics did the same with their insulin, they would all be dead. In short, wage-price controls are detested in the United

States. So why do we keep using them? Because the alternative way to fight inflation is far worse.

Only two policies can reduce the rate of inflation. On one hand, inflation can be reduced by cutting back the total rate of spending (aggregate demand) so severely that producers cannot raise their prices any longer. But such a severe cutback in aggregate demand also causes producers to lay off workers. The unemployment rate soars when inflation is fought in this way. And unemployment cripples our industrial economy, closes the door to the push from below, and causes widespread social disruption. Family formation slows down; divorce picks up. Alcoholism, drug abuse, juvenile delinquency, child abuse, and social pathology in general intensify as the personal impact of unemployment is felt by more and more of the general population. The labor force itself even declines as the discouraged unemployed give up looking for work and sink into the mire of drugs, crime, welfare motherhood, and anomie. Fighting inflation by cutting aggregate demand has become very costly. It may become even worse. Cutting aggregate demand increases unemployment and unemployment is socially disrupting. The grave danger we face is that reactionary political responses to the disruption will lead us to fascism, particularly if the increasingly strident demands of the "Moral Majority" result in new social legislation. Such legislation would be inherently repressive.

On the other hand, fighting inflation, in the only other way possible, runs against the grain of American ideology. Cutting aggregate demand is one thing. But controlling aggregate supply is another matter entirely. It requires wage-price controls, "interference" with the "free" market. More germane to the issue, perhaps, it requires government regulation of powerful economic interests rather than government repression of powerless unemployed blacks, browns, and welfare mothers. Yet wage-price controls are the only other way to fight inflation. We can cut aggregate demand or we can control wages and prices. These are our only alternatives, like them or not.

Major Control Programs

Three major wage-price control programs have been used since the Great Depression to control inflation. The most comprehensive program was used during World War II. The famous guidepost program was used in the Kennedy-Johnson years. Then the Nixon phases program was implemented in the early 1970s. Other control programs were also attempted. The Korean War saw wage-price controls. President Eisenhower used exhortations for responsible action and President Carter played with an ineffective voluntary program. Nevertheless, World War II controls, the guidepost program, and the phases program are the best known. Contrary to the conventional wisdom, these programs were not ineffective.[1]

Wage-price controls were initiated during the Second World War in April 1942 with the imposition of a wage-price freeze. The freeze was enforced by an inflexible "general maximum price regulation" which attempted to keep prices at a level not to exceed the prices charged in March 1942 for the same product. But inflexibility and evasion led to the frequent introduction of allegedly "new" products at higher prices. The major enforcement agency was the Office of Price Administration, which had been given the statutory power to control prices and rents in January 1942. Then in October 1942 the Office of Economic Stabilization was established by executive order. Comprehensive, slightly more flexible controls were used thereafter, bolstered by a "hold-the-line" order by President Roosevelt in 1943 and strengthened by extensive rationing of consumer goods. At the end of the war, the controls became ineffective and were officially removed in 1946.

The controls worked remarkably well. Unemployment fell from 9.9 percent in 1941 to a low of 1.2 percent in 1944 and then closed out the war period at 1.9 percent in 1945. Industrial production rose by nearly 50 percent from 1941 to the height of activity in 1944. Yet, in spite of the tremendous growth in employment and output, inflation was actually reduced. Consumer prices were rising by 5.0 percent in 1941; the rise accelerated to 10.7 percent in 1942. But then the controls took hold and inflation fell to 6.1 percent in 1943; hit a low of 1.7 percent in 1944; then back up to 2.3 percent and 8.5 percent in 1945 and 1946. Controls had been removed in 1946. Consumer prices rose at a 14.4 percent rate in 1947. The controls worked, until we removed them. The control program was quite effective in holding prices down during the fastest expansion of industrial output the world has ever witnessed.[2]

This price stability was not maintained at the expense of a decline in profit. In fact, profits actually rose during the period. Corporate profits after taxes rose from $7.2 billion in 1940 to a high of $11.2 billion in 1944. They closed out the war at $9.0 billion in 1945. Of course, when controls were dropped, profits after tax soared to $15.5 billion and $20.2 billion in 1946 and 1947.[3] But the unemployment rate also doubled. Nor was price stability maintained at the expense of workers. Total hourly compensation of manufacturing workers before taxes was 23 percent higher in 1945 than in 1940.[4] But the patriotism and cooperation of the war effort contributed a great deal to the wage-price control program's effectiveness. Peacetime controls cannot hope to be effective, according to the conventional wisdom in the U.S.

Finding an extended period of peace to test the conventional wisdom is not really possible. During the later Eisenhower years, peace broke out, but wage-price controls were not used. During the early Kennedy-Johnson years, however, relative peace was maintained and a wage-price control program was in force. The Vietnam war then expanded. Nevertheless, the effectiveness of wage-price controls during that war cannot be attributed to public support of the war effort. As the war ground on, Nixon finally implemented his own wage-price control effort. So the Kennedy-Johnson program and the Nixon program bear further investigation. They were not exactly peacetime programs but they did not exactly benefit from patriotic support and cooperation either.

The Kennedy-Johnson guideposts were initiated in 1962. The program, unlike World War II controls, was based on voluntary compliance, backed up by the moral suasion of the Office of the President. The guideposts were really quite simple. First, the President's Council of Economic Advisers calculated that the average rise in U.S. labor productivity was about 3.2 percent per year. If average wages also rose by 3.2 percent, average unit labor costs would remain constant, exerting no upward pressure on prices. A guidepost for wages was established — they should rise by no more than 3.2 percent per year. Of course, labor productivity rises faster in some sectors of the economy than in others so if wages were not allowed to rise above the wage guidepost in high productivity sectors, unit labor costs would fall in those sectors. Also, if wages were allowed to rise by the guidepost rate of 3.2 percent in low productivity sectors, unit labor costs would rise. For example, if labor productivity rose by 5.0 percent in high productivity sectors and by only 1.4 percent in low productivity sectors, with wages rising at the guidepost rate of 3.2 percent in both sectors, average unit labor costs would be constant for the economy as a whole even though sector by sector actual unit labor costs would not be constant. From this came the price guidepost: In high productivity sectors with falling unit labor costs, the above average productivity gains should be passed on to consumers in the form of lower prices. In low productivity sectors with rising unit labor costs the below average productivity gains would also be passed on to consumers, but in the form of higher prices. Some prices would be falling, others rising. Yet the average price level would be constant.

The wage-price guideposts did not freeze profits, as a casual glance at them might imply. High productivity sectors, even after passing on some of the productivity gains to consumers, could still earn higher profits, particularly with rising volumes. Conversely, low productivity sectors could still see their profits fall, even after passing higher unit labor costs on to consumers. So the profit incentive was maintained. So too was the scale of relative wages earned by workers in different sectors. With the wage guidepost of 3.2 percent applicable to all sectors, powerful unions or professional associations were discouraged from pushing up their wages or salaries faster than other groups. Such behavior often sets off very aggressive wage demands from the other groups who feel that they are falling behind. These aggressive demands can then trigger excessive demands across all sectors as a fiercely competitive game of "catching up" begins.

A flaw in the wage-price guideposts was the lack of any established sanctions for violators. As a result, the guideposts were enforced through "jaw-boning," extra-legal exercises of Presidential power. Moral persuasion and political pressure were brought to bear to enforce the guideposts. From the perspective of the Post-Watergate Era, jaw-boning has become one of the unacceptable political behaviors of the Imperial Presidency.

This flaw aside, how well did the Kennedy-Johnson guideposts work?[5] The answer to the question depends on what the guidepost designers wanted them to do. If the objective was to reduce the unemployment of the Eisenhower years with minimal inflation costs, then the guideposts worked. But if the objective was to stop inflation and keep it stopped, then the guideposts failed. An examination of Table 10.1 will explain. Unemployment fell steadily throughout the Kennedy-Johnson years, with some problems in 1961 and 1963. By 1968, unemployment had fallen to 3.6 percent. The inflation cost of reducing unemployment was very low until 1966-67, when inflation rose to 2.9 percent per year.

TABLE 10.1

Inflation and Unemployment 1960–1982

Year	Rate of inflation[a]	Rate of unemployment
1960	1.6	5.5
1961	1.0	6.7
1962	1.1	5.5
1963	1.2	5.7
1964	1.3	5.2
1965	1.7	4.5
1966	2.9	3.8
1967	2.9	3.8
1968	4.2	3.6
1969	5.4	3.5
1970	5.9	4.9
1971	4.3	5.9
1972	3.3	5.6
1973	6.2	4.9
1974	11.0	5.6
1975	9.1	8.5
1976	5.8	7.7
1977	6.5	7.0
1978	7.7	6.0
1979	11.3	5.8
1980	13.5	7.1
1981	10.4	7.6
1982	6.1	9.7

[a]Based on the Consumer Price Index.
Source: Bureau of Labor Statistics.

Such inflation rates appear astonishingly low when viewed from a 1980s perspective. But by 1968, inflation was clearly gathering momentum. In that year it rose to 4.2 percent and the wage-price guideposts crumbled. The guideposts did not stop inflation. But they were very successful in reducing unemployment with minimal inflation costs. For most of the guidepost period, inflation remained below 2.0 percent per year. Never did it get even close to the double digit rates that ravaged us in the late 1970s and into the 1980s.

In short, the guideposts bought more employment and growth and paid a very low inflation price for them. But the guideposts were not backed up by formal sanctions or inducements, so as the economy heated up with Vietnam war spending, the guideposts melted. Had the guideposts been made of sterner stuff, they could have withstood more inflationary heat.

President Nixon, after promising not to impose wage-price controls, did so in August 1971 by freezing for 90 days wages, prices, and rents all across the economy. Pragmatism, it seems, is stronger than ideology. The freeze became known as Phase I of Nixon's "New Economic Policy." In all, the Nixon wage-price control program had four phases and two freezes, and the program lasted until April 1974. Presidential authority for the program was established by the Economic Stabilization Act of 1970, passed by Congress in response to a public grown weary of both the Vietnam war and the war inflation of 5.4 percent and 5.9 percent in 1969 and 1970. Nixon's four phases were part publicity stunt, part attempt to ensure reelection in 1972, and part control program. Inflation was moderating in 1971 but the unemployment rate was the highest since 1961. Bringing unemployment down quickly before the Presidential election without rekindling inflation, even while devaluing the dollar, required controls. There was no other way: Balance of payments pressure downward on the dollar had become irresistible, but devaluation causes inflation as import prices rise. Austere fiscal policy had seen the unemployment rate rise by 1971 by 170 percent of the 1969 rate, and the unemployed vote *against* incumbent Presidents. Yet war inflation persisted and improving the employment picture while devaluing the dollar would have been highly inflationary. Nixon announced the freeze on August 15, 1971.

The freeze was replaced 90 days later with Phase II of the control program. In this phase, a Price Commission and a Pay Board were established to administer the program. The Pay Board adopted a wage guideline of 5.5 percent for all firms. This guideline was consistent with the Price Commission's goal of a 2.5 percent rate of price increase, as long as labor productivity was rising at 3 percent and as long as no raw materials or energy shortages arose. The Internal Revenue Service established spot enforcement procedures to ensure that the rules were followed. Furthermore, firms and bargaining units were classified into three tiers. Tier I contained, for price considerations, firms with sales of $100 million or more and, for wage considerations, collective bargaining units of 5,000 or more workers. Tier II contained firms with sales of $50 to $100 million and collective bargaining units of 1,000 to 5,000 workers. Tier III contained firms with sales under $50 million and collective bargaining units of under 1,000 workers. All tiers were subject to the same wage and price rules but to simplify administration of the program, each tier was subject to different reporting requirements. Since price and wage power is roughly related to size, Tier I units had to obtain Price Commission or Pay Board permission before price or pay increases were made. Tier II units merely had to submit reports of prices or wages. Tier III units had no reporting requirements.

Phase II of the program was ended in January 1973, shortly after the 1972 Presidential election. But while it lasted, the rate of inflation was brought down dramatically from 5.9 percent in 1970 to 4.3 percent in 1971 and down further to 3.3 percent in 1972. Phase II started out with the formulation of a set of simple price rules. Later on, unfortunately, the rules were needlessly complicated. Nevertheless, the early price rules centered on the allowable cost principle: Prices could be increased only by the amount of allowable cost increases. Pay increases greater than 5.5 percent were generally not counted as allowable costs.

A flaw developed in the application of the allowable cost principle when profit margins were taken into consideration. As the principle was applied by the Price Commission, allowable costs were passed through and then the firm's customary profit margin was applied to the new costs. The result was higher total profits but constant profit margins. If a firm's customary profit margin were 10 percent, a dollar increase in allowable cost would result in a $1.10 increase in price. This set up a perverse incentive structure. The higher the allowable costs a firm incurred, legitimately or otherwise, the higher the firm's total profits. So a firm found it profitable to incur higher costs. A far more effective application of the allowable cost principle would have been a dollar-for-dollar pass through of allowable costs. Then, if allowable costs rose by a dollar, price would rise by only a dollar. The profit margin then would shrink, giving firms a strong incentive to resist cost increases. Rather than improving its application of the allowable cost principle, the Price Commission began proliferating its rules with such gems as TLP ("term limit pricing") and CIPM ("customary initial percentage markup").

Then, to add to the growing confusion, Phase II was replaced by Phase III. The third phase of President Nixon's control program replaced the Pay Board and Price Commission with self-policed controls. The Nixon administration never stated clearly the purpose or the implementation of Phase III. Inflation quickly reemerged. With it rose the public demand for renewed controls. Prices and wages rose even faster in anticipation of Presidential action. A second freeze was imposed in June of 1973 and replaced in August with Phase IV. This last phase of the Nixon control program was very similar to Phase II. The allowable cost principle was applied more effectively and the wide coverage of Phase II was narrowed to more manageable proportions. But public support of both the control program and of the President's Administration collapsed. The program was scrapped in April 1974.

Phases I and II had been effective, but Phases III and IV were mediocre at best. From a low point of 3.3 percent in 1972, inflation rose to 6.2 percent in 1973 and 11.0 percent in 1974. OPEC price hikes added the *coup de grace* to America's last serious attempt to fight inflation without causing massive unemployment. The politically-inclined reader will also note that 1974 marked the beginning of an extended period of time during which the American voter consistently voted against incumbents and voted for outsiders who ran against Washington. President Ford failed in his run against an outsider from Georgia. Once Carter became an insider he lost to the perennial outsider of American politics. And now President Reagan follows in their footsteps?

But the problem runs deeper than incompetence in high office. The problem originates in the core of our economy. Dominated by huge corporate combines that are administered by short-sighted, profit maximizing, managerial bureaucrats, our economy now generates, by its inherent nature, a persistently high rate of inflation. Unless we come to grips with this powerful inflationary machine through an effective wage-price control program which is an integral part of democratic economic planning, the American economy will continue stagnating and the American voter will continue supporting political outsiders offering quack nostrums and anti-Washington slogans.

An Assessment of Control Programs

The control program of the Second World War was effective. In the face of a tremendous increase in demand pressure, the consumer price index of 44.1 in 1941 had risen to only 53.9 in 1945. In fact, consumer prices in 1945 were at the same level as in the late 1920s, right before the disastrous deflation of the Great Depression. Of course, the controls enjoyed strong patriotic support and were supplemented by extensive rationing of consumer goods.

The guidepost program of the Kennedy-Johnson years was not supported by patriotism, nor was it supplemented by any kind of rationing. In fact, the program was voluntary. Violators were not subjected to any formal sanctions. Discredited Presidential "jaw-boning" was the only enforcement. In spite of all this, the guideposts were fairly effective in holding inflation to a minimum during a very substantial decline in unemployment. The voluntary guideposts began to give way in 1967-68 as the Vietnam war became a major drag on the American economy. Even so, the rate of inflation for the period 1962-68 averaged well under 3 percent. Out of the four Presidential Administrations since then, only Nixon's Phase I and Phase II comes close to matching the achievement of the guidepost program.

Nixon's control program was a mixed bag. After the 1972 election, Phases III and IV were very disappointing. But before the election, Phases I and II had allowed a devaluation of the dollar and a decline in unemployment to take place with only minimal inflation. In the Watergate era all of government, not just the wage-price control program, came perilously close to collapse.

The conventional wisdom is wrong about wage-price controls, as it is about much else. Yet there is always just enough doubt to keep the myths alive. Economics, unfortunately, is not only an imprecise science but also a politically-sensitive social science. Disagreement, then, arises from two sources: imprecision of the results and political views of the practitioners. In conservative times, the imprecision of the science allows economists to swim with the current, suffering few pangs of scientific conscience. And these are conservative times. Nevertheless, a reassessment is on the way.

TYPES OF INFLATION

Introduction

Controlling inflation without punishing the American worker or the American poor requires that we first differentiate between the types of inflation. The different types of inflation require strikingly different types of remedies. Two basic types of inflation have plagued us at one time or another: *Sellers Inflation* and *Buyers Inflation*.[6] The remedy for one type of inflation is inappropriate for the other type. It is like giving polio vaccine to prevent rubella. The consequences are predictable — the patient gets sick. When repeated often enough, the patient stops trusting doctors (or dies). Contemporary economists, like the doctors in my little analogy, are prescribing the wrong remedy. Today the economy is suffering from Sellers Inflation. But the majority of economists are prescribing for Buyers Inflation. The economy continues to sicken.

Buyers Inflation

Buyers Inflation is often referred to as demand pull inflation. It is caused by buyers attempting to purchase more than 100 percent of the economy's output. Too much money chases too few goods and pulls up the price of everything. Shortages emerge. Potential customers cannot find sellers. Shoppers encounter long lines and empty shelves when they go to the market. Frustration and black markets spread as the insatiable demand cannot be met, even when producers work at top speed and full capacity.

In their attempts to meet the unmeetable demands for their products, producers scramble frantically to hire more workers. Unemployment falls to very low levels. Prices soar. The symptoms of Buyers Inflation are unmistakable — yet orthodox economists manage. Low unemployment, production rates at full capacity, and shortages are clear signs of Buyers Inflation.

The only cure for Buyers Inflation is a cut back in buying. The buying spree must be stopped. Three ways are available. First, buying can be prohibited unless the buyer has the appropriate rationing coupon. This was a method used in the Second World War. The rationing authority cut back on buying by issuing only a limited number of coupons. Second, buying can be cut back by taxing away the buyers' incomes or by reducing government buying. Very high tax rates were also used in the Second World War to reduce consumer spending. Third, buying can be cut back through higher interest rates and reductions in the money stock. This third way, monetary restraint, is not as simple as it appears. Further discussion of monetary policy will be reserved for a later chapter. In the absence of effective cutbacks, Buyers Inflation cannot be controlled.

Sellers Inflation

Sellers Inflation is often referred to as cost push inflation. But a cost is always somebody's sales revenue or income. A producer's cost is always a seller's receipt, so the term Sellers Inflation is more descriptive of the problem. Furthermore, in our vertically integrated industries most "costs" are not arrived at through arms-length bargaining, nor are most "costs" paid to independent suppliers. Instead, most costs are determined by internal accounting decisions and involve tranfers between a raw material supplying subsidiary and a finished product subsidiary of a conglomerate. The classic example of this is the "cost" of crude oil purchased from wholly or jointly owned subsidiaries of major oil companies. Sellers Inflation is caused by sellers attempting to appropriate receipts summing up to more than 100 percent of the total product. Since appropriating more than 100 percent of the product is impossible, the attempt to do so inflates the price of the product.

Sellers Inflation is relatively new and unrecognized. It is a product of the huge corporation's growing power to push up prices and, to a lesser extent, it is a product of the strong union's ability to push up wages. Sellers Inflation is usually diagnosed by orthodox economists as Buyers Inflation.The wrong diagnosis is due to a failure to recognize that the American corporation's power to raise prices has increased substantially, particularly since the conglomerate merger wave. Orthodox economists rely on a very narrow measurement of corporate power, one that has led them astray. They measure the corporate power to raise prices by specific market concentration ratios rather than by more appropriate measures of diversification. A specific market concentration ratio is the proportion of total market sales accounted for by the four largest firms in the market. Average corporate power, so measured, has not changed drastically since the mid-1960s. Since corporate power has changed little since then, orthodox economists conclude that our inflation cannot be due to corporate power. But the real power to raise prices and close plants in any one market comes from diversification into many different markets. With diversification the corporation can raise prices in one market, reap the short-term profit, and move into other markets before the long-term loss of profit from that one market occurs. And diversification has surged, particularly since the conglomerate merger wave of the 1960s.[7] Our inflation is Sellers Inflation, orthodox misdiagnosis to the contrary not withstanding.

The symptoms of Sellers Inflation, like the symptoms of Buyers Inflation, are also unmistakable. Prices rise in each, of course. But in Sellers Inflation, unemployment rises, plants are closed, the federal deficit soars as unemployment benefits and various welfare payments rise, and an intense struggle over income distribution spreads to all corners of the economy. These symptoms are strikingly different from the symptoms of Buyers Inflation. Figure 10.1 compares the two at a glance.

The only cure for Sellers Inflation is a curbing of sellers' power to appropriate more income through pushing up prices and wages. Two methods of curbing that power are available. First, the power can be dispersed by breaking up the power centers. Large corporations can be broken up through antitrust action. Powerful unions can be broken through right to work legislation. If only the unions are attacked, workers would be left defenseless and most of the inflation would persist. But if the huge corporations are broken up, all the efficiencies of large-scale, corporate-planned production would be lost. These efficiencies are substantial enough that treating the illness in this way would risk killing the patient. Curbing sellers' power can be done in a second way. Wage-price controls can cure Sellers Inflation by limiting

FIGURE 10.1

Buyers and Sellers Inflation

Symptom	Buyers	Sellers
Unemployment	Low	High
Plant Activity	Full Production	Widespread Shutdowns
Federal Outlays	Neutral*	Social Program Hemorrhage
Social Struggle	Over Goods	Over Income

*If the major Buyer causing the inflation is the federal government, spending on military and public works projects will be soaring. Otherwise, outlays will be normal.

corporate power to raise prices and by limiting union power to raise wages. Perhaps an ideological aversion to the best cure, wage-price controls, contributes to the orthodox economist's inappropriate diagnosis of the disease. I rather think so, for even a freshman economics student has little difficulty distinguishing between Buyers Inflation and Sellers Inflation on an exam.

Now it should be clear what kind of inflation plagues us and why it continues to do so. The current inflation is Sellers Inflation. Widespread plant shutdowns, high unemployment, hemorrhaging social programs, and the social struggle over income have all become very serious. The inflation drags on because we do not apply the cure. The cure is wage-price controls, not tax cuts and social program slashes. This simple error is incredibly costly. We will not cure the disease of Sellers Inflation by applying a quack cure for Buyers Inflation. Instead, we will cause even more difficulties.

It is time we faced two simple facts: (1) We have Sellers Inflation, (2) Wage-price controls are the prescription.

EFFECTIVE WAGE-PRICE CONTROLS

Preliminaries

First of all, wage-price controls cannot be effective against Buyers Inflation. As a supplement to rationing, high tax schedules, and tight monetary policy, wage-price controls can be helpful. But the objective of wage-price controls, by themselves, must not be the control of

Buyers Inflation. Failure and disillusionment would be the result. Since the current inflation is Sellers Inflation, wage-price controls are the cure. The first principle of controls is to stop inflation by ensuring free market wages and prices in those sectors of the economy where free markets have been replaced by corporate administered prices and by union negotiated wages.

This principle is very important. Ignoring it will have disastrous effects on the economy's flexibility. The principle also has several major implications for all aspects of an effective control program. The implications will become clear as we discuss the different aspects of controls, particularly wage and price guidelines.

The Kind of Controls

Corporate power will not go away, unless we cut off our nose to spite our face by breaking up America's huge corporations. So an effective wage-price control program cannot be an "on again, off again" program. It must be a permanent part of the American economy because the huge corporation has become a permanent institution. Drop the controls and inflation will resume. A control program is to our economy like insulin to the diabetic. Neither patient can stop taking their medicine lest they get sick.

Although wage-price controls must be permanent, they need not be comprehensive. In fact, controls probably should not be comprehensive because they may become needlessly cumbersome to administer. Comprehensive controls apply to all sectors of the economy. Nixon's first price freeze was comprehensive, needlessly so. Not all of the economy is dominated by huge corporations linked to powerful unions. The free market still exists in much of agriculture, retail trade, and services. Free market sectors do not generate Buyers Inflation because they cannot. In free market sectors the power to push up prices or wages does not exist so wage-price controls need not apply. Only those sectors dominated by huge corporate administrations and influenced by powerful collective bargaining units need to be under the jurisdiction of wage-price controls. But this includes all of the industrial core of the American economy. A simple but effective rule of thumb would be to include all of Fortune's 500 corporations under the control program's purview and to exclude the rest. Jurisdictional adjustments would have to be made as the program evolved, but this would be an excellent benchmark for the extent of the controls.

To ensure fairness and effectiveness, controls must be on both wages and prices. Effectiveness is lost if only wages are controlled because corporate power could still push up prices. The rising prices would then destroy fairness as well because real wages would fall as prices rose. Labor, clearly, would be the loser. Effectiveness would be threatened if only prices are controlled because powerful labor unions and powerful professional associations could push up wages and salaries. Corporate profits would shrink until continued losses led to capital strike — a drying up of capital accumulation. Then everyone would be the loser. Controls must be on both wages and prices because, in practice, one cannot be controlled for long without controlling the other.

Controls must not be in the form of permanent wage-price freezes because the economy gradually loses flexibility under a freeze. Yet a wage-price freeze is a very practical way to initiate a control program after an extended period of inflation. A freeze breaks the inflationary expectations built up over the course of the previous inflation. It is important to break inflationary expectations because, if people expect inflation to occur, they insist that the wages, prices, rents, and interest rates they receive contain an inflationary premium to protect them from the expected price rise. Such insistence on inflationary premiums then contributes to continued inflationary pressures. Inflationary expectations are a well known example of a self-fulfilling prophecy. Such expectations must be broken and the best way to do so is through a wage-price freeze. But the freeze must be removed as soon as the expectations are broken (say three to six months) to allow for flexibility. Price and wage flexibility is essential because changes in consumer habits, technology, and international relations must be reflected in changes in relative prices to avoid the emergence of shortages in some sectors and surpluses in others. The price system must be allowed to reflect changes in fundamental economic relations so permanent controls must be flexible.

The last characteristic of wage-price controls needing emphasis is the difference between voluntary and mandatory controls. Voluntary controls, like the Kennedy-Johnson guideposts, are not backed up by formal sanctions or inducements. Mandatory controls are. Lacking formal sanctions or inducements, voluntary controls are based on perverse incentives: A corporation, union, or professional association which breaks the guidelines is rewarded for its anti-social behavior with higher income. Yet if the guidelines are followed in line with social responsibility, the follower is punished with inflation eating away at its income. As a result, voluntary controls melt under strain. They rapidly become ineffective because they are unfair. They reward cheaters and punish the others. Controls must be mandatory.

To sum up, controls need to be permanent, cover both wages and prices, be limited to sectors where power has replaced the free market, be flexible, and mandatory. Controls with these characteristics can cure Buyers Inflation and do so without creating a disorder worse than the one cured.

Sanctions and Inducements

As a general rule, a society using democratic economic planning to improve its material well-being should not rely on sanctions to achieve objectives. Inducements are superior. Yet all general rules have exceptions. Faced with a very serious, intractable problem, the application of mild economic sanctions is justified. The case of Sellers Inflation is the exception. Sellers Inflation has become so serious and so intractable, sanctions are needed. Primary reliance should be made on inducements, but mild economic sanctions must be formally available if inducements fail. The reason is twofold: First, Sellers Inflation is very rewarding to those who originate it. If monetary incentives (inducements) are given to the originators to "bribe" them not to inflate their wages and prices, how large must the payment be to stop the action? The answer is simple. The payment must be at least as large as the gain from inflating. Then society still ends up paying the costs of Sellers Inflation. But the costs are borne by paying the higher taxes needed to fund all the "bribes" to the reformed inflaters rather than by paying their inflated prices in the first place. This is the fatal flaw in "TIP" and "MAP" schemes to buy-off inflaters. Hence, in the case of truly recalcitrant inflaters, sanctions are called for. The second reason for establishing formal sanctions is to avoid the temptation to use informal, *illegitimate* ones like the "jaw-boning" of the guidepost era. Formal open sanction procedures are far more desirable.

Wage-price controls could be backed up formally, in cases of extreme violation, by subjecting the inflater's income or profit to an excess income or profit tax. In the first instance of abuse only the income or profit earned by breaking the wage-price guidelines would be subjected to the very high excess tax rate. A second infraction would subject 100 percent of the inflater's income or profit to the high excess tax rate. Continued inflating would become very expensive, very fast, because a high tax rate on all of the inflater's income or profit would reduce after-tax income or profit by more than the inflater gained by the infraction. Inflating would not pay.

An alternative or additional sanction could also be employed. This sanction would be a strong drive to encourage imports of the inflater's products at a price within the control program's guides. For a union or professional association, an analogous move would be to lift immigration restrictions on those having the skills of the offending union's membership or on those having the credentials of the offending professional association's membership. Such action not only would get the inflater's attention in a hurry, but would also eliminate any real or imagined bottleneck in production or shortage of skill in the inflater's bailiwick. This particular kind of sanction is an extremely useful one because it is a sanction which is also an inducement. It makes antisocial behavior have detrimental consequences for the perpetrator while it encourages participation in socially acceptable behavior from those who previously were not participating.

Economic sanctions to encourage the inflater's foreign competitors should be used even more aggressively on the domestic front. In particular, a huge untapped potential exists in minority American businesses and workers and in the small business sector. Improved training opportunities would bring forth a huge supply of minority workers, willing and able to work for wages within the control guides. New producers from the minority business community and from the small business sector could be formed if the financial capital were available. We can make it as available as we choose. An aggressive public policy would be to buy half or more of the shares of stock of any new minority business that began production in sectors where price guides were broken, as long as the new corporation agreed to follow the guides. Interest-free or guaranteed loans could also be arranged. A large pool of equity capital and debt capital could be created for investment in those sectors where it was needed, either because of real or contrived bottlenecks. The public commitment required is well within our means. But is it within the limits of our hearts and imaginations?

A WAGE-PRICE COMMISSION

Unified Authority

The administration of wage-price controls must be under one roof. President Nixon's control program is an excellent reason why. Nixon's phases were administered by a Cost of Living Council, a Pay Board, and a Price Commission. This tri-partite arrangement was workable for a while but it became increasingly cumbersome and confusing to the public as the program continued. I suggest that a unified Wage-Price Commission be used instead. Then, responsibility for controlling both wages and prices rests in one place. Then, a Price Commission cannot blame the separate Pay Board for allowing costs (wages) to push up prices; nor can a Pay Board blame the separate Price Commission for allowing rising prices to exert upward pressure on wages. The authority to regulate both wages and prices should be unified in the same agency.

Unified authority over both wages and prices is also necessary to ensure that the Wage-Price Commission remain an independent, function-specific regulatory body. If independent units were to have authority over wages and prices, each independent unit would gradually come to resemble an industry-specific regulatory agency. A separate unit for regulating wages, though it may not become captured by the AFL-CIO, may become very sympathetic to the private interests of powerful collective bargaining units. The same holds for a separate unit regulating prices: though it may not become captured by, say NAM (the National Association of Manufacturers), it may become very sympathetic to the private interests of powerful corporate price-setters. Unified authority, in one regulatory unit, over both wages and prices will help ensure regulatory independence from the private interests being regulated.

Composition of the Commission

The members of a unified Wage-Price Commission must represent the major economic interests being regulated. This means that the same number of Commissioners must represent wage and salary setters as represent corporate price setters. The traditional way representatives of such groups have been selected is through Presidential appointment. But this selection process is faulty, particularly for a body such as the Wage-Price Commission proposed here. In the past, renegade labor leaders and their unions could be manipulated by an astute Administration to serve as token labor representatives. (Recall the Nixon pardon of James Hoffa and subsequent Teamster participation on the Pay Board.) The same could be done to renegade business interests. To avoid token representation, labor interests and business interests should choose their own representatives through democratic elections held by the AFL-CIO and by NAM, or by some other open, democratic procedure. Lacking that, the head of the AFL-CIO and of NAM should be automatically included on the Commission. Then, the third member of the five-member Commission should be chosen by an organized consumer group. The best would be the Consumers Union.

With labor, business, and consumer interests all choosing their own representatives, the Commission would be truly representative of the groups whose interests are at stake. However, a labor-business coalition against the consumer interest would not be unlikely if the Commission had only three members. So I suggest a five-member Commission. The fourth member would be selected by the President as a formal representative of the federal government interest. The fifth representative would be chosen by the governors of the fifty states as a formal representative of the state government interest. The importance of the fourth Commissioner, representing the federal government, is obvious. Yet the need for a fifth Commissioner, representing state government, is also very real. The state governments are strongly affected by trends in collective bargaining contracts and by rising prices. So their interests need to be represented as well as the interests of the federal government, labor, business, and the consumer.

After some experience with the Commission, we may find that its membership should be broadened even further to include a representative chosen by the small business sector, a representative chosen by minority workers, a representative chosen by minority businesses, and a representative chosen by the struggling family farmer. As with all of the concrete proposals made in this book, the composition of the Commission is merely a suggestion, a place to begin rational discourse.

The Commission and the Corporate Public Director

Wage-price controls must be flexible. Wages and prices must change to reflect changes in underlying economic conditions. Otherwise, shortages occur in some sectors, surpluses in others. Avoiding unjustified price increases, but also avoiding the emergence of shortages when prices in one sector really need to rise, requires reliable, detailed information from within the corporation. This is an important function for the Corporate Public Director. Rather than placing the burden of information gathering and reporting on the corporation itself, and rather than relying on corporate credence, the Public Director(s) will be asked by the Wage-Price Commission to make a price report whenever a corporation requests a price increase above the Commission's guideline.

The price report will contain the information needed by the Commission to act on the corporate price request. Such information would include the amount of unused capacity, if any, held by the corporation, ownership interests in suppliers, if any, and the amount the corporation plans to invest in the sector where the corporation wants to raise its price. This information will help the Wage-Price Commission to determine if the price increase really is needed because of the higher raw material costs of independent suppliers or if the higher price really is needed because demand for the product has outstripped the corporation's capacity to produce. A price increase is not justified otherwise. Financing corporate diversification or enlarging the profit margins of subsidiary raw material suppliers are not justifications for price increases. Corporatons asking for price increases will not use these reasons as their justifications, of course. That is why the Corporate Public Director must supply the information needed by the Wage-Price Commission to ascertain the real reason for the price increase.

The Commission and the Democratic Planning Process

Quite frequently, a newly-initiated planning process results in the formulation of goals that are far too high. Over optimism is to be expected in the early stages of democratic planning, American style. But the Wage-Price Commission can play an important role as a counterbalance to the over optimism. In particular, the Commission should prepare a wage-price impact statement for use in the planning process. Starting with sector-by-sector goals given to it by the major planning bodies, the Commission should explain what the wage and price consequences of achieving those goals are likely to be in each sector and for the economy as a whole.

Of course, the Wage-Price Commission will probably be pessimistic in its wage-price impact statement. This pessimism is to be expected, for the Commission will try to make its own job easier by pushing for lower output and employment goals. Generally speaking, the lower these goals, the easier it would be to hold the line on wages and prices. Nevertheless, through a give and take process, the employment and output goals formulated through the planning process will be tempered by the caveats of the Wage-Price Commission while, at the same time, the Commission will be encouraged to do its best to ensure that wage and price increases do not rob the democratic planning process of its goals.

Wage-Price Guidelines

The Kennedy-Johnson guideposts and the Nixon phases both tried to link wage increases to productivity increases. At first glance, such a linkage makes sense. But careful reconsideration is definitely in order. Such a linkage will not work. Such a linkage violates the first principle of controls, to wit: the first principle of controls is to stop inflation by ensuring free market wages and prices in those sectors of the economy where free markets have been replaced by corporate administered prices and by union negotiated wages. In free markets, wages rise in occupations with low rates of unemployment. The higher wages attract workers into the areas where they are needed the most. Wages stagnate where unemployment is high, telling workers to go elsewhere if possible. In free markets, prices rise in industries where production is close to full capacity. The higher prices attract new entrants into the industry and finance the needed capacity expansion of the existing producers. Prices stagnate in industries with excess capacity, telling potential new businesses to go elsewhere. So, wage and price increases should be linked to sector-by-sector unemployment rates and capacity utilization rates, not to productivity. Productivity may be rising in an area where both wages and prices are too high, or it may be falling in an area where both wages and prices are too low. Hence, it provides an improper guideline for setting wages and prices.

This is not to say that productivity is unimportant. Quite the contrary, it is crucial. The U.S. economy is suffering from a productivity crisis. New ideas and new people are no longer flowing into American industry to provide the yeast needed to raise productivity. This is why corporate reform is so essential and why several chapters of this book have been devoted to the internal workings of the corporate bureaucracy. The push from below of new people and new ideas must be encouraged, peacefully. Otherwise, productivity will continue to stagnate.

However, wage and price guidelines cannot be based on productivity because our allocation of resources would become more and more distorted as productivity trends continued diverging in different sectors of the economy. Instead, wage and price guidelines must be based on unemployment and capacity utilization rates in different sectors. Quite frequently, such a base will yield the same result as a productivity base, but it need not. For example, suppose consumers begin buying more skilled services than physical goods. (They have been doing so for some time.) As a general rule, productivity has been rising very slowly in skilled service areas. Should the wages of skilled service workers not rise, the supply of skilled service workers would dry up and service shortages immediately emerge. The frustration over shortages would destroy the wage-price guidelines. However, if wages were linked to unemployment rates, shortages of skilled service workers would lead to higher wages and more workers would be attracted into skilled services.

So, rather than base the wage guideline on the average growth of labor productivity, base it on a realistic goal for the unemployment rate and relate it indirectly to labor productivity. Suppose we can count on labor productivity growing at an overall rate of two percent per year and suppose we can achieve a four percent overall unemployment rate as our goal. Then, the wage guideline for sectors with unemployment of six percent or more would be no increase in wages at all. Sectors with a five percent unemployment rate could increase wages by one percent. Sectors with a four percent unemployment rate could receive two percent higher wages. Three percent unemployment sectors could receive three percent higher wages. Two percent unemployment or lower in a sector would allow a four percent wage hike. The average wage hike, for the economy as a whole operating at a four percent rate of unemployment, would be two percent: The same as the growth in labor productivity, so upward pressure on prices from unit labor costs would be eliminated. This kind of wage guideline would work very effectively. Wages would rise, on average, at the same rate as labor productivity. But where workers were scarce, higher wages would attract additional labor and where workers were plentiful, wages would not rise.[8]

A very similar kind of guideline could be applied to prices. Prices could rise only in bottleneck sectors or only where a price request was justified by an uncontrollable increase in raw materials costs. Excessive wage or salary increases would never be justification for a price increase. Falling prices in other sectors would roughly compensate for the rising prices in bottleneck sectors. Furthermore, an adequate national reserve of crude oil and strategic raw materials could be used to mitigate the impact of higher material costs caused by international instabilities.[9]

CONCLUDING REMARKS

Equality

Bringing Sellers Inflation under control would go a long way toward improving the plight of many poor Americans. Stabilizing the price level would stop the erosion of the real income of aged Americans living on fixed incomes. Social Security benefits have been adjusted upward for the rising price level, but private pension payments and other sources of retirement income have fallen further and further behind. The resulting squeeze on the aged has been scandalous. Wage and price controls are the only sure way to bring cost of living relief to the aged. Higher and higher Social Security benefits funded by higher and higher payroll taxes will be inadequate as long as the price level is free to soar to unprecedented heights.

Bringing Sellers Inflation under control would also improve the plight of the unemployed. President Reagan's large tax cut has resulted in very few new jobs. Instead, the ever higher cost of living absorbed the higher after-tax incomes before the ink could dry on the Reagan budget. Instead of higher employment we have higher prices. And the experts — the facile supply-side economists — tell us the same thing that Andrew Mellon told our grandparents during Herbert Hoover's Administration: The tax cuts were needed to stimulate saving (of the rich). The social cuts were necessary to encourage hard work (of the poor). It did not work then. It will not work now. We believed it then. Do we believe it now? Putting the unemployed back to work today requires the control of wages and prices so that higher incomes mean higher employment figures, not higher prices and wages.

Wage and price controls, buttressed by inducements for small and minority businessmen to enter sectors where prices are rising, would also improve the position of the small and minority businessmen. With the federal government providing access to financial capital, these formerly excluded businessmen could give a few corporate Goliaths, at least, a good run for their money. But not too much should be hoped for too soon on this front. The huge corporation has the benefit of economies-of-scale and the benefit of carefully planned, vertically integrated production processes.

Freedom

Critics of wage-price controls never tire of fearful pronouncements that controls destroy individual freedom. They never tire of innuendos linking controls to creeping socialism or to even worse — dare I even write it? — yes, to the International Communist Conspiracy! But like the old water fluoridation scare (remember when we were warned that fluoridation was a Communist Plot?), experience gives the lie to fearful pronouncements and hair-raising innuendos. World War II controls did not rob us of our freedoms. They kept the inflation rate down. The Kennedy-Johnson guideposts did not enslave us. They allowed employment to grow at a minimal inflation rate. The Nixon controls did not destroy our freedoms. They reduced inflation.

But wage-price controls do reduce the freedom of economic power blocks to set their own wages and prices above free market levels, generating inflation and unemployment as they do. And this kind of freedom, the rest of us can do without. So, too, can the power blocks. Under a free market system, they would not possess the power to set their own prices in the first place. Instead, they would have to survive with the price set by the free play of supply and demand in the market. Instead of being price and wage makers, participants in a free market are price and wage takers. They take what the market gives them because they lack the power to dominate the market. Wage and price controls that restrict the power of huge corporations and unions to make prices and wages do not deprive them of any freedoms possessed by competitive businessmen. Instead, such controls return the power blocks to their proper market role — that of price taker instead of price maker. This will strengthen the market system, not weaken it.

Profits

An important function of high profit is to attract new firms into industries where they are needed and to finance expanded facilities of the existing firms in very profitable industries. Price controls, it is often feared, would destroy this function of profits. Yet the price controls proposed here would do no such thing. Instead, the controls proposed here would restore this profit function in areas of our economy where it no longer exists. In those sectors dominated by huge corporations, particularly the conglomerates, high profits do not finance expansion of existing facilities. Instead, high profits finance corporate diversification — movement into new markets. Even the most casual reader of newspapers knows where high oil and steel profits go, for example. (They do *not* go into the oil and steel industry, at least the lion's share does not.) Nor does the lure of high profits to be earned in sectors dominated by huge corporations result in a flood of new firms into those sectors. The risks to the new entrant are too high because the power of the entrenched producers is too great. In the absence of government guarantees and government capital, new entrants are not forthcoming. The controls proposed here would offer such government guarantees and government capital to new entrants willing to take on the giants who abuse their price making and profit appropriating power, restoring the proper role of high profits. The opportunity to make profits should not be restricted to the corporate elite.

Nor should the corporate elite's opportunity to make profits be restricted, unless their profits are appropriated rather than earned. Profit is earned when a producer cuts costs through more efficient use of resources. Profit is earned when a producer innovates, introduces a new product or a new process for making an old product more efficiently. Profit is also earned when a producer cuts his profit margin but more than makes up for it with higher volume. Price controls would not restrict these ways of earning profit in the least.

But profits can also be appropriated. Profit is appropriated when economic power is used to force down wages or raw material prices. Profit then is reaped at the expense of workers or suppliers. Labor unions and some antitrust legislation arose because of this kind of profit appropriation. Profit is also appropriated when economic power is used to drive up the price of one's product. Profit then is reaped at the expense of the consuming public. Price controls are needed to control this kind of profit appropriation. Price controls, it should be emphasized, do not restrict earning profits. Price controls only restrict appropriating profits at the public expense by forcing up prices.

Equity

Wage-price controls are often referred to as "incomes policy" because controls protect the price level from the scramble to appropriate more and more income. The income scramble, of course, is the cause of Sellers Inflation. So controlling Sellers Inflation requires controlling the income scramble itself.[10] This leads directly to the question of equity in the distribution of income. Following the line of equity reasoning, most observers conclude that wage-price guidelines should link wages and prices to productivity. We believe that people should earn more only if they produce more, and linking wages and prices to productivity allows them to do so. But an effective wage-price control program must link specific wages to the unemployment rate for that particular occupation and it must link specific prices to the capacity utilization rate for that particular industry.

I do not propose that we give up our goal to create an equitable distribution of income. But I do suggest that a wage-price control program is not the best way to bring about equity in our income distribution. Instead, tax reforms, transfer programs, affirmative action plans, democratic planning, and corporate reforms are the best ways to pursue an equitable distribution of income. A wage-price control program, to be effective, must focus on stopping Sellers Inflation. Of course, once it is stopped, the aged will find that their incomes are no longer eroded by inflation and the unemployed will find that a growing economy generates jobs for them instead of higher prices and wages for those with entrenched economic power. So wage-price controls deliver a more equitable distribution, but only if the controls do their primary task. That task is to stop Sellers Inflation.

11 MONETARY AND FISCAL POLICIES

INTRODUCTION

Since the late 1960s, each business cycle has worsened the U.S. economy's deepening stagflation. Recoveries get slower; recessions deeper. Each recovery has been welcomed by Wall Street as a light at the end of the tunnel. Each recovery has been hailed by the President and his men as a new era of prosperity. But the light always faded as each recovery turned into recession. At long last, the public has begun to realize that permanent prosperity is not just around the corner. Something is fundamentally wrong with the American economy. It has not been getting better, just more erratic, more unstable. For in addition to a revamped wage-price control program, the U.S. economy desperately needs revitalized monetary and fiscal policies at the federal level. Yet federal retrenchment has been prescribed with increasing disregard for the disastrous consequences by first the Nixon Administration, then by the Ford, Carter, and Reagan administrations.

What the economy increasingly needs is federal leadership. What it increasingly gets is federal abandonment. And when the economy gags on its medicine, instead of changing the prescription, the good doctors order larger doses. It is time to remove the doctors from the case. We have listened to the orthodox and ultra-orthodox economists long enough to know that their medicine does not work. It gives, at best, a temporary fillip to the rich. But the poor, and the economy, and society at large all deteriorate. Before they kill us, fire the monetarists and the supply-siders. Their orthodox prescriptions are for an economy and society that no longer exist. They have become quacks because their theories are outmoded. Both their monetary quackery and their fiscal quackery must be rejected and replaced.

MONEY AND HISTORY

The Monetarist Misinterpretation

"*Monetarism*" is the accepted orthodoxy of academic economists when it comes to regulating banks, interest rates, and the money supply. The monetarists have modernized an ancient doctrine known as the quantity theory of money. According to their modernized version of the quantity theory, controlling the money supply will eliminate inflation, recession, and excessive unemployment. Faith in the quantity theory of money was threatened for a few years after the Great Depression by the followers of John Maynard Keynes.[1] Nevertheless, the Keynesian heresy quickly was squelched in the bastions of academic propriety and conservatism. Arthur Burns, President Eisenhower's Chairman of the Council of Economic Advisers, and Burns's star pupil Milton Friedman of the University of Chicago were early leaders in the good fight against unconventional thought. Burns as a policymaker and Friedman as a theoretician both contributed to the resurgence of the old quantity theory of money as a defense against the new economic heresy.[2] The quantity theory of money was formulated in an earlier time when money was commodity money instead of credit money, and this is why the monetarist quackery must be rejected once and for all. It is hopelessly outmoded. The quantity theory of money, upon which monetarism is based, was relevant for an economy which used commodity money. But it is no longer relevant for our economy because our economy has evolved beyond the commodity money stage of development to the credit money stage of development.

Virtually all economies, primitive and advanced, have used something as a medium of exchange or means of payment. Very few economies have relied exclusively on barter. Almost all have used some kind of money. Primitives and ancients alike have used shells, cattle, tobacco, and precious metals. These were commodity moneys. When the quantity of the commodity used for money in these economies rose, the quantity of money rose. Conversely, when the quantity of the commodity fell, the quantity of money fell. Such rises and falls were due primarily to acts of God. Drought, crop failure, or the exhaustion of a mineral deposit caused a decline in the quantity of money. Ample rain, good crops, or the discovery of new mineral deposits caused an increase in the quantity of money. These fortuitous events had immediate economic impacts. Good fortune meant an immediate increase in the income and money-wealth of mine-owners, herders, or farmers. Their higher incomes and money-wealth were spent and a round of inflation often followed. Too much money chased too few goods. On the other hand, bad fortune meant an immediate decrease in the income and money-wealth of mine-owners, herders, or farmers. A round of deflation often followed as too little money was available to spend on too many goods. It took early thinkers very little time to realize that if the quantity of the commodity money could be stabilized, the rounds of inflation or deflation could be stopped. This was the commodity-money birth of the quantity theory of money. It was perfectly correct, as far as it went.

But once economies evolved beyond using commodities as money, things became more complicated and the quantity theory of money became less relevant. The first step away from commodity money was the use of commodity-reserve money. The most well-known kind of commodity-reserve money is the gold standard. On the gold standard, gold served as a reserve for issues of banknotes. Banks issued banknotes to borrowers and depositors, backing the notes with a fractional reserve of gold. The complication introduced by this new practice was that acts of God were no longer the only determinants of the quantity of money. In addition, acts of man affected the quantity of money. Money was no longer independent of economic pressures. Most importantly, increases and decreases in the demand for credit led to increases and decreases in the quantity of money. High credit demand induced banks to issue more banknotes. Low credit demand led to a decline in banknote issuance. The link between the quantity of money and the quantity of the monetary commodity was weakened dramatically. The quantity of money became, in Economese,[3] endogenous. It became partially linked to the demand for credit.

Modern, twentieth century economies use credit money, money that is based exclusively on credit. Modern money has no link to the quantity of gold or to the quantity of any commodity. Acts of God affect it not. It is determined exclusively by acts of man, by the actions of our Federal Reserve System, bankers, bank competitors, and credit customers. In particular, the Federal Reserve System attempts to control the creation of credit money while bankers, bank competitors, and the credit-hungry public all try to avoid the control of the Federal Reserve. The banks and other financial intermediaries try to grant as much credit as possible at the highest interest rate possible. The public tries to get as much credit as it can to finance homes, cars, plants, and capital equipment at minimal cost. When the Fed (short for Federal Reserve System) tries to restrict the creation of credit money, interest rates soar and the search for new forms of credit money accelerates. In the last century when the U.S. Comptroller of the Currency clamped down on the issuance of banknotes, banks began using new credit money — demand deposits (checking account money). And today, after more than a decade of tightening up by the Fed, the same kind of thing is occurring. N.O.W. accounts, bank credit cards, and money market mutual funds are proliferating. Even more sophisticated forms of credit money surely are on the way.

The point of this brief discussion of commodity money, commodity-reserve money, and credit money is simple. As money evolved, it lost its tight link to the quantity of any particular commodity and became more tightly linked to the demand for credit. Becoming linked to credit, money became "endogenous." Its quantity began to increase and decrease with increases and decreases in the demand for credit. Since the demand for credit rises and falls with the level of economic activity, the quantity of money rises and falls with the level of economic activity. A recession is caused by a decline in investment (the Keynesian heresy). But the drop in investment is accompanied by a decline in the demand for credit. This results in a decline in the quantity of money, or a decline in its rate of growth, during a recession. A recovery, on the other hand, is fueled by new investment and new demands for credit. As a result, the quantity of money expands during a recovery in economic activity. So economic recessions generally are accompanied by declines in the quantity of money and economic recoveries generally are accompanied by increases in the quantity of money.[4]

These coincidental increases and decreases in the quantity of money, or in its rate of growth, have been occurring along with the business cycle for at least a century, setting the stage for the most tragic misinterpretation of the historical record ever made by orthodox economists. Note the recessions are accompanied by falls in the quantity of money; recoveries by rises in the quantity of money. Both the fall in the economy and in the money stock are caused by a decline in spending, investment spending primarily. Also, both the rise in the economy and in the money stock are caused by an increase in spending. But these rises and falls are only accompanied by rises and falls in money, not caused by fluctuations in money. Nevertheless, one who learned the old quantity theory of money at the feet of his academic mentors could easily misinterpret the historical record by reading it through the "lens" of the quantity theory.

This is exactly what happened in the case of Milton Friedman and his co-workers at the University of Chicago. Beginning in the early 1950s, Friedman and his co-workers have tirelessly argued that the business cycle, and later the stagflation, which plague the American economy are due to wide swings in the quantity of money. If only the quantity of money were controlled, Friedman argued relentlessly, the economy would be stable. And, unfortunately, the historical data backs him up, at least superficially. From the end of the Civil War to the present, recessions have been accompanied by declines in the quantity of money or in its growth rate and recoveries have been accompanied by increases in the quantity of money or in its growth rate. Friedman and the Monetarists, interpreting the data through the lens of the quantity theory of money, conclude that monetary instability has been the cause of our economic instability.[5] If they are correct, then controlling the quantity of money will stabilize the economy. But they are incorrect because, in fact, the instability of our economy has been the cause of the instability of our money, not the other way around.

The Monetarist Experiment

By the late 1960s, people began to believe Friedman and the growing ranks of young Monetarists. The author was one of those people, for even the unorthodox began to believe that control of the quantity of money could be an effective means to help stabilize the U.S. economy. But events were soon to demonstrate the gross error of Monetarism. In 1970 President Nixon appointed Arthur Burns Chairman of the Board of Governors of the Federal Reserve System. Milton Friedman had been the star pupil of Professor Burns. Rather than appointing the student, Nixon appointed the teacher himself. Burns was not as rabid as Friedman, but under Burns the Federal Reserve System immediately changed its strategy for conducting monetary policy. Rather than regulating money market conditions, as was done under

Burns' predecessor, William McChesney Martin, Jr., the Fed adopted a Monetarist strategy of controlling the quantity of money.[6] Although Burns was not the hard-nosed Monetarist that Milton Friedman is, he tried for eight years to control the U.S. money stock. At first, I thought he could do it. At first, I thought controlling money would help stabilize the economy. But Burns could not control the money stock, nor could controlling it have stabilized the economy.[7]

Burns' technical tactic involved using the "Reserves available to support Private Deposits" (RPDs) and the Fed fund rate as month-to-month "targets" in the actual control of the money stock. When Burns was replaced with Paul Volcker by President Carter in 1978, much hoopla was made by the business press about putting Monetarism into practice, for Volcker is a hard-nosed Monetarist. But Burns had been putting Monetarism to the test since 1970.[8] The only thing that Volcker changed was the *technical tactic* used by the Fed. *There was no change in strategy, only in tactics.* Volcker's tactic is no better than Burns'. Neither has been successful in applying a Monetarist strategy, yet Monetarism refuses to die out. First Burns and now Volcker have been running the American economy through the Monetarist ringer for 13 years and the economy continues getting worse. They have not been able to stabilize the quantity of money because it is so strongly influenced by the changing demand for bank credit. Instead, their misguided attempts to control the money stock have destabilized interest rates and weakened once-sound financial institutions. Savings and Loan Associations have been particularly hard hit by over a decade of Monetarist machinations.

Under the Burns-Volcker Monetarist regime, the changing credit needs of the economy and the increasing financial sophistication of multinational banks and of huge megacorps have resulted in soaring interest rates, severe distortions in credit flows, and the rapid creation of "near-moneys" and "money-substitutes." The damage caused by Monetarism has been spreading for over a decade. The Monetarists, with their simplistic faith in controlling the quantity of money, have failed to understand the changing nature of our financial system. The results have been catastrophic.

If the Monetarists could just agree on what the quantity of money is, they could try to control it. Unfortunately, there are nearly as many definitions of the quantity of money as there are Monetarists.

The following exercise in monetary definition-making from the *Federal Reserve Bulletin* illustrates my point. Currency in circulation plus demand deposits held by the public and by state and local governments comprise the narrowest definition of the quantity of money. This definition is denoted M_{IA}. To M_{IA} add "negotiable order of withdrawal and automated transfer service accounts at banks and thrift institutions, credit union share draft accounts, and demand deposits at mutual savings banks" and you get M_{IB}. To M_{IB} add "savings and small denomination time deposits at all depository institutions, overnight repurchase agreements at commercial banks, overnight Eurodollars held by U.S. residents other than banks at Caribbean branches of member banks, and money market mutual fund shares" and you get M_2. To M_2 add "large-denomination time deposits at all depository institutions and term RPs at commercial banks and savings and loan associations" and you get M_3.[9] We could keep on adding more items, but the point has been made. Besides, since this was originally written the Fed has redefined money to cover its tracks. Neither the Fed nor the Monetarists can make up their minds.

Small wonder too; for suppose they decided that money was M_{IA}. So, control M_{IA}. But controlling M_{IA} leads to the expansion of M_{IB}. Well then, money must *really* be M_{IB}. So, control M_{IB}. But controlling M_{IB} leads to the expansion of M_2. Well then, money must *really* be M_3, so control it. The problem with the Monetarist strategy should now be clear. Controlling any particular "monetary aggregate" leads to growth in some other "monetary aggregate." The Monetarist strategy has turned out to be little more than a shell game. You cannot find the pea under any of the shells. But since the Monetarists can pull more shells out of their sleeves as fast as you can turn them over, you will never be able to prove that there is no pea. Worse yet, as the Monetarists have been playing this shell game with the public, attention has been diverted from the distortions in our financial system which have been growing since the game was started by Burns in 1970.

Since 1970, interest rates have climbed to levels matching those reached during the financial and economic chaos of the Civil War. Interest rates have never been even close to these levels during peace time in the entire history of the United States. These astronomical interest rates have resulted in a massive redistribution of income away from small businessmen, farmers, entrepreneurs, new home buyers, and other credit hungry groups, to bankers, insurance companies, coupon-clippers, and other monied groups. Under Monetarism, those who have, received more and those who have not, received less.

The high interest rates have not reduced the flow of credit into financing corporate mergers. Quite the contrary. Recent years have witnessed a resurgence in the conglomerate merger wave which first crested in the 1960s. Huge conglomerates are always first in the line for credit. Quite often they do not even need it. Corporate profits and accelerated depreciation allowances ensure a cash flow adequate for most purposes. If that falls short, the huge conglomerate has access to easy credit in the Eurodollar market. Only if that fails, will a truly powerful corporation rely on the currently expensive U.S. credit market. Even then, the large corporation taps first into the prime commercial paper market or the long-term bond market for credit at rates usually far below the prime rate charged by banks. Then, as a last resort, the large corporation will borrow from banks at the prime rate of interest. If any bank credit is left over, other groups get a shot at it. But other groups usually pay effective rates of interest significantly higher than the prime rate. The result of all this has been a diversion of credit flows away from small business, family farming, and similar activities. Large corporations are flush, the rest of the economy anemic.

The distortion of credit flows in the economy since the shell game began in 1970 has been reinforced by a drastic weakening of our Savings and Loan Associations. As interest rates ratcheted upward under Burns and Volcker, large commercial banks offered attractive new forms of investments for large depositors. Sophisticated large depositors quickly withdrew their funds from the S&Ls and placed their funds in banks. The S&Ls retaliated with their own new, high-interest investments for large depositors. But the S&Ls were no match for the banks because the S&Ls held most of their assets in the form of long-term, fixed-rate mortgages. Banks, on the other hand, held short-term commercial loans that were constantly rolling over to higher interest rates. So the banks could outbid the S&Ls by offering higher interest rates to large depositors than S&Ls could offer. As the S&Ls lost deposits to the banks, they had to cut back on mortgage credit to home buyers. S&Ls also were forced to grant new mortgage credit at a variable rather than fixed rate of interest.

In spite of massive credit aid to the S&Ls by the Government National Mortgage Association and by the Federal Home Loan Mortgage Corporation, the S&Ls have continued to reduce their mortgage lending. With a continuation of the Monetarist shell game, the outlook for housing is very bleak. A new home is simply not in the realm of the possible for most young families in the United States. Reasonable cost credit will not be available if the Federal Reserve System continues its Monetarist attempt to control the quantity of money. The Fed is bound to fail. Each time it fails, the Fed drives interest rates even higher. Each time interest rates rise, the dream of owning their own home slips farther away from the financial capacity of the average American family.

At a time when so much attention is focused on strengthening the family, the results of Monetarism are truly ludicrous. At a time when so much attention is focused on strengthening the small businessman, the family farmer, and the independent entrepreneur, the results of Monetarism are equally ludicrous. These groups are all credit-hungry. And Monetarism is starving them all to death. The megacorp can avoid the control obsession of the Monetarists. The others cannot.

A MONETARY POLICY THAT WORKS

The Tobin Strategy

For nearly 13 years we have tried to control the quantity of money in the United States, even though we were not sure what it was. It is time to stop. The side-effects have become far too costly and we are no closer to controlling it than we were when Arthur Burns took the helm of the Fed in 1970. Yet in a sense the Monetarist experiment has not been a failure. The experiment has shown us what we *cannot* do. That is an important lesson to learn. Now, what *can* we do with monetary policy?

As the Monetarist wave was rising among economists in the 1960s, a few economists remained skeptical. One of them was James Tobin.[10] Tobin proposed a monetary strategy radically different from the Monetarist strategy which was adopted.[11] He was many years ahead of his time, however, and his proposal received very little attention. With modifications appropriate to the new conditions of the 1980s, I propose that we replace the failed Monetarist strategy with the Tobin strategy. Before doing so, however, the extremism of the Federal Reserve system should be curbed. The Tobin proposal will make the Fed a very effective instrument of public policy. Before adopting it, the Fed should be reformed so that the policy it conducts is really in the public interest. Otherwise, we may make the Fed more effective at conducting monetary policy only to find that the policy it adopts runs against the public interest.

The Federal Reserve System is the central bank for the United States. Central bankers have always been a curious lot, a kind of subculture in miniature. Central bankers have always held opinions and shared values that are different from those of the larger society. A central banker's world is a gentlemen's world, a world of high finance and of monied families. The work-a-day world of the middle classes and the working classes is far away. Central bankers do not belong to unions, worry about lay offs, or strive to please their bureaucratic superiors. They are the superiors. They do not fear unemployment, recession, and cuts in social security. Instead, they fear inflation, falling interest rates, and "government interference" in their affairs. They are honorable, God-fearing men who love their families and their country. Nevertheless, their interests as central bankers are not the same as the interests of the common man. When free of "government interference," central bankers always see a need to fight inflation with tight money and they always see a need to encourage thrift with high interest rates.[12] Independence of the central bank is their rallying cry. The Fed must be protected against political interference lest "unsound" economic policies be forced on the central bank. Yet, as Galbraith remarks, "what is called sound economics is very often what mirrors the needs of the respectably affluent."[13] Expressed even more frankly, the concern of the central bankers with keeping interest rates high and with fighting inflation at all costs is extremism, when viewed from the interests of the common man. This extremism must be curbed.

It can be done quite simply. The Board of Governors of the Federal Reserve System is composed of seven Presidential appointees. A Governor's term of office is fourteen years, however, so only one Governor's appointment expires every two years. The President of the United States, with a four-year term, can appoint only two Governors in one term, barring resignations. Obviously, since they serve for fourteen years, Governors cannot be removed by incoming Presidents. This makes them relatively independent from the President, who is supposed to be the democratic representative of the people. Furthermore, one of the Governors is designated the Chairman of the Board by the President. The Chairman serves, as Chairman, for four years. But the Chairman's term does not coincide with the President's. President Nixon, for example, had to wait for two years before he could appoint his own Chairman — Arthur Burns — in 1970. Carter also had to wait before appointing Volcker in 1979, so Reagan was stuck with Volcker for the first two years of his term. To simplify this mess and to make the Board a servant of the duly-elected officials of the Federal government, we should have the members of the Board appointed differently.

In particular, the Board of Governors should reflect the interests of the society at large, not the interests of just one segment. Toward that end, three members of the Board should be appointed by the President and three by Congress. Then the Chairman can either be chosen by the six appointees or be appointed by the President as well. Furthermore, rather than serving a fourteen-year term, each Board member should serve at the discretion of the Branch that appointed him (either Presidential or Congressional). Such a proposal is always shocking to those who want an independent central bank. But an independent central bank often conducts a monetary policy that conflicts with the fiscal policy worked out by Congress and the President. Such is the case now. The tight monetary policy of the Fed is holding down spending while the Reagan tax cuts are increasing spending. The two policies cancel each other out, crippling the Federal government's over-all ability to influence the rate of spending, and needlessly delaying our recovery from the 1981 recession. The Fed needs to become a member of the Presidential-Congressional team so that fiscal and monetary policies do not offset each other.

In addition to becoming a team player, the Fed needs to adopt a monetary strategy that works. It cannot control the quantity of money but it can control the cost of credit. The Tobin proposal would strengthen the Fed's ability to do so. As Tobin put it, "those who believe that a democratic society should seek to control its own economic destiny will wish the government to have the means to carry out its will."[14] Creating the means to control the cost of credit would be quite easy. First the Federal Reserve System should allow all financial intermediaries under its reserve requirement jurisdiction to borrow from it freely at the usual Federal Reserve discount rate. Second, the Federal Reserve should pay the discount rate to all financial intermediaries under its reserve jurisdiction for any excess reserves they hold at the Fed. Third, the Fed should then use the discount rate as a direct means of controlling the prime rate of interest and as an indirect means of controlling other interest rates.

Suppose the Fed were purged of its Monetarist madness by replacing the current Board of Governors with a Presidentially and Congressionally appointed Board committed to bringing down the cost of credit. Using the Tobin strategy, the Fed could do so quickly and efficiently. By lowering the discount rate to, say, four percent, the prime rate of interest would immediately come down with the discount rate. As long as financial intermediaries can borrow from the Fed at four percent and lend at more than four percent, they would do so. Credit would immediately begin flowing again. As credit flows expanded, the increased supplies of credit would drive the borrower's cost of credit down to four percent (the discount rate) plus the cost incurred by financial intermediaries in extending credit to their customers. This cost would include administering or processing the loan, the risk premium on the loan, and a reasonable rate of profit for the intermediary making the loan. This cost would be the financial intermediary's "spread" between the interest rate it pays for credit from the Fed and the interest rate it charges a credit customer. As long as the large financial intermediaries in the U.S. are not allowed to buy up their competitors, this spread would be minimal. Competition would keep it that way.

If the economy entered a period of Buyers Inflation, with "too much money chasing too few goods," rather than a futile attempt at controlling the quantity of money, the Tobin strategy would result in a successful control of the cost of credit. The Fed would raise the discount rate to, say, ten percent. Immediately, financial intermediaries that used to lend at the old four percent discount rate plus their spread, would cease doing so. Instead, they would hold excess reserves at the Fed and earn a risk and cost-free ten percent. The flow of credit would dry up, driving up the cost of credit to ten percent plus the spread. The Buyers Inflation, to the extent that it was fueled by excessive use of credit, would come to a halt using the Tobin strategy. Under the Monetarist strategy, the Fed would play a shell game, controlling one definition of the quantity of money only to discover that another definition of money soared out of control, continuing to fuel the Buyers Inflation. In short, the Tobin strategy for conducting monetary policy would work efficiently whether we needed to increase or decrease the cost of credit.

Supplementing the Tobin Strategy

For use in the 1980s, the Tobin strategy must be supplemented in two ways. First, competition among financial intermediaries must be encouraged to keep the spread as low as is consistent with a healthy financial system. Second, the flow of credit from the financial system into the different sectors of the economy needs to be directed by the social benefits received as well as by the profit earned.

The U.S. financial system is characterized by a very large number of different financial intermediaries. Although a few banks have reached immense size and a few Savings and Loan Associations have followed their example, thousands of independent banks and S&Ls still compete vigorously. Yet if the recent trend is allowed to continue, the merger movement among financial intermediaries will result in a dramatic decline in competiton. That decline will result in a widening of the spread. So mergers among financial intermediaries should be blocked by antitrust. Financial intermediation enjoys few, if any, of the economies of scale or economies of planning enjoyed by most other economic activities. Huge size is simply not justified for financial intermediaries. The financial system, therefore, should be kept as decentralized and competitive as practical. This will keep the spread at a minimum.

Even if we maintain a competitive financial system, the flow of credit through it will not always correspond to social priorities. The flow of credit will correspond to private profit, however, because activities yielding high profits can pay high interest rates for credit. Since profitability is not an adequate indicator of social desirability, democratically-determined social priorities should be used to supplement the profit criterion. A major step in that direction has already been taken with passage of the Community Reinvestment Act of 1977.[15] Although the Act has been only weakly implemented, it forms the framework of social priorities needed to supplement the profit criterion in directing the flow of credit through our economy. The basic objective of the Act is to ensure that financial intermediaries, particularly banks, serve the varied credit needs of their communities.

To do so will require that two fairly common financial practices be curtailed. The first practice is *red-lining*, the practice of marking certain neighborhoods (black) or communities as off-limits for new credit. Although financial intermediaries usually deny the practice, in many urban neighborhoods and rural communities credit is not available from legitimate institutions at any price. The second practice is *funneling*, the practice of using the deposits of smaller independent banks or of branch banks to finance large corporate customers. Funneling diverts credit out of smaller neighborhoods and communities into large regional and national financial centers. The result is an abundance of credit for large national and international corporations but a real credit scarcity for family farmers and local businessmen, not to mention minority entrepreneurs and new community housing.[16]

Tobin's monetary strategy can be combined very neatly with implementation of the Community Reinvestment Act by allowing financial intermediaries unrestricted access to borrowing from the Fed, only if they agree to abide by the objectives of the Act. Bank examiners would then verify that they do so. Most intermediaries will agree to do so in order to gain access to Fed credit. But no intermediary would be forced to do so, only induced. In this way, we would be adopting a monetary strategy that works and we would be inducing financial intermediaries to supplement the profit criterion with social criteria for directing the flow of credit through our economy.

THE GOVERNMENT BUDGET AND THE ECONOMY

Trends in Government Finance

The growth of government spending and debt in recent years is well known. Nevertheless, a few details and trends need to be highlighted. First we will examine the federal fiscal scene, then look at the state and local governments.

Table 11.1 contains federal expenditures, receipts and surpluses or deficits for the years 1960 to 1981. In absolute dollars, federal receipts and expenditures have grown tremendously. Each has increased about

TABLE 11.1

The Federal Budget (national income and product accounts)

	Receipts		Expenditures		Surplus or Deficit (-)	
Year	In billions of dollars	As a percent of GNP	In billions of dollars	As a percent of GNP	In billions of dollars	As a percent of GNP
1960	96.1	19.0	93.1	18.4	3.0	0.6
1961	98.1	18.7	101.9	19.4	-3.9	-0.7
1962	106.2	18.8	110.4	19.5	-4.2	-0.7
1963	114.4	19.2	114.2	19.1	0.3	0.1
1964	114.9	18.0	118.2	18.5	-3.3	-0.5
1965	124.3	18.0	123.8	17.9	0.5	0.1
1966	141.8	18.8	143.6	19.0	-1.8	-0.2
1967	150.5	18.8	163.7	20.5	-13.2	-1.7
1968	174.4	20.0	180.5	20.7	-6.0	-0.7
1969	196.9	20.9	188.4	20.0	8.4	0.9
1970	191.9	19.3	204.3	20.6	-12.4	-1.2
1971	198.6	18.4	220.6	20.5	-22.0	-2.0
1972	227.5	19.2	244.3	20.6	-16.8	-1.4
1973	258.6	19.5	264.2	19.9	-5.6	-0.4
1974	287.8	20.1	299.3	20.9	-11.5	-0.8
1975	287.3	18.5	356.6	23.0	-69.3	-4.5
1976	331.8	19.3	384.8	22.4	-53.1	-3.1
1977	375.1	19.6	421.5	22.0	-46.4	-2.4
1978	431.5	20.0	460.7	21.4	-29.2	-1.4
1979	494.4	20.5	509.2	21.1	-14.8	-0.6
1980	540.8	20.6	602.0	22.9	-61.2	-2.3
1981	624.8	21.4	686.4	23.5	-61.6	-2.1

Source: *Economic Report of The President* (Washington, D.C.: GPO, 1982), p. 320, and my own calculations.

fivefold. But in relative terms, receipts and expenditures have been remarkably constant over the 22 years covered by Table 11.1. Receipts have averaged 19.4 percent and expenditures 20.5 percent of Gross National Product (GNP). Receipts have ranged from a high of 21.4 percent of GNP in 1981 to a low of 18.0 percent in 1964 and 1965. Expenditures have ranged from a high of 23.5 percent of GNP in 1981 to a low of 17.9 percent in 1965. Neither receipts nor expenditures have deviated much from their average proportions of GNP. Expenditures have deviated more than receipts because many federal expenditures automatically rise when the economy slides into a business cycle recession and then they fall during recovery. The severity of the recession in 1980–81 caused expenditures to rise to unusually high proportions of GNP in those years. Also, in 1980–81 the high rate of inflation pushed many taxpayers into higher tax brackets, causing federal receipts to rise to their peak proportions of GNP.

Since receipts have generally been slightly less than expenditures, the federal government usually ran a deficit. The average deficit has been quite small though, 1.1 percent of GNP for the 22 years covered by Table 11.1 The major expenditure determinants of the deficit have been war expenditures and economic recessions. The high deficit in 1967 was due to an acceleration of Vietnam war spending. The rising deficits in 1970–71 were due to economic recession, as were the high deficits of 1975 through 1977. The high deficits of 1980–81 were also due to a depressed economy. The record deficits of 1982–83 (not shown in Table 11.1) are due to a number of factors: the worst recession since the 1930s; a resumption of the arms race; and the Reagan tax cuts.

Nevertheless, the Reagan tax cuts are not new. For several years now, tax loopholes have been opened wider and wider by new tax laws. Tax loopholes are referred to officially as "tax expenditures," because such loopholes have the same effect on the federal budget as actual expenditures — a larger deficit. The opening-up of tax loopholes for affluent individual taxpayers and corporations actually has contributed more to the federal deficit than any other factor. By 1980, loopholes for corporations and the affluent resulted in well over $100 billion of tax expenditures.[17] Had the loopholes been closed, rather than opened wider in recent years, deficits would have disappeared.

Of course, the deficit has not disappeared so the result has been an increase in the national debt. Table 11.2 shows the absolute and relative size of the debt for the years 1967–81. The absolute size of the debt has tripled, but no sustained trend has occurred in the relative size of the debt. Debt as a percent of GNP ranged from a high of 25.6 in 1967 to a low of 17.8 in 1974, then it rose unsteadily to 22.8 in 1981. The federal debt has not been exerting a heavier and heavier burden on the American taxpayer, conservative rhetoric to the contrary. Furthermore, had loopholes been closed rather than widened in recent years, the debt as a percent of GNP would have declined substantially, in spite of the recent recession-induced deficits.

TABLE 11.2

Net* Debt of the Federal Government, 1967-1981

Year	Debt in Billions of Dollars	Debt as a Percent of GNP
1967	204.4	25.6
1968	217.0	24.8
1969	214.0	22.7
1970	217.2	21.9
1971	228.9	21.2
1972	243.6	20.5
1973	258.9	19.5
1974	255.6	17.8
1975	303.2	19.6
1976	376.4	21.9
1977	438.6	22.9
1978	488.3	22.6
1979	523.4	21.7
1980	589.2	22.4
1981	665.4	22.8

*Total debt minus debt held by government accounts and the Federal Reserve System.

Source: *Economic Report of the President* (Washington, D.C.: GPO, 1982), p. 325 and my own calculations.

So far, the trends we have unearthed in federal government finance yield no evidence whatsoever that a growing federal government has imposed an increasing burden on the private sector. Private incentives simply have not been reduced by the growing financial activities of the federal government. In fact, the effective tax rate paid by the vast majority of affluent Americans to their federal government has declined substantially over the last several years. For example, a married couple with two dependents and an adjusted gross income of $25,000 paid an effective tax rate of 21.3 percent in the years 1954-1963. That effective rate declined to 16.4 percent in 1975 and declined further to 14.0 percent in 1979-1980.[18] Although Social Security taxes rose substantially during those years, millions of affluent Americans still paid lower effective tax rates, even after Social Security boosts.[19] To conclude and to emphasize, the new right rhetoric about rising tax burdens and declining individual incentives is mostly hot air. There is little substance to it. Nevertheless, most affluent people want to believe it. The new right rhetoric helps them hide their greed from themselves. The truth is, the federal government has not been taking more from the well-to-do. Instead, they simply want more for themselves so they insist on giving less to the federal government.

But how about the state and local governments? What kinds of trends and details can be discerned in state and local finances? Table 11.3 presents the pertinent data. In terms of dollars, state and local expenditures

TABLE 11.3

State and Local Government Budget (national income and product accounts)

	Receipts		Expenditures		Surplus or Deficit (-)	
Year	In billions of dollars	As a percent of GNP	In billions of dollars	As a percent of GNP	In billions of dollars	As a percent of GNP
1960	49.9	9.8	49.8	9.8	0.1	0.0
1961	54.0	10.3	54.4	10.4	-0.4	-0.1
1962	58.5	10.4	58.0	10.3	0.5	0.1
1963	63.2	10.6	62.8	10.5	0.5	0.1
1964	69.5	10.9	68.5	10.7	1.0	0.2
1965	75.1	10.9	75.1	10.9	0.0	0.0
1966	84.8	11.2	84.3	11.2	0.5	0.1
1967	93.6	11.7	94.7	11.8	-1.1	-0.1
1968	107.3	12.3	107.2	12.3	0.1	0.0
1969	120.2	12.7	118.7	12.6	1.5	0.2
1970	135.4	13.6	133.5	13.4	1.9	0.2
1971	153.0	14.2	150.4	14.0	2.6	0.2
1972	178.3	15.0	164.8	13.9	13.5	1.1
1973	195.0	14.7	181.6	13.7	13.4	1.0
1974	211.4	14.7	204.6	14.3	6.8	0.5
1975	237.7	15.3	232.2	15.0	5.5	0.4
1976	267.8	15.6	251.2	14.6	16.6	1.0
1977	298.0	15.6	270.0	14.1	28.1	1.5
1978	327.4	15.2	298.4	13.8	29.0	1.3
1979	351.2	14.6	324.4	13.4	26.7	1.1
1980	384.0	14.6	355.0	13.5	29.1	1.1
1981	416.8	14.3	380.3	13.0	36.5	1.2

*Preliminary data.

Source: *Economic Report of the President* (Washington, D.C.: GPO, 1982), p. 320, and my own calculations.

and receipts rose by nearly eight-fold over the period 1960–1981. Federal expenditures increased by five-fold over the same period. State and local government expenditures and receipts have grown markedly faster than federal. This is reflected in the gradual increase in the proportion of GNP represented by state and local government expenditures and receipts. Expenditures and receipts steadily rose as a percent of GNP through 1971, fell off, rose again through 1975, and dipped slightly since then. In 1981, state and local governments accounted for about one-third more GNP than they did in 1960. Even so, they ran gradually larger surpluses beginning in the early 1970s and continuing into the 1980s.

A large part of these trends at the state and local level is due to the very substantial increase in federal grants to state and local governments. In 1960, such grants amounted to $6.9 billion, only 13.8 percent of state and local government receipts. By 1981 they were $90.1 billion, 21.6 percent of state and local government receipts.[20] In the absence of federal grants, state and local governments would have run very large deficits throughout the period, or they would have had to cut expenditures and/or raise taxes. With this in mind, most state and local governments have viewed their recent surpluses as illusory. Of course, most of the large cities ran deficits in spite of the federal aid, but the aid was large enough to give state and local governments, on a consolidated basis, a slowly growing surplus.

By function, about 36 cents of every dollar of state and local government expenditures go for education; about 13 cents for public welfare; 9 cents for highways; and the rest for miscellaneous functions such as police and fire protection, health and hospitals, and parks and recreation.[21] These functions would almost certainly have to be reduced if additional ones are added by the federal government or if federal aid were eliminated. With continued public resistance to higher state and local taxes in the wake of "Proposition 13," few alternatives to cut backs exist.

In short, state and local governments are in no condition to shoulder the larger burdens so eagerly urged upon them by Dixiecrats and states-righters posing as "New Federalists." Without expanded federal aid, state and local expenditures will be very hard-pressed to meet their existing obligations for expenditures in our local communities and states. A cut back in federal aid or an expansion of state and local obligations will spell disaster. Needs simply will not be met.

The Economics of Deficits

Conservatives have been holding their breaths for years now, waiting for the federal government to collapse under the weight of what they misperceive to be a crushing burden of debt. The facts have been most unkind to their expectations, but facts have never had any impact on the paranoic anyway. So still they fear and they direct their fear, not toward a movement to tighten up loopholes, and cut military spending, but to a movement to cut social expenditures. The extremely paranoid also call for a constitutional amendment forcing the federal government to balance its budget. To the extent that their statements rely on logic, they fall back on two logical supports for their fears: an incorrect analogy, and a theoretical possibility.

The analogy used by the balanced budget zealots is a simple comparison drawn between a single individual's budget and a sovereign nation's budget. Since a single individual who constantly spends more than he earns will eventually have his assets seized and his salary garnisheed by creditors, individuals should not run such constant budget deficits. By analogy, the balanced budget zealots conclude that a sovereign nation should never run a deficit. But the analogy they draw is incorrect in several respects. Most obviously, the fact that a single individual cannot constantly spend more than he earns does not mean that a sovereign state must *never* run a deficit. Properly drawn, the analogy would mean that a sovereign state must not run *constant* deficits. A more subtle mistake is also contained in the analogy: a single individual's income, if it is rising over time, can easily sustain current account deficits because the rising income can support a higher debt burden. The same holds, in the properly drawn analogy, for a sovereign nation. As long as the nation's GNP is rising as fast as its debt, constant current account deficits in the budget can be sustained. Refer back to Table 11.2 In spite of recent heavy deficits, the national debt is still a lower percentage of GNP than it was in 1967. Had Table 11.2 included years previous to 1967, the reader would see that the debt as a percentage of GNP had been falling since the Second World War. Only since the last half of the 1970s has it risen slightly because of stagnating economic growth. Recent deficits easily can be sustained.

The simplistic analogy drawn by the balanced budget zealots between an individual's budget and a sovereign nation's budget is also incorrect because a sovereign nation is very different from a single individual. An individual's creditors can seize his assets. But since we are the federal government's creditors and since we already "own" the federal government's assets as U.S. citizens, why should we seize our own government? Furthermore, an individual does not have the rights to levy taxes and to regulate credit conditions. A sovereign state does and can use such powers, if necessary, to finance its activities. Now we have run the balanced budget zealots to earth, for their harping on the deficit is another Trojan Horse in a long line of conservative Trojan Horses. If the least bit intelligent, they do not really fear deficits. Instead, they fear the possibility of higher taxes and lower costs of credit that sovereign nations bring about, if and when a deficit really gets out of hand. The central bankers and creditor special interest groups do not want national policies which drive down interest rates to ease the burden of the national debt. Yet such policies are inevitable if a deficit becomes really burdensome. Nor do high income taxpayers want to pay more taxes. Yet they will have to do so if a deficit becomes really burdensome.

Note the different conservative responses to a deficit run, on one hand, because of higher military spending and larger tax loopholes versus, on the other hand, a deficit run because of social program spending. Before becoming President, Ronald Reagan viewed deficits with alarm bordering on hysteria. Those deficits were due, in large part, to social program spending. After becoming President and enlarging both military spending and tax loopholes, Ronald Reagan now views *his* deficit with more complacency. This complete reversal reveals the harping about deficits for what it really is—another conservative Trojan Horse, another excuse for economic retrenchment.

In addition to an incorrect analogy, proponents of economic retrenchment also use a theoretical possibility to support their fear of deficits. The theoretical possibility is the "crowding out hypothesis." Balanced budget zealots hypothesize that government deficit spending crowds out private investment spending. This crowding out leaves the total amount of spending constant and, therefore, leaves the total GNP and the total unemployment rate constant as well. Government deficit spending merely replaces the private sector with the public sector, according to the crowding out hypothesis. But the crowding out hypothesis is valid only under very special circumstances. Otherwise, government deficit spending "fills in" for private investment spending rather than crowds it out.

Crowding out occurs if the supply of credit to the economy is fixed. With a fixed (perfectly inelastic in Economese) credit supply the government drives out private borrowers as it borrows to finance its deficit spending. The problem with this theoretical possibility is that the supply of credit is not fixed. Financial intermediaries of all kinds are astonishingly innovative when it comes to creating new forms of both credit and money. Recall the problems the Federal Reserve System has had in defining the money supply. As soon as the Fed defines credit money in one way and controls that set of things included in its definition, financial intermediaries create new forms of credit money to avoid the Fed's control. With such an innovative financial system, the supply of credit is not fixed, so crowding out remains a theoretical possibility with little practical import.

Crowding out could also occur if our supply of economic resources is fixed and being fully utilized. Then, an increase in government deficit spending would crowd out private spending because resources would be diverted from private uses to public uses by the deficit spending. This diversion of resources would leave total resource use unchanged, but government use would replace (crowd out) private use. The problem with this theoretical possibility is that our supply of resources is not fixed in any permanent sense nor have we fully utilized those resources for any extended period outside of war. Some crowding out began to occur in the most active phase of the Vietnam war. Crowding out also occurred during the Second World War, and perhaps during the Korean War. During war time, government deficit spending on war materials quickly crowds out civilian purchases, if the economy is close to full employment, because civilian needs take a backseat to military needs. Such crowding out is also accompanied by Buyers Inflation. When civilian and military demands on the GNP are added together, total demands exceed total GNP. Crowding out and inflation result.

Nevertheless, outside of war time, crowding out is merely a theoretical possibility. Our economy has not operated at the full employment level during peace time, so room for more spending and output frequently exists. In fact, rather than crowding out private investment, deficit spending fills in for private investment. Practical businessmen, bankers, and politicians have known this for many years. Whenever a community suffers a major plant shut down, practical community leaders know that the unemployment benefits and other forms of federal and state aid received by affected members of the community will help fill in for the lost payroll. In the absence of the aid receipts, retail sales would collapse, rent receipts would plummet, mortgage defaults accelerate, and economic decline would spread quickly through the entire community. But the various forms of federal and state aid keep the collapse from spreading by partially filling in for the lost private spending.

Without this filling in for the cut backs in private spending that occur in communities all over the country, the recessions we have suffered in recent years would have deepened into depressions. Rather than retrench on entitlement programs such as unemployment insurance, food stamps, aid to families with dependent children, and Social Security, these programs should be enlarged so that they fill in a larger proportion of the loss of private spending which occurs during recessions. If such programs were enlarged, recessions would be milder. But government deficits, induced by recession, would be larger and balanced budget zealots use the larger deficits to argue against such programs. Nevertheless, their arguments are groundless. Crowding out is only a theoretical possibility in peace time. Government deficit spending actually fills in for private spending rather than crowds it out. And the analogy balanced budget zealots draw between the deficit spending of an individual and the deficit spending of a sovereign nation is simply incorrect. The conservatives' fears about federal deficits are unfounded and should be discounted accordingly in the democratic process of planning federal fiscal policy.

Military Spending

In Economese, the cryptic language used by economists, national defense is a "public good." While the public has slowly come to recognize it as, at best, a necessary evil, economists refer to it as a public good. In the economist's lexicon, there are "public goods" and "private goods." A private good is something that individuals can buy for themselves, and a private good yields all its benefits to the individual who buys it. A public good, on the other hand, is something that individuals find difficult to buy for themselves, and a public good yields its benefits to everyone, not just to one person. Public goods should be purchased by the government for the benefit of all. Private goods should be left to the free play of supply and demand in the private sector. "National defense" is a public good because each one of us cannot buy, for our own protection, defense against foreign invasion.

We must pool our resources together for the common defense. So, according to conventional wisdom in economics, we must pay taxes to provide the "public good" of national defense.

However, our military spending does not provide for the national defense. It is not a "public good." Rather, it is an "international bad." Our military spending is for *international offense* rather than *national defense*. The need for national defense is very real and has grown every year since the bomb was dropped on Hiroshima. But our military spending has not met the growing need for national defense against nuclear destruction. We are more at risk today than we were 30 years ago and, if current trends continue, we will be even further exposed in the future. The MX missile is not a defensive weapon. It is an offensive missile system. The neutron bomb is not a defensive weapon. It is an offensive, anti-personnel bomb designed for killing people in Europe without killing Europe. The cruise missile is not defensive. It is offensive. Weapon system after weapon system, they are all offensive systems. None defend us from foreign attack. In fact, defending the civilian population is not the purpose of our military spending at all.

The purpose of our military spending is to enhance our ability to destroy the Soviet Union, her satellites, and her puppet states in the third world. That is an offensive purpose, not a defensive purpose. In the topsy-turvy world of our War Department, now called our Defense Department, offense has become defense. The game played is called deterrence. The outcome of each round of the game is an increased risk of nuclear destruction for the bystanders. The game players, after each round, charge the bystanders a larger game fee so that the players can go another round for higher stakes. The principal game players are the Soviet military hierarchy and the American militaryindustrial complex. The bystanders are the underlying civilian populations of the two superpowers and their allies.

Each round of the game commences with the discovery of a "missile gap," a "window of vulnerability," or some other alleged imbalance in the balance of power. The side discovering the vulnerability gets to play first. Since each side wants to play first, the players try very hard to discover (create?) a vulnerability in their game plan. The first play is made by building up new offensive weapons with which to threaten the other side. The other side takes their turn by retaliating in kind. As the play progresses, each side keeps track of the kill ratios—how many times over can the civilian population of the opposing superpower be killed? The higher the ratio of overkilled bystanders the greater the alleged deterrence effect on the opposing players. But as the game intensifies, the players pay less and less attention to the fate of the bystanders and more and more attention to winning the game. If the game runs much longer, the players will be so mesmerized by their moves that they may forget entirely about the bystanders.

It is time the bystanders stopped the game. Neither group of civilian populations has gained anything from it. Quite the contrary, they have everything to lose if the game continues. This is no longer just an analogy. It has become the real thing. The arms race has not increased U.S. security. It has merely intensified the military efforts of an increasingly paranoid, aged, alcoholic, military hierarchy in the Soviet Union. The probability that the Soviet Bear will suffer a mental breakdown increases every time the arms race speeds up. And we have no defense against a nuclear attack from the Soviets. All we have is more and more offensive weapons, the effect of which is to drive the Soviet Bear deeper into paranoia.

National defense of the United States has not been obtained and cannot be obtained through more military spending. The Soviets, weakened though they are, will match us and then some. Step-by-step multilateral disarmament, backed by ironclad safeguards and unhindered international inspection teams, is the only possible national defense; the only true "public good." It is the only rational fiscal policy. The billions we have spent for military purposes have not yielded one iota of national defense. It has all been wasted. After thirty years of it, we should have learned our lesson. The irrationality of cutting back social programs, for fear of deficits, while increasing military spending, in the name of national defense, boggles the mind.[22] It will yield less economic stability and more international insecurity.

TOWARD EFFECTIVE FISCAL POLICY

The Tax Side

For years now, every President and every Congress has promised us tax reform. They give us enlarged tax loopholes instead. During recessions such promises come one after another as the President and the Congress fall all over themselves in an attempt to do the impossible — cut deficits and give tax relief at the same time. All that results is more loopholes for special interests. We desperately need to reform the federal tax structure once and for all, then leave it alone. Every time minor "reforms" are made in it, the reform turns out to be another loophole. So effective tax rates keep falling for those taxpayers who can take advantage of the loopholes. The rest of us keep proclaiming the need for more tax reform. Enough of this.

I propose that we (1) close all the loopholes, (2) treat all forms of income the same way, and (3) adopt a lower set of progressive tax rates. With the loopholes closed and all forms of income treated the same, the rates in each progressive tax bracket can be lowered without losing tax revenue. These proposals are in addition to the elimination of the corporate profits tax as a quid pro quo for federal corporate chartering.

First, as noted earlier in this chapter, closing all tax loopholes would increase tax revenues by well over $100 billion a year. This increase in revenue would occur even after dropping the corporate profits tax. Tax loopholes include excessive depletion and depreciation allowances, investment tax credits (these alone resulted in nearly $20 billion in lost tax revenue in 1980), expensing of various capital outlays, and exclusion of interest on state and local bonds. Closing these loopholes would make the tax structure much more simple and fair; simpler because a large number of special loophole provisions and procedures would no longer apply, fairer because those of us unable to take advantage of the loopholes would no longer have to take up the slack left by those able to do so. Second, treating all forms of income in the same way would also add to federal tax revenues. If capital gains and corporate shareholder earnings were taxed like other income, revenues would not only rise but the unfair burden placed on other forms of income could be reduced. In particular, income from financial capital should be treated the same as income from human capital. Currently, income from financial capital generally pays a lower effective tax rate than income from human capital. Third, the higher revenues gained by closing loopholes and treating all income the same way would allow a lowering of the rates in all tax brackets. Progressivity would be maintained, but overall rates could come down.

A tax system is progressive when a higher effective tax rate is paid as the taxpayer's income rises; conversely, as the taxpayer's income falls, a lower effective tax rate is paid. Tax equity and economic stability are both served by a progressive income tax. Equity is served because a progressive tax ensures that taxpayers most able to shoulder the tax burden, shoulder the major portion of it. A progressive income tax helps to maintain economic stability because, as the economy slides into a recession, taxpayers' incomes fall into lower tax brackets. They pay lower effective tax rates as a result, leaving them with more after-tax income than otherwise so they are able to maintain their consumption spending at higher levels. This works to stop further economic decline. If the economy were to expand too quickly into a period of Buyers Inflation, taxpayers' incomes would rise into higher tax brackets and pay higher effective tax rates. This progesssivity would leave them with lower after tax income than otherwise, forcing them to cut back on their inflation-causing buying binge. So a progressive income tax is a kind of automatic stabilizer. It softens recessionary declines and weakens Buyers Inflation.

Once we have closed the loopholes, treated all income in the same way, and established lower progressive tax brackets, we will have a tax system which is fair, simple, and an aid to stability.[23] Once such a tax system is in place, we should stop tinkering with it. For every time we tinker, special interest groups use the opportunity to open loopholes in the tax system. The only tinkering required might be a periodic adjustment, equal in all tax brackets, to eliminate the possibility of "fiscal drag." Fiscal drag can occur with a progressive tax system because economic growth slowly pushes more and more taxpayers into higher tax brackets, increasing the total tax take. If government expenditures are not rising as fast as tax revenues, a growing budget surplus will emerge. The growing surplus will act as a drag on the economy because it will "sterilize" private income. But fiscal drag is a remote possibility for the 1980s. Public needs are immense, and government expenditures show no tendency to fall below tax revenues, even if the revenues were increasing at a healthy pace.

The Expenditure Side

Once a fair, simple, and stability-enhancing tax system has been established, and a multilateral disarmament process has begun, federal expenditures can be determined by long-term socioeconomic goals worked out through the democratic economic planning process. Furthermore, once our Federal Reserve System has been tamed, the Monetarist obsessions of our central bankers will no longer be allowed to work at cross purposes with the rest of our economic policies. Then we will be free to determine our own economic future because then we will be able to link federal expenditure programs to the goals of democratic planning.

I have no predetermined plan, no set of specific objectives, no detailed blueprint to offer for the future. Rather, I have offered a series of reforms which will make the future ours, help us free ourselves from the blind drift of events, the sway of vested interests, and the intellectual chains of outmoded theories. In keeping with that spirit, no specific expenditure priorities will be offered. Instead, several general guidelines will be discussed.

It is essential to avoid wide swings in expenditures. The stop and go policies of the past have often contributed to economic instability and stagnation. Democratic planning should take the long view, and continuity should be a major guide. The principal cause of federal expenditure swings has been military spending. Vietnam war spending contributed very significantly to the overheated economy of the 1960s and early 1970s. That war cost the U.S. over $120 billion.[24] The current rapid arms buildup may cost even more. President Reagan's Council of Economic Advisers, while downplaying the impact of the accelerating arms race, admits that Reagan's planned increase in military spending involves a faster annual rate of increase than occurred during the peak years of the Vietnam buildup.[25] Multilateral disarmament, with safeguards, is not only a moral imperative; it is an economic imperative.

With the principal cause of wide swings in federal spending eliminated through international treaty, federal spending will no longer be a source of instability. Nevertheless, the federal government will still run deficits and occasional surpluses in its budget. The balanced budget zealots will continue to worry, yet the decifit or surplus actually will be beneficial. With expenditures stabilized, determined by long-run democratic objectives, and a truly reformed tax system, the federal budget becomes a powerful economic stabilizer. If the economy grows too quickly, taxpayers rapidly rise into higher tax brackets, pay higher taxes, and the federal government runs a surplus. If the economy slides into recession, the reverse happens to tax revenues and the federal government runs a deficit. Government surpluses automatically drain spending power out of the economy, keeping it from overheating. Government deficits automatically fill in for declines in spending, keeping the economy from receding further. Keynesian economists have been trying to convince their orthodox and Monetarist colleagues of the beneficial results of deficits in recessionary times for years. Their colleagues have not listened. Perhaps the public will.

The Human Side

An effective fiscal policy involves more than just fair tax systems and planned expenditures. It involves "investment" in people. Clarence Ayres, an underground economist, elevated "investment" in people to a principle of economic development.[26] He realized that people are the fundamental strength of an economy. Their welfare is also the *raison d'etre* of the economy. So a fiscal policy that shortchanges programs that "invest" in people, or a fiscal policy that shortchanges welfare programs is not only an inhumane fiscal policy but also a debilitating one. Yet greed and confusion dominate public thought in the United States to such an extent that "welfare" has become a dirty word. Welfare programs support people, keep them from going without food, shelter, clothing, and medical care. Welfare programs give welfare children a chance to join the mainstream of life as full participants. Today that chance is taken away by the permanent stigmata placed on welfare recipients by confused and greed-crazed public thought. Purveyors of the conventional wisdom even argue that poor people and minorities would be better off without welfare or affirmative action because then they would be free of their stigmata. But the stigmata was put on them in the first place by those very purveyors of the conventional wisdom! Welfare is a dirty word only because we have been taught to think it so, and our teachers are wrong. The welfare of people is the purpose of our economy and it is the essence of our humanity.

We allow the politicians and their opportunists to apply the budget ax to "welfare" programs because, in our confusion, we have lost sight of the purpose of our economy and in our greed, we have lost our humanity. Welfare programs encourage the push from below that provides our basic institutions with new ideas and people. Without this flow of vitality our institutions rigidify and stagnate into closed little worlds of homosocially-reproducing elites. The corporation has already begun to do so. Declining productivity has been the economic result. A bottling up of the desires and drives of those who are excluded has been the individual and sociological result. The world of the Corporado has become increasingly more self-righteous and self-satisfied while the world of the excluded has become increasingly more angry and frustrated. We can reduce the pathology of the two worlds only by bringing them together. But they must be brought together on equal terms. This will require a substantial increase in "welfare" spending. We must invest far more in people who have not been able to invest enough in themselves. Such investment can only be financed by the federal government because it alone has the financial wherewithal to shoulder the massive investment program called for.

CONCLUSION

Since 1970 our Federal Reserve System has been using a Monetarist strategy to control the U.S. money supply. The strategy was directed first by Arthur Burns. He failed. Paul Volcker changed the Federal Reserve System's tactics in 1979. But he still followed the Monetarist strategy, so he too has failed. The Monetarist experiment has lasted long enough. We need a new strategy. Nobel laureate James Tobin's strategy shows a real promise of working. Although we cannot control the quantity of credit money, we can regulate the cost of credit with the Tobin proposal. We can also break the big bankers' hold on the Federal Reserve System by changing the appointment procedure and the term of office of the members of the Board of Governors. Then we would have a democratically determined monetary policy that worked. Combined with the objectives of the Community Reinvestment Act, such a monetary policy not only would be more effective in stabilizing the economy, it would also revive our declining communities and our Savings and Loan Associations.

Fiscal policy, freed from outmoded theories and overblown fears about deficits, and relieved of mushrooming military expenditures, could also contribute to economic stability and to economic development. State and local governments lack the financial capacity to expand their roles much further. Taxpayers already are in revolt against rising state and local taxes. Yet state and local expenditures have been absorbing a larger and larger proportion of GNP. (See Table 11.3.) Increased federal aid to state and local governments has had to make up the difference. As noted earlier in this chapter, federal grants accounted for over 20 percent of state and local receipts in 1981. A revitalizing of federal fiscal policy is in order, but what we get is retrenchment; a Dixiecrat and states' rights retreat labeled the "New Federalism."

On the tax side, federal fiscal policy should rely on a simple progressive tax on individual income. All income should be treated the same and all loopholes should be eliminated. Such a tax system would ensure fair tax treatment of all taxpayers and would also ensure economic stability. On the expenditure side of fiscal policy, the major source of wide swings in federal expenditures has been military spending. We have received in return, not national defense, but increased exposure to nuclear annihilation. Multilateral disarmament, with safeguards, would free us and our fiscal policy from a growing burden. Then our expenditure priorities could be determined through democratic economic planning, which takes the long view of our social and economic needs. On the human side of fiscal policy, "investment" in human beings should be elevated to the first principle of economic development. The politics of greed, created by the current grab for tax loopholes, has distorted our vision. Instead of more tax breaks for the already affluent who can invest in themselves and in their children, our society should invest more in the poor and excluded, those who cannot invest in themselves. The dispossessed and the wretched of the earth have a drive and a vitality that the affluent have failed to comprehend. Lacking in comprehension but not in fear, the affluent of the United States have turned their backs on the poor and the excluded. Not only has this cost us our humanity. It has also cost us the vitality of our basic institutions. The corporation, in particular, has evolved into a rigid bureaucratic organization, sealed off from the new people and ideas pushing up from below. Small wonder that American productivity is beginning to lag further and further behind.

More tax cuts for the affluent and a "New Federalism" which turns our national problems back to the state and local governments certainly will not turn things around. Federal investment in the poor will.[27]

12 REVITALIZATION, NOT RETRENCHMENT

AMERICA AT THE CLOSE OF THE TWENTIETH CENTURY

The New Landscape

The United States at the close of the twentieth century is remarkably different from what it was at the close of the nineteenth. The market system has drifted away from the price mechanism toward a new administrative system. That is, price changes have equated supply to demand less and less while administrative changes have equated supply to demand more and more. In the labor market, an excess supply of labor in a particular occupation is not likely to drive that occupation's earnings down, encouraging people to go elsewhere for jobs. Instead, administrative changes are made in the qualifications required of new job applicants. The qualifications are raised to equate the supply of, now over-qualified, applicants to the demand. The "underqualified" are now filtered out of the applicant pool. In the capital market, individual capitalists no longer invest the bulk of the country's financial capital in new ventures. Instead, conglomerate administrators appropriate funds from one corporate subsidiary for investment in some other subsidiary. In the product market an excess supply of a product is less and less likely to drive the price of the product down. Instead, it is more and more likely to result in an administrative adjustment in advertising, credit terms, services, or product image. An excess supply of a product is almost certain to result in quick cut backs in production, for the old intermediate product market network of individual wholesalers and retailers has been replaced in most of our economy by vertically-integrated corporate giants. The giants have learned to calibrate production very closely to their rate of sales. The independents never did. Economic evolution, particularly the growth of the corporation, has transformed our economic system into a new species. Corporate capitalism has replaced market capitalism in much of our economy.

The producers in our economy are now entrenched corporate conglomerates. They used to be dynamic individual entrepreneurs. In the nineteenth century the push from below of new people met little effective resistance from American entrepreneurs, some of whom were formerly excluded people in the first place. Opportunity for them required free markets with no government interference, except to return run away slaves and to remove native Americans. But today, the push from below meets very effective resistance in the corporate practices of filtering and homosocial reproduction. Opportunity for the excluded of today is no longer served by laissez-faire. On the contrary, if the federal government keeps its hands off, the push from below will be blocked by the practices of entrenched corporate bureaucracies.

Furthermore, if the federal government keeps its hands off, another corporate practice wreaks havoc on the economy. The havoc is unintentional, but real nonetheless. Corporate diversification into many different markets has freed the corporate conglomerate from the constraints of any one market. So the conglomerate, treating each market division or subsidiary as a profit center, can increase prices, shut down plants and reap the resulting short run profits, knowing that the long run losses will come long after the conglomerate has moved into new markets. Besides, the managers of each profit center know that future losses will come out of the bonuses of their successors but immediate profits will add to their own bonuses. The results of this conglomerate practice are higher short-term profits for the conglomerate and higher bonuses for the profit center managers. But, the results are also plant closings, unemployment, inflation, and a hemorrhaging of the federal budget through social programs designed to fill in for declines in private payrolls. In the absence of an effective wage-price control program, stagflation spreads. And when the federal government and the Federal Reserve System try to fight inflation, the unemployment costs of doing so soar.

In addition to the evolution of a new species of American producer – the conglomerate corporation – The American Consumer at the close of this century is also a very different animal than at the close of the last century. Consumers used to really need the products they purchased. Now the affluent have become jaded and fickle. This is not to say that our affluence has reduced our greed, far from it. But only the poor really *need* today. The rest of us *want*. Affluent consumers work for corporate bureaucracies or for institutions dependent upon the corporation. In this corporate world, the status scramble is pervasive. Corporados seek desperately to climb up the status ladder faster than their peers. This requires a rapid rise in income and expenditure. Affluence has actually intensified the struggle for more income among the Corporados. To earn more, we must spend more in order to demonstrate our higher status. Then the more we demonstrate our higher status, the more we must earn to pay the bills. There is never enough, particularly after Uncle Sam takes his. Besides, he gives it away to black people and ne'er-do-wells. Or so we think, as we try to rationalize away our greed.[1]

While the affluent consumers have become obsessed with their wants, the poor are deprived of their needs. Impoverished American consumers still find it impossible to meet all their needs for food, clothing, shelter, medical care, and education. They underinvest in themselves. The result is a gross misallocation of resources. The affluent chase their status phantoms with buying sprees while the poor deprive their children of life's necessities. The result is also a gross distortion of social and political life. The poor are easy prey for the dream peddlers – the pushers and the preachers. The affluent are easy prey for the greed rationalizers – the racists and the tax revolters. The push from below is deflected into a quagmire of drugs or into a vision of the hereafter. When not deflected, the push from below is misinterpreted by the greed-crazed as a demand for "something for nothing," while in fact it is a demand for full participation in work and life. This class division between consumers is reaching crisis proportions at the close of the twentieth century.

The close of the century is also witnessing the emergence of a new king of regulator. The old industry-specific regulator's influence has been reduced by President Carter's deregulation push. By and large, the public has benefited from the weakening of these co-opted regulators in transportation and finance. But we will not benefit from a weakening of the new function-specific regulators. The Environmental Protection Agency, the Equal Employment Opportunity Commission, and the Occupational Safety and Health Administration perform crucial functions not linked to any specific industry. More immure to cooptation, these new regulators have been far more effective than the old ones. Hence the sustained outcry against them and the appoint-

ment of opportunists to head them. Though largely immune to cooptation, the new regulators are far less immune to the damage caused
by opportunism at their highest levels. If they survive President Reagan's appointees, EPA, OSHA, and EEOC will be potent forces for future reforms. If they do not survive, they can be rebuilt.

A far more subtle change can also be detected in America at the
close of the twentieth century. Hegemony is replacing plurality. This
trend must be reversed, if democracy is to survive. In the nineteenth
century, our major institutions were largely independent of each other.
Today they are less so. Our religious institutions, when content to remain poor, used to be independent of political and economic institutions. This is changing. Our families used to be the foundations of our
lives. Now they are "springboards" for economic success. Our political
institutions were built on the ideals of The Enlightenment. Now we
want to apply "sound business principles" to government. In the process, we are losing sight of Plato's *justice* as the purpose of the state.
Our educational institutions, once in need of both the guidance and
finance of other institutions, no longer need the guidance but get it
anyway because most educational institutions still need the finance.
Our public school system, divided up into "Independent" School Dis-
tricts, is abjectly dependent upon the fears and fancies of self-righteous
local groups with their book-burning, their scientific creationism, their
racism, and their xenophobia. Not just public school teachers need to
curtail free inquiry in their classrooms lest offense be given to the locals.
Even university professors often must rein in the enthusiasm of their
students and themselves lest offense be given to potential contributors.
Free inquiry is full of surprises, and it does not pay. Vocational training is not and it does. In short, institutional plurality is being lost in
America as our formerly independent institutions, with the exception
of educational institutions which were never independent in the U.S.
to begin with, become more dependent on the growing financial and
cultural strength of our corporate institution.

Stagflation and Relative Decline

The newest and most startling change in the American economy is
the emergence of stagflation – the stagnation of employment combined
with the inflation of prices. To bring a complete stop in inflation now
takes a double-digit unemployment rate, or wage-price controls. Since

the 1960s the economy has become sick, very sick, but not because of government interference. The economy has become sick because of the growth and use of conglomerated corporate power and because of our failure to deal with that power. Rather than turning the corporate system to account through democratic economic planning, we cut taxes. Rather than limiting price and wage increases through wage-price controls, we cut back on social program spending. And our decline accelerates.

The U.S. economy was never a poor economy, relative to others. But we are becoming one. We started out with an incredible bonanza of resources. So we should stand head-and-shoulders above other western nations. But when compared with our peers, we are now second rate. According to the World Bank, our GNP per capita is now fourth among major industrialized market economies. (Refer back to Table 1.1.) It should be first. It used to be first. Also according to the World Bank, our GNP growth rate is now ninth among major industrialized market economies. We are falling further and further below our potential. Our decline is not due to too much government "interference." In all of the major industrialized market economies, the economic role of government is larger than in the United States. The only possible exception to that is the United Kingdom under Margaret Thatcher, and they are in steeper decline than we are.

The U.S. is undergoing a productivity crisis, but not because of government interference. Most of Western Europe has adopted code-termination and has a strong labor movement. Japanese management is far more participatory than U.S. management. The push from below brings new people and new ideas into European and Japanese managerial circles. And their productivity rises. The push from below in the United States has met with entrenched managerial resistance. And our productivity stagnates. When the EEOC attacks discrimination in the workplace the familiar refrain about government "interference" is heard once again.

Americans blame government deficits on logrolling, patronage, and social programs. Big government, not big business is to blame. Americans blame inflation on government deficits and regulation. Americans also blame lagging productivity on government. In fact, government has become the scapegoat for all our problems. In a new knee-jerk response, educational decline is also blamed on big government – federal interference with neighborhood schools. Perhaps we cannot help ourselves. Perhaps we have become knee-jerk reactionaries in our frustration over our second rate performance. No longer able to deny our relative decline, but not yet able to take positive action about it, we blame the decline on something distant from ourselves. With the American left destroyed by McCarthyism in the 1950s, with open racism now considered in poor taste, and with the stench of Watergate still in our noses, the federal government, which seems distant to most of us, is the best scapegoat we have, barring a new war. Even the war front is not too promising. Who can blame tiny El Salvador or bizarre Libya, for all our problems? Besides, blaming big government for all our problems is in keeping with our escape into nostalgia about the good old days of frontier American individualism and dynamism. And who better to lead us into nostalgia than Ronald Reagan? We have scapegoated and romanticized ourselves into retrenchment. But the effects will be real.

WHY WE CHOSE RETRENCHMENT

We chose retrenchment for more reasons than the romanticizing of our past and the scapegoating of our federal government, however. The retrenchment was also due to a failure of politics and to a failure of economics. Our political system let us down and our economics profession has not grasped the nature of our problems.

The Failure of Politics

Politics has not presented us with alternatives to retrenchment. The full alternative to economic retrenchment involves democratic economic planning to turn the corporate administrative system toward the public purpose; it involves wage-price controls to limit the corporate adminstrative system's power to raise prices; it involves corporate reform and the strengthening of EPA, OSHA, and EEOC; it also involves a multilateral disarmament treaty to ensure national security. But, to date, no major candidate for national office has run on anything even approaching such a platform. The reason is not hard to find. In the 1976 presidential campaign, the democrats spent $62.9 million and the republicans spent $48 million. The bulk of the expenditures were made in the primaries. In spite of the $67.9 million of U.S. Treasury funding provided the major presidential candidates, $46.1 million of private campaign contributions were still made. A total of $99 million was spent by campaigners for the U.S. House and Senate in 1975-76.[2] Running for national office has become so expensive, a candidate cannot afford to alienate any major group of potential contributors. Since a real alternative to economic retrenchment would require a reduction of corporate power, a candidate who campaigned on such a platform would find it very difficult to fund his or her campaign. He or she would alienate the Big Money. Then he or she would not be able to take their message to the national electorate.

As a result, the voters usually get to choose between a conservative and a reactionary (Carter and Reagan) or between two conservatives (Carter and Ford). A choice between a liberal and a conservative (Kennedy and Nixon) was possible in 1960, but since then such a choice usually required an open public revolt against the reactionary policies of an incumbent (McGovern versus Nixon). Yet even liberals who make it through the primaries very seldom attack entrenched corporate power in the general election. They can run on a peace ticket (McGovern), but not on an economic reform ticket. Apparently they can afford to go without the contributions of the military-industrial complex. But they cannot afford to lose the whole corporate system.

Furthermore, unlike other major industrial nations in the West, the U.S. does not have a labor party. In other nations, the labor party is the only mainstream party which is independent from the corporate system. It plays a vital political role, as a result. Yet in the United States, that role is not played because an independent labor party never evolved here. This absence contributes significantly to the failure of American politics to present real choices to the national electorate.

An election involves a choice between at least two different alternatives. What we usually have is more a plebiscite, more a ratification or a legitimation of political nonalternatives, than an election. Our politicians have failed us. The extent to which we do not vote is an indication of the failure. In fact, refusing to vote has become a kind of vote, a vote of no confidence in the political process. When the choice is between Tweedledum and Tweedledee, nearly half of voting age Americans "vote" by not voting for either. In the 1980 presidential election only 52.5 percent of the voting age population voted for a candidate. In the Congressional elections that year, only 45.4 percent voted for a candidate.[3] Whether we call it voter apathy or votes against the "choices" offered, this nonvoting indicates a political failure of real importance.

The Failure of Economics

Our mainstream economists have failed us as well as our mainstream politicians. Neither have developed alternatives to economic retrenchment. The reasons for the politicians' failure are fairly obvious. The reasons for the economists' failure are far more subtle: First is the ahistorical nature of mainstream economics itself; second is the Monetarist misinterpretation of the U.S. historical record; third is the historical origin of the American university.

Societies have histories, so most of the social sciences are historical in nature. That is, much of sociology, anthropology, and political science is devoted to the evolution of different aspects of social life. But economics is different. Although economics is a social science, very little of economics deals with the evolution of economies. Some economists are historians. Some renegade institutional economists even formed an Association for Evolutionary Economics. Nevertheless, mainstream economics is an *ahistorical* discipline. To make a contribution to pure theory, void of any practical application or historical context, has long been the dream of all aspiring young economists who wished to make it in the mainstream. So economics, unlike the other social sciences, has developed along hypothetical rather than historical lines. Economists build models of hypothetical markets or economies. They do not study the evolution of real markets and of actual economies. At least mainstream economists do not. When they venture into history, if they do so at all, it is to establish the "parameters" of their models, not to explore the evolution of their economies.

When that evolution is explored, some real surprises are discovered. Economic historian Alfred D. Chandler, Jr. has found that the visible hand of corporate management has replaced the invisible hand of the market in much of our economy. Institutional economists have found similar remarkable changes in American consumers, producers, and regulators. In fact, our economy has been transformed from market capitalism to corporate capitalism in the brief span of one century. The mainstream has failed to take note of the transformation.

Worse than that, the Monetarist part of the mainstream has applied the quantity theory of money, a theory relevant to the *commodity* money system, to the historical record of the U.S. *credit* money system. This Monetarist misinterpretation is the second reason that mainstream economists have failed to provide an alternative to economic retrench-ment. Remember that with a credit money system like ours, an eco-nomic boom results in an increase in the demand for credit money. Banks and other financial intermediaries supply more credit money to the eager demanders, at higher interest rates, of course. Then an eco-nomic slump results in a decrease in the demand for credit money. Banks subsequently reduce the quantity supplied as interest rates and demand fall. So over the course of a complete business cycle of boom and then slump, the quantity of credit money rises in the boom and falls in the slump. Booms and slumps are caused by fluctuations in in-vestment. Nevertheless, the Monetarists misinterpret the historical re-cord because they see it through their own little model – the quantity theory of money.

Following their misinterpretation, the Monetarists argued that all we needed to do to stabilize the economy was control the money stock. Booms and busts would be eliminated. So since 1970 we have put our economy through the Monetarist wringer, first under Arthur Burns, then under Paul Volcker. Booms and busts, obviously, have not been eliminated. Monetarism does not work, but still the Monetarists try to convince us that *this* time stability is right around the corner. Instead of basic reform, the mainstream economists give us one more dose of the Monetarist nostrum. I suggest that we stop the Monetarist experi-ment before it kills us. The Monetarists will never admit defeat. Their model is so far removed from reality that each time their medicine fails, they blame the patient for not adhering to their preconceived model of the good patient. They will never accept the fact that the blame lies with the medicine not the patient. The patient is a historical reality; their medicine a hypothetical abstraction which, for over a decade now, has been tried in reality and found wanting.

Not all economists are mainstream economists. A few dissenters survive here and there in academe. Their status often is similar to that of a token black or woman on a corporate board of directors. Every good board needs a black to demonstrate the corporation's belief in affirmative action. Likewise, every good university's economics depart-ment needs a dissenter to demonstrate belief in academic freedom. I overstate my case to make my point – the American university has a long way to go before free inquiry is not only tolerated but encouraged;

no, more than that, demanded. But until free inquiry is demanded, most academicians will take the easy way. The easy way in economics is merely to expound on the old verities of laissez-faire economic theory. As more and more economists have followed the easy, traditional way, the discipline has entered a baroque period, a period of intellectual stagnation. This seldom offends powerful lay members of university governing boards, but it seldom results in the development of alternatives to the sterility of the conventional wisdom either. The conventional wisdom in economics is designed for sterility, for it is purposefully ahistorical. It is not designed to deal with historical economic reality. Yet it is academically fruitful for it ruffles no feathers; it discourages no donors; it does not question the status quo of corporate America.

Instead, when mainstream economists do venture out of their ivory towers into the real world, their sorties smooth feathers, encourage donors and apologize for the status quo. Cost-benefit studies of government "interference" in the hypothetical free market buttress the mounting attack on the new regulators. The Monetarist misinterpretation quiets misgivings about the demonstrated instability of corporate capitalism – if we just controlled the quantity of money all would be well. And the "new" supply-side economists act as the shock troops in this *attack* on reality. It *is* an attack on reality, not an attempt to understand reality. Rather than redesigning received economic theory to fit reality, the supply-siders are trying to redesign reality to fit received theory. The poor, the excluded, and the ideals of America are all being sacrificed in the process. But corporate capitalism grows fat, at least for now.

Today, more than ever, we need economists who will question the status quo of corporate America in terms of American ideals. A few home-grown critics exist. An underground economics has been developing in the U.S. for some time now. Underground American economists call themselves all kinds of things: institutionalists, evolutionary economists, heterodox economists, Post-Keynesians, or social economists. This book has drawn on most of their works in presenting their, and my, alternative to economic retrenchment. The one thing they all have in common is their attempt to change economic theory to fit the change in economic reality. But to do so, they have had to reject the bulk of received theory. Their rejection brands them as heretics and places them beyond the pale of "sound" academic discourse. This exclusion has not stopped the development of alternative economics. Instead, it has ensured the sterility of mainstream economics.

It is no longer appropriate to call the economic dissenters underground economists, for they are no longer just an underground movement in economics. They have developed into alternative economists, economists with viable alternatives to sterile theory and workable alternatives to economic retrenchment. Alternative economic theory begins with the facts of corporate capitalism. The corporation now dominates our economy. It has replaced the free market with corporate administration. The replacement occurred because corporate administration proved to be more efficient than the free play of supply and demand. But corporate efficiency does not benefit the public. It benefits entrenched corporate elites. Corporate efficiency has not been turned toward the public purpose. Mainstream economists and the supply-side shock troops do not recognize this corporate dominance. Instead, they blame our stagnation on vague "government interference" with the free market and they propose economic retrenchment as the cure for stagnation. Alternative economists argue that corporate administration should be turned to public account through democratic economic planning.

This would not destroy or revolutionize our economy. Quite the contrary. Democratic economic planning would humanize and democratize it. As it stands now, the corporate system is predatory. Corporate power and efficiency serve corporate interests. Corporados are not evil men. Nevertheless, the system they have built serves evil purposes. It excludes many of us from full participation in economic life. As a result, the invigorating push from below is thwarted. It maximizes corporate short-term profits appropriated from the different sectors of our economy. As a result, prices rise and plants close; the economy stagnates. It creates a status panic in increasingly bureaucratic organizations. As a result, anxiety and greed spread among the affluent, status-striving bureaucrats while the real needs of the poor go unmet.

The system is powerful and efficient but it has no direction, no channels through which the public purpose can be made known to the private managers of corporate America, no channels through which the public can hold the private managers accountable for pursuing the public purpose. The main thrust of alternative economics is to emphasize the need for such channels and to suggest ways to meet the need. The main thrust of supply-side economics, on the other hand, is to deny that the need exists and to destroy those few channels already constructed to meet the need. I recognize that my criticism of the supply-siders is very harsh. But it is fully justified. Mainstream economists have failed us because they have become irrelevant. Supply-siders are worse. They are destroying the small efforts made to humanize and democratize corporate capitalism at the very time those efforts could be forged into a real rejuvenation of the American economy.

THE SIGNIFICANCE OF THE REAGAN PRESIDENCY

New Federalism, Old States' Rights

The Reagan Presidency, though a reactionary one, is not a political aberration. Reagan's election was not a mere fluke, but the political result of deeply-rooted social trends primarily in the South and in the West. Conservative white Southerners have objected to federal social programs since the Dixiecrats refused to support Harry Truman in the 1948 Presidential election. The Southerners formed the States Rights Democratic party and nominated Strom Thurmond as their Presidential candidate. Their smoldering resentment broke out into open rage with President Eisenhower's support of school integration in Little Rock, Arkansas. But it was not until the Goldwater campaign of 1964 that the South had a chance to vote for a major candidate who clearly echoed the South's anti-federal sentiments. Nevertheless, Johnson was too much for Goldwater. The reaction in the South seemed doomed to third party status with George Wallace's Presidential campaigns. But then in 1976 the South elected one of their own – Jimmy Carter – only to be bitterly disappointed with his conservative rather than reactionary stand on federal social programs. Carter had run against Washington, but he was not a racist or a sexist.

During all this time that the South had been going it alone, against the Federal government, the West was also changing. The influence of energy and minerals corporations grew rapidly in the West and quickly became anti-federal in tone as environmental concerns were reflected in federal regulations. The states' righters in the South gained an ally and the political balance in the country tipped from conservatism to reaction. Ronald Reagan rode the wave of reaction into the White

House. Once there, he immediately began cutting back both the social programs detested by White Southerners and the environmental controls restraining Western lumber, mineral and energy interests. The old Dixiecrats and states' righters were finally triumphant. They could, and did, throw off their old stigma of being regional special-interest groups. Instead, they placed the special-interest group stigma on environmentalists, women, and blacks.

This is the historical significance of the Reagan Presidency: The values most central to the American tradition have been cast out of the political center of balance. Now out of balance the country lurches to the far right. In its lurch, the old Dixiecrat position can be passed off as a "New Federalism." A bloodless coup d'etat of American values has taken place, leaving supporters of the old values speechless. The New Right has become the New Middle. But the situation clearly is unstable. It can move even farther right into repression and a police state, or the supporters of the American Dreams of equality and quality of life can reassert their position.

Reasserting equality and quality of life as central values instead of special interests will not be easy because Reagan's Presidency has already weakened very significantly the primary vehicle for pursuing equality and quality of life. The federal government's effectiveness has been reduced through deregulation, decentralization, defunding, and opportunist appointees at the highest levels. This weakening of the only effective countervailing power to that of the corporation will take years to repair.

The Politics of Fear and Greed

Tax cuts for the rich, program cuts for the poor, retreat from civil rights and affirmative action for the Dixiecrats, deregulation for the energy and minerals corporations, billions for the Southern and Western military-industrial complex, and continued high interest rates for the bankers: These are the fruits of the politics of fear and greed. Stagnation will not be cured by such as these. In the few years ahead, the economy may slowly recover from the 1980–81 slump. But it will not recover to anything near its potential. The savings of the rich will not trickle down into the millions of new jobs needed by the unemployed. The poor will not be able to invest enough resources in their needs for food, shelter, clothing, medical care, and education. The excluded minorities will not become full participators in the social, political, and economic life of the nation. The environment will not be protected from the mining, oil, and lumber corporations. The nation will not be secured against nuclear destruction by the military-industrial complex. Small businessmen, farmers, entrepreneurs, and home buyers will not find the low-cost credit they need. In short, economic retrenchment will not revitalize America, only make it meaner, greedier, and more insecure. This is the American nightmare, not the American dream.

BACK ON COURSE

The Push From Below

The push from below will continue, as it has done since at least the time of Christ, but it will turn sour, as it has done before, when the excluded find that their aspirations are blocked by vested interests. Deprived of new people and new ideas, America's corporate elite will continue to stagnate, to turn inward upon itself and to look outward with selfrighteous indignation at the depravity and the lack of appreciation shown by "their" women and by "their" blacks. This is not the America that I love. These are not the people I learned to admire in my history books. In fact, I admit quite emphatically that the process of retrenchment offends me personally. Economists are not supposed to admit things like that. Economists are supposed to be purely objective scientists. Nevertheless, we are *social* scientists and this is *my* society, and *yours*.

More and more Americans, as the retrenchment continues, will also find it offensive. And as they do, they too will want to put America back on course. We have always been, or claimed to be, the land of opportunity. To get back on course does not mean to give more and more opportunity to those who already have it. To get back on course means to give opportunity to those who do not have it. The push from below, when it meets with the opportunity to expand, revitalizes the institutions into which it flows. The new people bring new ideas, insights, drives. These things used to make our economy and society vibrant and alive. But the man on the make used to need very little (if he was white) to make it. The people trying to make it today, however, need good health, college diplomas, geographic mobility, low-cost credit, and much more that they do not have. Unless federal programs (not state, because the states lack either the wherewithal or the will) are designed to provide these needs, the new people pushing up from below will not make it. Then the vitality our basic institutions need will not be forthcoming. Stagnation will intensify as entrenched corporate elites solidify their positions.

American Ideals

Our history books tell us of liberty, equality, and the pursuit of happiness. These, we learned, were the American ideals. Now we read of individual incentive, reverse discrimination, and over regulation. Have our ideals really changed, or have we temporarily wandered off course? It must be the latter. Surely, liberty means more than pursuing our greed. Surely, it means full participation as citizen, worker, consumer, and human being. Furthermore, the meaning of equality is incredibly distorted when equality is used as justification for reverse discrimination suits brought by the advantaged against the disadvantaged. Equality is not served by such legalistic sleight of hand. Quite the reverse; homosocial reproduction and discriminatory filtering are protected instead. Is our pursuit of happiness *really* hampered by federal regulation? When was the last time a federal regulation stopped an individual's legitimate pursuit of happiness? When EPA initiated regulations that reduced the pollution of our air and water? When automobile safety standards were raised? When sex and race discrimination in employment were banned? When OSHA began requiring a safer environment for us to work in? When the integration of public schools was initiated? Only when an individual is distorted by fear or cruelty or envy so that he pursues happiness by hurting others does the federal government restrict his pursuit of happiness. Otherwise, the individual's pursuit of happiness is often enhanced, not restricted. What is restricted is the corporate pursuit of profit when that profit is at the public's expense.

The present deformation of American ideals can be overcome. We do not have to believe that individual incentives equal liberty, that reverse discrimination suits equal equality, or that deregulation equals the pursuit of happiness. Currently, many of us do believe these things because of the growing influence of the corporate institution on our other institutions, our lives, our symbols, and our values. Yet corporate hegemony is not complete. To most of us, liberty still means more than getting more money; equality still means helping the underdog and the pursuit of happiness means individual growth. But we are confused by the growing mystification of our symbols and values explained in Chapter Four.

An Alternative to Retrenchment

When we return to our senses, we can begin to deal with our problems in a positive way, with an alternative to retrenchment. Corporate reform must be first on the agenda. To facilitate the push from below into the higher corporate circles, to revive lagging productivity with new people and new ideas, and to humanize the corporate bureaucracy will take sweeping changes. Replacing state chartering with federal chartering of all corporations will allow all of the needed reforms to be instituted in one step. Eliminating the corporate profit tax could be a sufficient quid pro quo for such a step. The step should include a new board of directors, ombudsmen, advisory councils, an employee bill of rights, and supervisor election from below in place of supervisor selection from above. The new board of directors should include public directors and worker directors. A strengthened EEOC should work with corporations in their adoption and implementation of affirmative action plans to replace discriminatory filtering and homosocial reproduction. Education for citizenship should replace vocational training in our schools and universities.[4]

Democratic economic planning is the second reform on the alternative to retrenchment agenda. Planning at the federal level, within our democratic traditions, will be required if the reinvigorated corporation is to be turned toward the public purpose. Planning is also necessary to maintain balanced, full-employment growth and to plan the role of small and minority business in the American economy, to provide for enhanced environmental quality, and to implement affirmative action in the economy at large. Corporations already plan, but their private planning needs to be channeled into meeting these public needs by democratic planning.

Wage-price controls are an integral part of the alternative agenda. Without them, our economy cannot attain price stability without an unacceptably high rate of unemployment. Nor can our economy grow to full employment without an unacceptably high rate of inflation. Our economy, in the late 1970s and into the 1980s suffers from Sellers Inflation. The symptoms are undeniable — rising prices, plant closings, spreading unemployment, and a hemorrhaging of the federal budget as social programs fill in for the loss in payrolls. Cutting back on federal spending and controlling the quantity of money will not cure Sellers Inflation, outside of a depression-level unemployment rate. On the other hand, wage-price controls that reimpose free market wages and prices where the free market no longer exists *will* cure Sellers Inflation.

Next on the alternative agenda is an effective monetary policy conducted by a democratically responsible Federal Reserve System. Once relieved of its big bank bias through a restructuring of its Board of Governors, the Federal Reserve System should drop its experiment in Monetarism, first put into practice by Arthur Burns in 1970. The experiment has been a dismal failure. The Monetarists now cannot even agree on what the money stock is, let alone control it. The Tobin monetary strategy should replace the Monetarist strategy. Using Tobin's strategy, the Fed should bring the cost of credit down *immediately* to reasonable levels. Combined with the Community Reinvestment Act, the Tobin strategy can ensure adequate flows of credit at reasonable costs into the communities and sectors that need it most, rather than into areas that can pay the most.

Improved fiscal policy measures are also on the alternative agenda. A constitutional amendment forcing the federal government to balance its budget would be a disaster, for government deficits generated through entitlement programs fill in for declining private payrolls during recessions. Such programs and recession deficits do not crowd out private spending as argued by the advocates of a balanced budget. If we can finally put the balanced budget obsession to rest, the democratic planning of tax policy and expenditure policy will be possible. On the tax side, the alternative agenda must include a progressive income tax to provide economic stability and equity. Stability is served because, if the economy expands too rapidly, tax receipts rise even faster, dampening the expansion. On the other hand, if the economy begins contracting, tax receipts fall quickly and the government deficit reverses the economic contraction. A progressive tax is an equitable tax because those most able to carry the tax burden carry the largest portion of it and those least able carry the smallest portion. Equity also requires that the gaping loopholes be closed and that all forms of income be treated equally. On the expenditure side, programs should be determined by the long-term socioeconomic goals which emerge from the democratic planning process. Wide swings in expenditure totals will be avoided if the long view is emphasized and if the arms race is stopped. On the human side of fiscal policy, a massive increase in federally funded investment in people is a major priority of the alternative agenda. Making it in America today takes far more than it did in the last century. The cost of an adequate education, of adequate nutrition, health care, and housing are beyond the means of over 30 million Americans.[5] This failure in the land of opportunity must be changed because our humanity demands it and because our institutions, particularly our corporations, need the vitality of new people with new ideas.

Investment in people, on the scale needed, will not be forthcoming if federal resources are siphoned off by a speed-up of the arms race. Hence, multilateral disarmament with safeguards is another priority on the alternative agenda. The billions spent for "defense" and the billions more planned are not for defense at all. They have not and will not make us secure from nuclear obliteration. Our security requires that the arms race be stopped through international treaty. For thirty years our leaders have sought international superiority through building up their capacity to kill Russians. The Russian leaders have reciprocated by building up their capacity to kill Americans. Both sets of leaders justified their murderous activites on the grounds of national security. It is finally beginning to dawn on both the Russian and the American people that they are more insecure than ever as a result of the international bully-boy game played by their leaders. The alternative agenda must capitalize on this groundswell of popular awakening to put an end to the game.

Strengthening federal regulation in the job discrimination, environmental and workplace safety areas is the last major item on the alternative agenda. Co-opted, industry-specific regulation is not the issue here. The initiatives started during the Carter administration have gone a long way toward dismantling the co-opted regulators. It should have been done long ago. But the new function-specific regulators are different. More immune to co-optation, the EPA, OSHA, and EEOC do not serve the interests they regulate. Hence the sustained corporate outcry against them. The issue before us now is whether we allow the needed dismantling of co-opted regulators to spread to the dismantling of the effective new regulators.

As explained in Chapter Four, with the corporation becoming an increasingly dominant institution, outlines of a new social reality in

America have clearly emerged. The pluralism of the nineteenth century is yielding to corporate hegemony in the twentieth. As this has occurred, *the mystification of American symbols and ideals has become so extensive that the old symbols and ideals of the public interest have been labeled as "special interests."* Conservation of resources and preservation of wilderness areas used to be in the public interest. Conservation and preservation used to be valued as measures intended to pass on our national heritage to future generations. The Great Outdoors was a symbol of great importance to mainstream America. Now the conservationists and preservationists are labeled "environmental extremists" by our country's leadership. The ideas for which they strive are denigrated and their symbols ridiculed. The corporate interest in mines, wells, tree farms, and park concessions has replaced the public interest in the Great Outdoors, and conservationists have been replaced by "environmental extremists." The old public interest in equality, in helping the underdog, is now manifested in reverse discrimination suits. The old belief that everyone who worked for a living deserved a safe, nontoxic workplace has been replaced with cost-benefit studies: If the corporate cost of reducing employee death and disability is greater, as calculated by the corporation or by its hired experts, than the employee benefits of life and health, then the death and disability should continue. So the corporate experts would have us believe. And if our work kills or disables us, it must be our fault — we forgot to wear our ear plugs, safety glasses, steel-toed boots, respirators, and radiation dosage meters.

Confused by the mystification of our symbols and values, we allow Presidentially-appointed opportunists to gut our Environmental Protection Agency, Equal Employment Opportunity Commission, and Occupational Safety and Health Administration. It is done in the name of freedom and individual incentive — too much government interference, you see. In a sense, the government *is* interfering too much. The new regulators were becoming effective in protecting the public interest in environmental quality, racial and sexual equality, and safe working conditions. But their effectiveness was at the expense of corporate power and profit. So from the corporate point of view, the dominant point of view today, government was interfering too much.

To strengthen the new regulators, as required by the alternative agenda, they must be protected against the destructive capacity of opportunistic appointees. An *opportunistic appointee* is one who seeks to lead a regulatory agency in order to destroy it and parlay the destruction into personal gain. If a significant portion of the agency's leadership were elected by the professionals within the agency itself, the agency could be protected, partially at least, from such opportunism. For then the opportunists, if appointed, would have to share the top power with committed career professionals. Neither the career professionals nor the political appointees could dominate, and neither should.

Also to strengthen the new regulators, adequate levels of funding must be provided. Currently, the defunding of federal regulators has left them grossly under-staffed and the staff that has survived has been thoroughly demoralized by the purge. Furthermore, salaries have begun to fall further and further behind salaries for comparable jobs in the private sector. A career in public service now requires considerable financial and personal sacrifice. Adequate funding for full staffs at comparable salaries must be established.

The new regulators will be strengthened further when their activities are coordinated by democratic economic planning. Now each regulatory body works independently. Because our regulatory agencies were created helter-skelter in response to particular public needs, and because no democratic economic planning process exists in the United States, actions of one agency, which could be made complementary to the goals of other agencies, are often contradictory. The net or overall impact of regulation is significantly lowered by the lack of planning.

In summation, the alternative to economic retrenchment should include the following: (1) Sweeping corporate reforms to vitalize and humanize the corporate bureaucracy, (2) Democratic economic planning to turn corporate planning to the public purpose, (3) Wage-price controls to stop Sellers Inflation from making it impossible for us to achieve price level stability and full employment at the same time, (4) Effective monetary policy to ensure adequate flows of credit at low cost to the sectors that need credit the most in addition to the sectors that can pay the most for it, (5) Fiscal policy that ensures equity and stability and that ensures adequate investment in people, (6) Multilateral disarmament to ensure the security of the American people, (7) Strengthened new regulators to safeguard the public interest in environmental quality, human equality, and worker safety.

Such an alternative agenda is not utopian, but well within our grasp. This is important to emphasize because in our current confusion and retreat, the realm of the possible seems to have shrunk. Yet we are still a people of great potential. Before the growing corporate dominance of all our institutions, symbols, and ideals is completed, reform rather than revolution is still possible. Practical, workable changes can still be initiated peacefully, through the democratic process. The changes discussed here in detail are all within the realm of the possible. So are other specific reforms. The details were discussed, not to draw up my own blueprint for the future, but to demonstrate that real reforms are indeed very practical. Viable alternatives to retrenchment exist. My purpose has been to bring them into the public arena as a way to begin the inquiry into an alternative agenda. We are not incapable of reform, not yet.

But the old remedies no longer work like they were supposed to. Our economy has been transformed into corporate capitalism. Policies appropriate for an earlier age are no longer appropriate. In the pluralistic society of nineteenth century America, the best government may have been the one which governed the least. Such a government was democratic, then. In the close of the twentieth century, pluralism is fading and the corporate institution is dominant. The least government is no longer the best. It no longer serves to promote democracy and pluralism. Instead, such a government abandons the field to the dominant corporation. Democracy and pluralism are now served by an activist federal government which promotes diversity and equality. We can never return to the good old days of frontier America. Nevertheless, we can forge new ways of pursuing democratic ideals. Retrenchment is not the answer. Alternatives should be explored more seriously. Perhaps this book will be a beginning.

Appendix

Employment in all Private Nonagricultural Sectors and the Extent
of Bureaucratization 1947–1981

Year	Thousands of Nonproduction Employees	Thousands of Production or Nonsupervisory Workers	Ratio of Production or Nonsupervisory to Nonproduction Workers
1947	4,635	33,747	7.28
1950	4,821	34,349	7.12
1955	6,227	37,500	6.02
1960	7,320	38,516	5.26
1965	8,411	42,278	5.03
1970	10,169	48,156	4.74
1975	11,268	50,991	4.53
1980	13,765	60,106	4.37
1981	14,126	60,300	4.27

Sources: For 1980 and 1981, March data of each year from *Employment and Earnings,* BLS (May, 1981). All other years are
annual averages from *Employment and Earnings, United States,
1909-78,* Bulletin 1312-11, BLS, 1979. Nonproduction Employees were found by subtracting Production or Nonsupervisory
Workers from All Employees.

TABLE 2A

The Extent of Bureaucratization in Private Employment by Industry 1947-1981 (in thousands)

Year	Mining		Construction		Manufacturing		Transportation and Public Utilities		Trade		Finance Insurance Real Estate		Services	
	Production	Non-Production	Production	Non-Production	Production	Non-Production	Production	Non-Production	Production	Non-Production	Production	Non-Production	Production	Non-Production
1947	871	84	1,786	223	12,990	2,555	n.a.	n.a.	8,241	714	1,436	292	n.a.	n.a.
1950	816	85	2,101	263	12,523	2,718	n.a.	n.a.	8,742	644	1,565	323	n.a.	n.a.
1955	680	112	2,477	362	13,288	3,594	n.a.	n.a.	9,675	860	1,889	409	n.a.	n.a.
1960	570	142	2,497	429	12,586	4,210	n.a.	n.a.	10,315	1,076	2,145	484	n.a.	n.a.
1965	494	138	2,749	483	13,434	4,628	3,561	475	11,358	1,358	2,388	589	8,295	741
1970	473	150	2,990	598	14,044	5,323	3,914	601	13,375	1,665	2,879	766	10,481	1,067
1975	571	181	2,808	717	13,043	5,280	3,894	648	15,023	2,037	3,173	992	12,479	1,413
1980	740	256	3,213	937	14,727	6,066	4,296	847	17,737	2,489	3,844	1,241	15,549	1,929
1981	809	279	3,168	961	14,138	6,116	4,232	869	17,909	2,585	3,954	1,299	16,090	2,017

Sources: For 1980 and 1981, March data from *Employment and Earnings*, BLS (May, 1981). All other data are annual averages from *Employment and Earnings, United States, 1909–1978*, Bulletin 1312–11, BLS, 1979. Nonproduction Employees were found by subtracting Production or Nonsupervisory Workers from All Employees. The nonbureaucratic category of workers is composed of production workers in mining and manufacturing, construction workers in construction, and nonsupervisory workers in all other industry classifications.

Notes and References

Chapter 1

1. Further discussion is in Frederick Jackson Turner, *The Frontier in American History* (New York: Henry Holt, 1921).

2. Malcolm Sawyer, "Income Distribution in OECD Countries," *OECD Economic Outlook, Occasional Studies* (July, 1976), pp. 3-36. See his Table 10 and 11, p. 19. The eleven countries were Australia, Canada, France, Germany, Japan, Netherlands, Norway, Spain, Sweden, United Kingdom and United States.

3. Further discussion of inequality in the United States is in Lester C. Thurow, *Generating Inequality* (New York: Basic Books, 1975); Christopher Jencks et al., *Inequality* (New York: Basic Books, 1972); Christopher Jencks et al., *Who Gets Ahead* (New York: Basic Books, 1979). The latest manifestation of the old genetic determination theory is "sociobiology." See William M. Dugger, "Sociobiology for Social Scientists: A Critical Introduction to E.O. Wilson's Evolutionary Paradigm," *Social Science Quarterly*, 62 (June, 1981), pp. 221-233.

4. The perceptive reader will have noticed an anomaly in Table 1.3: Japan has the highest life expectancy but the fewest physicians, while Germany with the most physicians has the lowest life expectancy. Perhaps physicians are hazardous to health? The Surgeon General should be alerted. (Obviously, I have no explanation of the anomaly.)

5. *Economic Report of the President* (Washington, D.C.: GPO, 1983), p. 199.

6. Board of Governors of the Federal Reserve System.

7. Further discussion is in Simon Kuznets, *Toward a Theory of Economic Growth* (New York: W.W. Norton, 1968).

Chapter 2

1. For Reagan's program itself see David A. Stockman, "How to Avoid an Economic Dunkirk," *Challenge*, 24 (March/April, 1981), pp. 17–21; Lyle E. Gramley, "The Role of Supply-Side Economics in Fighting Inflation," *Challenge*, 23 (January/February, 1981), pp. 14–18; and Joseph A. Pechman, ed., *Setting National Priorities: The 1982 Budget* (Washington, D.C.: Brookings Institution, 1981). The general political-philosophical background of Reagan's program is discussed in Alan Crawford, *Thunder on the Right* (New York: Pantheon Books, 1980); Milton and Rose Friedman, *Free to Choose* (New York: Avon Books, 1980); George N. Nash, *The Conservative Intellectual Movement in America* (New York: Basic Books, 1979); Peter Steinfels, *The Neoconservatives* (New York: Simon and Schuster, 1979); and Jude Wanniski, *The Way the World Works* (New York: Simon and Schuster, 1978).

2. The following discussion relies on Pechman, editor, *Setting National Priorities* and on Walter W. Heller, "Kennedy's Supply-Side Economics," *Challenge*, 24 (May/June, 1981), pp. 14–18.

3. See Pechman, editor, pp. 70–71.

Chapter 3

1. The viewpoint taken in this chapter is that of an "underground economist." Most U.S. economists are members of the orthodox Neoclassical school, but the ideas drawn on in my discussion come from the heterodox schools known as Institutional Economics and Post-Keynesian Economics. Heterodox thought is very seldom taught in schools and universities and is seldom discussed in the mass media so the interested reader may wish to investigate the following sources from which I have drawn. For the leading Post-Keynesian see Alfred S. Eichner, *The Megacorp and Oligopoly* (White Plains, N.Y.: M.E. Sharpe, 1980), and Eichner, "Reagan's Doubtful Game Plan," *Challenge*, 24 (May/June, 1981). For the best known Institutional Economist see John Kenneth Galbraith, *Economics and the Public Purpose* (Boston: Houghton Mifflin, 1973). For a harsh attack on economic orthodoxy see William M. Dugger, "Ideological and Scientific Functions of the Neoclassical Theory of the Firm," *Journal of Economic Issues*, 10 (June, 1976).

2. The best historical account of this replacement is Alfred D. Chandler, Jr., *The Visible Hand: The Managerial Revolution in American Business* (Cambridge: The Belknap Press of Harvard University Press, 1977).

3. Calculated from *Economic Report of the President* (Washington, D.C.: GPO, 1981), p. 260.

4. If interested in the origins of this intellectual outlawry see Clarence Ayres, *The Theory of Economic Progress;* 3rd ed. (Kalamazoo, Mich.: New Issues Press, 1978); Ayres, *Toward a Reasonable Society* (Austin: University of Texas Press, 1961); Thorstein Veblen, *The Place of Science in Modern Civilization and Other Essays* (New York: B.W. Huebsch, 1919); Veblen, *Essays in Our Changing Order*, edited by Leon Ardzrooni (New York: Augustus M. Kelley, 1964); and John R. Commons, *The Economics of Collective Action*, edited by Kenneth H. Parsons (New York: Macmillan, 1950).

5. Further discussion is in Marc R. Tool, *The Discretionary Economy* (Santa Monica: Goodyear, 1979).

6. The classic statement of this theory is in Joseph A. Schumpeter, *The Theory of Economic Development*, translated by Redvers Opie (New York: Oxford University Press, 1934).

7. See John M. Blair, "Market Power and Inflation: A Short-Run Target Return Model," *Journal of Economic Issues*, 8 (June, 1974), pp. 453–478.

8. Arthur M. Okun, *Equality and Efficiency: The Big Tradeoff* (Washington, D.C.: The Brookings Institution, 1975).

9. Marc R. Tool, *The Discretionary Economy*, p. 293 (italics added).

10. Clarence Ayres, *Theory of Economic Progress*, p. 233.

11. Sheldon Danziger and Robert Haveman, "The Reagan Budget: A Sharp Break with the Past," *Challenge*, 24 (May/June, 1981), p. 7. A recent "guesstimate" of some of the leaks from Okun's bucket is in Sheldon Danziger, Robert Haveman, and Robert Plotnick, "How Income Transfers Affect Work, Savings, and the Income Distribution," *Journal of Economic Literature*, 19 (September, 1981), pp. 975–1028. They guesstimate that 23¢ leaks out of the bucket for every dollar put into the bucket.

12. For "an economic audit of the price that America has paid for twenty years of cold war," see Seymour Melman, *Our Depleted*

Society (New York: Dell, 1965). See also his later *The Permanent War Economy: American Capitalism in Decline* (New York: Simon and Schuster, 1974) and his presidential address to the Association for Evolutionary Economics, "Decision Making and Productivity as Economic Variables," *Journal of Economic Issues,* 10 (June, 1976), pp. 218-250 and The Boston Study Group, *The Price of Defense* (New York: Times Books, 1979).

13. The following is drawn from John McCarron's articles of October 31, 1981 and November 8, 1981 in the *Chicago Tribune.*

14. James O'Connor, *The Fiscal Crisis of the State* (New York: St. Martin's Press, 1973), pp. 82-91.

15. See Allan G. Gruchy, "The Concept of National Planning in Institutional Economics," *Southern Economic Journal,* 6 (October, 1939); pp. 121-144, Allan G. Gruchy, *Modern Economic Thought* (1947; New York: Augustus M. Kelley, 1967), pp. 541-628; J. Ron Stanfield, *Economic Thought and Social Change* (Carbondale: Southern Illinois University Press, 1979), pp. 76-88.

16. Karl Polanyi, *The Great Transformation* (1944; Boston: Beacon Press, 1957), pp. 46-55.

17. Further discussion is in Daniel M. Berman, *Death on the Job: Occupational Health and Safety Struggles in the United States* (New York: Monthly Review Press, 1978), and Jeanne M. Stellman and Susan M. Daum, *Work is Dangerous to Your Health* (New York: Vintage Books, 1973).

Chapter 4

1. See Hans Gerth and C. Wright Mills, *Character and Social Structure* (New York: Harcourt, Brace and World, 1953), pp. 26-29.

2. John Kenneth Galbraith, *The New Industrial State* (Boston: Houghton Mifflin, 1967), pp. 198-218.

3. Thorstein Veblen, *The Higher Learning in America: A Memorandum on the Conduct of Universities by Business Men* (New York: B.W. Huebsch, 1918). Veblen, founder of institutional economics and iconoclast par excellence, is like a fine wine. He improves with age. Read his *The Theory of the Leisure Class* (New York: Macmillan, 1899) and *The Theory of Business Enterprise* (New York: Charles Scribners Sons, 1904).

4. Further discussion is in C. Wright Mills, *The Sociological Imagination* (New York: Oxford University Press, 1959).

5. In addition to John Kenneth Galbraith's *New Industrial State*, see his *The Affluent Society;* 2nd ed. (Boston: Houghton Mifflin, 1969).

6. The best history is Alfred D. Chandler, Jr., *The Visible Hand: The Managerial Revolution in American Business* (Cambridge: The Belknap Press of Harvard University Press, 1977).

7. Although his interpretation differs from mine, the following is excellent: John M. Blair, *Economic Concentration* (New York: Harcourt, Brace, Jovanovich, 1972).

8. In Economese (the technical language of economics) the elasticity of demand is a function of time. In the short run demand is generally inelastic; in the long run, elastic.

9. Gabriel Kolko, *The Triumph of Conservatism* (New York: Quadrangle, 1967).

10. Larry Reynolds, "Foundations of an Institutional Theory of Regulation," *Journal of Economic Issues*, 15 (September, 1981), pp. 641-656.

Chapter 5

1. Adam Smith, *An Inquiry into the Nature and Causes of the Wealth of Nations*, ed. by Edwin Cannan (1776; New York: Modern Library, 1937), p. 609.

2. The following draws from Tom Hadden, *Company Law and Capitalism* (London: Weidenfeld and Nicolson, 1972); E.A.J. Johnson, *An Economic History of Modern England* (New York: Thomas Nelson and Sons, 1939); H.A. Shannon, "The Limited Companies of 1866-1883," *The Economic History Review*, 4 (October, 1933); H.A. Shannon, "The Coming of General Limited Liability," *Economic History*, 2 (January, 1931); and Geoffrey Todd, "Some Aspects of Joint Stock Companies, 1844-1900," *The Economic History Review*, 4 (October, 1932).

3. Adam Smith, *The Wealth of Nations*, p. 710.

4. *Ibid.*, p. 714.

5. John R. McCulloch, *The Principles of Political Economy* (1864; New York: Augustus M. Kelley, 1965), pp. 360-366.

6. John Stuart Mill, *Principles of Political Economy*, rev. ed. Vol. 1 (1848; New York: P.F. Collier and Son, 1900), p. 134.

7. H.A. Shannon, "The Limited Companies of 1866-1883," p. 312.

8. Adolf A. Berle and Gardiner C. Means, *The Modern Corporation and Private Property*, rev. ed. (New York: Harcourt, Brace and World, 1967), p. 14.

9. Reinhard Bendix, *Work and Authority in Industry* (New York: Harper and Row, 1963), p. 229.

10. *Ibid.*, p. 214.

11. *Ibid.;* Seymour Melman, "The Rise of Administrative Overhead in the Manufacturing Industries of the United States, 1899-1947," *Oxford Economic Papers*, III (1951).

12. Alfred Marshall, *Industry and Trade*, 4th ed. (1923; New York; Augustus M. Kelley, 1970), p. 310.

13. Alfred Marshall, *Principles of Economics*, 8th ed. (London: Macmillan, 1938).

14. See, for example, Thorstein Veblen, *The Place of Science in Modern Civilization and Other Essays* (New York: B.W. Huebsch, 1919).

15. A collection of recent works is in Joseph S. Roucek, editor, *Social Control for the 1980s* (Westport, Conn.: Greenwood Press, 1978). See also John R. Commons, *The Economics of Collective Action*, ed. by Kenneth H. Parsons (Madison: University of Wisconsin Press, 1950).

16. See Alfred S. Eichner, *The Megacorp and Oligopoly* (White Plains, N.Y.: M.E. Sharpe, 1980); John Kenneth Galbraith, *Economics and the Public Purpose* (Boston: Houghton Mifflin, 1973) and "Symposium on Price Formation," *Journal of Post Keynesian Economics*, 4 (Fall, 1981), pp. 81-116.

17. See Allan G. Gruchy, *Contemporary Economic Thought* (Clifton, New Jersey: Augustus M. Kelley, 1972), and J. Ron Stanfield, *Economic Thought and Social Change* (Carbondale: Southern Illinois University Press, 1979).

18. Adolph Lowe, "What is Evolutionary Economics?" *Journal of Economic Issues*, 14 (June, 1980), p. 253. See also his classic, *On Economic Knowledge;* 2nd ed., (White Plains, N.Y.: M.E. Sharpe, 1977), and his *The Path of Economic Growth* (New York: Cambridge University Press, 1976).

19. Milton Friedman, *Essays in Positive Economics* (Chicago: University of Chicago Press, 1953), pp. 3-43; and Ludwig von Mises, *The Ultimate Foundation of Economic Science;* 2nd ed., (Kansas City: Sheed Andrews and McMeel, 1978).

20. Milton Friedman, *Essays in Positive Economics*, pp. 277–300.

21. Further explanation is in Adolph Lowe, "What is Evolutionary Economics?"

22. Mises, *Ultimate Foundation of Economic Science*, p. 41.

23. *Ibid.*, p. 42.

24. Milton Friedman and Rose Friedman, *Free to Choose*, (New York: Avon Books, 1979).

25. The political implications of government non-intervention in twentieth century capitalism are discussed in Rick Tilman, "Ideology and Utopia in Milton Friedman," *Dissent*, 26 (Winter, 1979), pp. 69–77. Further discussion of Austrian "radical individualism" is in Paul D. Bush, "A 'Radical Individualist's' Critique of American Institutionalism," *American Journal of Economics and Sociology*, 40 (April, 1981), pp. 139–147 and Paul D. Bush, " 'Radical Individualism's' Philosophical Dualisms as Apologetic Constructs," *American Journal of Economics and Sociology*, 40 (July, 1981), pp. 287–298.

Chapter 6

1. Charles Dickens, *Little Dorrit* (New York: Dodd, Mead and Company, 1951), pp. 97–117.

2. The classical work on bureaucracy is by Max Weber. See his *From Max Weber*, translated and edited by H.H. Gerth and C. Wright Mills (New York: Oxford University Press, 1946); and *Max Weber: The Theory of Social and Economic Organization*, translated by A.M. Henderson and Talcott Parsons, edited by Talcott Parsons (New York: Oxford University Press, 1947).

3. C. Wright Mills, *White Collar* (New York: Oxford University Press, 1951), p. 81.

4. Max Weber, *From Max Weber*, p. 233.

5. C. Wright Mills, *White Collar*, p. 78.

6. Reinhard Bendix, *Work and Authority in Industry* (New York: Harper and Row, 1963) and Seymour Melman, "The Rise of Administrative Overhead in the Manufacturing Industries of the United States, 1899–1947," *Oxford Economic Papers*, 3, 1951.

7. U.S. Bureau of the Census, *Statistical Abstract of the United States*, 1980 (Washington, D.C.: GPO, 1980), pp. 566-567.

8. Christopher Jencks et al., *Who Gets Ahead* (New York: Basic Books, 1979), pp. 301-303. This is a reinvestigation of Christopher Jencks et al., *Inequality* (New York: Basic Books, 1972).

9. Jencks et al., *Who Gets Ahead*, pp. 224-225 and 115-121. See also Lester C. Thurow, *Generating Inequality* (New York: Basic Books, 1975), pp. 77-81.

10. Thurow, *Generating Inequality*, p. 76.

11. W. Lloyd Warner and James C. Abegglen, *Occupational Mobility in American Business and Industry* (Minneapolis: University of Minnesota, 1955), pp. 115-126.

12. The following draws upon Rosabeth Moss Kanter's excellent case studies. However, her use of the term homosocial reproduction is more restrictive than mine. See her *Men and Women of the Corporation* (New York: Basic Books, 1977), pp. 47-68.

13. Warner and Abegglen, *Occupational Mobility in American Business and Industry*. Although a bit out-dated, their study is still one of the most useful and comprehensive, and their essential findings are not contradicted by more recent works such as Jencks et al., *Who Gets Ahead*.

14. Bernard Sarachek, "American Entrepreneurs and the Horatio Alger Myth," *Journal of Economic History*, 38 (June, 1978), p. 454. See also his related work, "Jewish American Entrepreneurs," *Journal of Economic History*, 40 (June, 1980), pp. 359-372.

15. Hans Gerth and C. Wright Mills, *Character and Social Structure* (New York: Harcourt, Brace and World, 1953), p. 83.

16. Ronald Corwin, Marvin J. Taves, and J. Eugene Haas, "Social Requirements for Occupational Success: Internalized Norms and Friendship," *Social Forces*, 39 (December, 1960), p. 139.

17. C. Wright Mills, *White Collar*, Chapter 11.

18. Rosabeth Moss Kanter, *Men and Women of the Corporation*, p. 54.

19. Wilbert Moore, *The Conduct of the Corporation* (New York: Vintage, 1962), p. 109, as quoted by Kanter.

20. Talcott Parsons, *Max Weber*, p. 73.

21. Michael Maccoby, *The Gamesman* (New York: Simon and Schuster, 1976), p. 7. Page references to Maccoby are from the readily available Bantam Books edition.

22. *Ibid.*, p. 202.

23. *Ibid.*, p. 122.

24. Thorstein Veblen, *The Theory of the Leisure Class* (New York: Augustus M. Kelley, 1975), p. 223.

25. *Ibid.*, p. 103.

26. John Kenneth Galbraith, *The New Industrial State* (Boston: Houghton Mifflin, 1967). But, see his, *The Anatomy of Power* (Boston: Houghton Mifflin, 1983).

Chapter 7

1. Further discussion, from a different perspective, is in Lester C. Thurow, *Generating Inequality* (New York: Basic Books, 1975), pp. 81-86.

2. For the best Libertarian critique see Joel H. Spring, *Education and the Rise of the Corporate State* (Boston: Beacon Press, 1972) and Joel H. Spring, *The Sorting Machine: National Educational Policy Since 1945* (New York: David McKay, 1976). The Marxist classic is, of course, Samuel Bowles and Herbert Gintis, *Schooling in Capitalist America* (New York: Basic Books, 1976). The Institutionalist classic is Thorstein Veblen, *The Higher Learning in America* (1918; reprint ed., New York: Augustus M. Kelley, 1965). See also Upton Sinclair, *The Goose-Step: A Study of American Education*, rev. ed. (Los Angeles: Upton Sinclair, 1923).

3. John Dewey, *Intelligence in the Modern World*, ed. by Joseph Ratner (New York: Random House, 1939), p. 724.

4. *Ibid.*, p. 428.

5. Hans Gerth and C. Wright Mills, *Character and Social Structure* (New York: Harcourt, Brace and World, 1953), p. 252.

6. Dewey, *Intelligence in the Modern World*, pp. 473-474.

7. Richard H. Hofstadter in Hofstadter and Walter P. Metzger, *The Development of Academic Freedom in the United States* (New York: Columbia University Press, 1955), pp. 7-8.

8. *Ibid.*, p. 41.

9. *Ibid.*, p. 223.

10. Further discussion is in Robert M. MacIver, *Academic Freedom in Our Time* (New York: Columbia University Press, 1955), pp. 67-120.

11. Hofstadter, *The Development of Academic Freedom in the United States*, p. 120.

12. William O. Douglas, *Democracy and Finance*, 1940. Quoted in Ralph Nader, Mark Green, and Joel Seligman, *Taming the Giant Corporation* (New York: W.W. Norton, 1976), p. 121. For further discussion of corporate reform see Christopher D. Stone, *Where the Law Ends: The Social Control of Corporate Behavior* (New York: Harper and Row, 1975).

Chapter 8

1. Ralph Nader, Mark Green, and Joel Seligman, *Taming the Giant Corporation* (New York: W.W. Norton, 1976), pp. 34–61.

2. Lester C. Thurow, *The Zero-Sum Society* (New York: 1980), p. 100.

3. Two outstanding popular works are Michael Maccoby, *The Leader* (New York: Simon and Schuster, 1981), and William G. Ouchi, *Theory Z* (New York: Avon Books, 1982).

4. Ouchi, *Theory Z*, p. 68.

5. Maccoby, *The Leader*, pp. 40–54.

6. Further discussion of the effectiveness of participative management is in Ronald E. Mueller, *Revitalizing America* (Simon and Schuster, 1980).

7. Ouchi, *Theory Z*, p. 78.

8. An excellent section of readings from the period are in *The Government and the Economy: 1783–1861*, edited by Carter Goodrich (New York: Bobbs-Merrill, 1967).

9. Quoted in Ralph Nader, Mark Green, and Joel Seligman, *Taming the Giant Corporation* (New York: W.W. Norton, 1976), p. 70.

10. For an excellent account see Arthur M. Schlesinger, Jr., *The Age of Jackson* (Boston: Little, Brown and Company, 1945).

11. For a stirring history of the transition to national-scale business see Ida M. Tarbell, *The Nationalizing of Business*, 1878–1898 (Chicago: Quadrangle Books, 1971).

12. Chris Argyris, *Personality and Organization* (New York: Harper and Brothers, 1957), p. 233.

Chapter 9

1. Further discussion is in Alfred D. Chandler, Jr., *The Visible Hand: The Managerial Revolution in American Business* (Cambridge: The Belknap Press of Harvard University Press, 1977), pp. 315-339.

2. An excellent critical study is Anthony Sampson, *The Sovereign State of ITT* (New York: Stein and Day, 1973).

3. A listing of large industrial mergers, 1952 to 1977, is in William G. Shepherd and Clair Wilcox, *Public Policies Toward Business*, 6th ed. (Homewood, Ill.: Richard D. Irwin, 1979), pp. 190-193.

4. Chandler, *The Visible Hand* and his *Strategy and Structure: Chapters in the History of the Industrial Enterprise* (Cambridge: The M.I.T. Press, 1962). Chandler's organization and presentation of the historical record are superb. But his interpretation of the social, political, and economic impacts of corporate evolution is quite limited.

5. Chandler, *The Visible Hand*, p. 364.

6. A more detailed account is in Chandler, *Strategy and Structure* and in Chandler, *The Visible Hand*, pp. 456-464.

7. *Ibid.*, p. 477.

8. Oliver E. Williamson, *Markets and Hierarchies: Analysis and Antitrust Implications* (New York: Free Press, 1975); and Oliver E. Williamson, "The Modern Corporation: Origins, Evolution, Attributes," *Journal of Economic Literature* (December, 1981), pp. 1537-1568. See also William M. Dugger, "The Transaction Cost Analysis of Oliver E. Williamson: A New Synthesis?" *Journal of Economic Issues* (March, 1983), pp. 95-114.

9. See, for example, William M. Dugger "The Reform Method of John R. Commons," *Journal of Economic Issues* (June, 1979), pp. 369-381; and William M. Dugger, "Property Rights, Law and John R. Commons," *Review of Social Economy* (April, 1980), pp. 41-53.

10. John R. Commons, *Institutional Economics* (1934; Madison: University of Wisconsin Press, 1961), pp. 1-124.

11. Thorstein Veblen, *The Theory of Business Enterprise* (1904; Clifton, N.J.: Augustus M. Kelley, 1975), p. 49.

12. The classic on corporate planning is John Kenneth Galbraith, *The New Industrial State* (Boston: Houghton Mifflin, 1967).

13. Further discussion of economic planning is in Allan G. Gruchy, *Contemporary Economic Thought* (Clifton, N.J.: Augustus M. Kelley, 1972), pp. 237–339.

14. Further discussion is in Gerhard Colm and Peter Wagner, *Federal Budget Projections, A Report of the National Planning Association and the Brookings Institution* (Washington: Brookings, 1966).

15. Further discussion is in William M. Dugger, "The 'Long Run' and Its Significance to Social Economy," *Review of Social Economy*, 37 (October, 1979), pp. 199–210.

16. See J. Ron Stanfield, *Economic Thought and Social Change* (Carbondale: Southern Illinois University Press, 1979).

17. Further discussion is in Charles R. Spruill, *Conglomerates and the Evolution of Capitalism* (Carbondale: Southern Illinois University Press, 1982).

Chapter 10

1. The best recent treatment of wage-price controls is Jerry E. Pohlman, *Inflation Under Control?* (Reston, Virginia: Reston Publishing Co., 1976). I have relied heavily on Pohlman.

2. Inflation and unemployment data are from the Bureau of Labor Statistics. Industrial production is from the Board of Governors of the Federal Reserve System.

3. Bureau of Economic Analysis.

4. National Bureau of Economic Research.

5. Economists still debate this question. An excellent discussion of the debate is in Pohlman, *Inflation Under Control?*, pp. 182–187.

6. These labels and the following definitions were first proposed by Abba P. Lerner in his excellent *Flation* (Baltimore: Penguin Books, 1973).

7. See Charles H. Berry, *Corporate Growth and Diversification* (Princeton: Princeton University Press, 1975) and Charles R. Spruill, *Conglomerates and the Evolution of Capitalism* (Carbondale: Southern Illinois University Press, 1982).

8. Abba P. Lerner suggests a similar wage guideline in his *Flation*, pp. 66–67.

9. An excellent discussion is in Barry P. Bosworth and Robert Z. Lawrence, *Commodity Prices and the New Inflation* (Washington, D.C.. Brookings, 1982).

10. Excellent discussions of various control programs are in Michael P. Claudon and Richard R. Cornwall, editors, *An Incomes Policy for the United States: New Approaches* (Boston: Martinus Nijoff Publishing, 1981).

Chapter 11

1. See Robert Lekachman, *The Age of Keynes* (New York: McGraw Hill, 1966). For the original, read the heretic himself: John Maynard Keynes, *The General Theory of Employment, Interest, and Money* (1936; New York: Harcourt, Brace and World, 1964).

2. See Milton Friedman, editor, *Studies in the Quantity Theory of Money* (Chicago: University of Chicago Press, 1956).

3. The technical language of orthodox economists, a mixture of Pidgin English and mathematics.

4. An excellent explanation of these processes, by a very conservative but unorthodox economist, is in Joseph A. Schumpeter, *The Theory of Economic Development*, translated by Redvers Opie (1934; New York: Oxford University Press, 1969).

5. Friedman's major monetary works, in chronological order, are: "A Monetary and Fiscal Framework for Economic Stability," in his *Essays in Positive Economics* (Chicago: University of Chicago Press, 1953), pp. 133–156; *Studies in the Quantity Theory of Money* (Chicago: University of Chicago Press, 1956); with Anna Jacobson Schwartz, *A Monetary History of the United States 1867–1960* (Princeton: Princeton University Press, 1963); *The Optimum Quantity of Money* (Chicago: Adline Publishing Company, 1969).

6. William M. Dugger, *Federal Reserve Open Market Strategy in Transition* (Dissertation, University of Texas at Austin, 1974).

7. An excellent account of this change in strategy, written by a member of the Board of Governors who served under both Martin

and Burns, is Sherman J. Maisel, *Managing the Dollar* (New York: W.W. Norton, 1973). Also, see my dissertation, with which I now disagree.

8. Burns should be given his due. See his *Reflections of an Economic Policy Maker* (Washington, D.C.: American Enterprise Institute, 1978).

9. *Federal Reserve Bulletin*, 67 (April, 1981), p. A3.

10. See his review of the Friedman-Schwartz Monetarist interpretation of U.S. economic history: James Tobin, "The Monetary Interpretation of History," *American Economic Review*, 55 (June, 1965), pp. 464-485.

11. James Tobin, "Towards Improving the Efficiency of the Monetary Mechanism," *Review of Economics and Statistics*, 42 (August, 1960), pp. 276-279.

12. Further discussion is in John Kenneth Galbraith, *Money: Whence It Came, Where It Went* (Boston: Houghton Mifflin, 1975).

13. *Ibid.*, p. 86.

14. James Tobin "Towards Improving the Efficiency of the Monetary Mechanism," p. 279.

15. An excellent discussion of the act is in F. Gregory Hayden with Larry D. Swanson, "Planning through the Socialization of Property Rights: The Community Reinvestment Act," *Journal of Economic Issues*, 14 (June, 1980), pp. 351-369.

16. An excellent case study is in David Leinsdorf and Donald Etra, *Citibank* (New York: Grossman Publishers, 1973), pp. 81-116.

17. Calculated from Table No. 445 in the *Statistical Abstract of the United States*, 1980 (Washington, D.C.: GPO, 1980), pp. 266-267.

18. Table No. 454 in *Ibid.*, p. 272.

19. Table No. 455 in *Ibid.*, p. 272.

20. *Economic Report of the President* (Washington, D.C.: GPO, 1982), p. 321.

21. *Ibid.*, p. 323.

22. Further discussion of the arms race is in Alva Myrdal, *The Game of Disarmament* (New York: Pantheon Books, 1976).

23. Numerous discussions with my friend and colleague Hugh Garnett were very helpful in writing this section.

24. Table No. 594 in *The Statistical Abstract of the United States,* 1980, p. 366.

25. *Economic Report of the President,* 1982, p. 86.

26. C.E.Ayres, *The Theory of Economic Progress;* 3rd ed. (Kalamazoo: New Issues Press, 1978), p. xxix.

27. See also Robert Lekachman, *Greed Is Not Enough* (New York: Pantheon Books, 1982).

Chapter 12

1. Further discussion of the affluent consumer is in John Brooks, *Showing Off in America* (Boston: Little, Brown, and Company, 1981); and Christopher Lasch, *The Culture of Narcissism* (New York: W.W. Norton, 1978.

2. U.S. Federal Election Commission.

3. *Statistical Abstract of the United States,* 1980 (Washington, D.C., GPO, 1980), p. 515.

4. For an excellent discussion see Ronnie Dugger, *Our Invaded Universities: Form, Reform, and New Starts* (New York: W.W. Norton, 1974).

5. In 1979, according to the U.S. Bureau of the Census, 26.1 million people lived below the official poverty level. During 1980 and 1981 an additional 5.7 million fell below the poverty level. By the end of 1982 a total of 34.4 million people were living below the poverty level. Retrenchment continued to take its grim toll in 1983. By the end of our experiment with retrenchment, we will have probably pushed at least six million people into poverty, a large number of them children.

Index

Abegglen, James C., 121
Advisory council, 145-147
Affirmative action, 44, 143-144, 191
Age of bureaucracy, 100
Age of enlightenment, 53
Aggregate demand, 20, 87; Keynesian
    control of, 88, 191, 203
Aggregate supply, 20, 203
Agriculture, 130
Alternative agenda, 276-281
Alternative economic theory, 28-32.
    See also Institutionalism;
    Underground economics
American Association of University
    Professors (AAUP), 140
American dream, 187, 273-274;
    immigrant participation in, 3;
    as illusion, 4
American ideals, 275
Antitrust, 86-87, 157, 214
Apology, American: and reality,
    11-12; for retarded growth, 7.
    See also Conventional wisdom
Arbiter cities, 42-43
Argyris, Chris, 168
Arms race, 202, 251-253. See also
    Militarization
Arnold, Thurman, 1
Association for Evolutionary
    Economics, 268
Auchter, Thorne G.: head of
    OSHA, 17; deregulation of the
    workplace, 18
Austrian school, 87-88, 90-93

Authoritarian romanticism, 168.
    See also Reaganomics
Ayres, Clarence, 36-37, 257

Balanced budget, 248-251, 256
Bank credit, 26
Bankers, 191; central, 238-239.
    See also Monetary policy
Banknotes, 231-232
Bendix, Reinhard, 80, 106
Bill of rights, bureaucrat's, 145,
    147-148
Block grants, 18-19, 42
Board of Directors: corporate, 145,
    148-151; worker directors,
    149-150; public director,
    149-151, 161-162
Board of Governors of the Federal
    Reserve System, 238-239. See also
    Burns, Arthur; Volcker, Paul;
    Martin, William McChesney, Jr.;
    Monetary policy
Boston Manufacturing Company, 80
Bottleneck, 197
Bracket creep. See Fiscal drag
Bubble Act, 75-76, 78
Bureaucracy: extent of, 80-81,
    105-114; corporate, 99, 124-130;
    defined, 100-105; and democracy,
    102; uses of, 103-104; formal
    structure of, 104; informal
    structure of, 104-105. See also
    Corporado

Bureaucrat, 105; number of, 106-114; character of corporate, 124-130; or technocrat, 129-130

Bureaucratization, 105-114; in private sector, 108-109; in manufacturing, 109-110; in other sectors, 110-114; index of, 108-112; in government, 112-114; in the labor market, 114-118

Burns, Arthur, 230, 233-234, 236, 239, 258

Business cycles, 229, 269

Capacity utilization rate: and stagflation, 11; and price guidelines, 223-225

Capital: human, 116, 122, 127, 257, 259; market, 179

Career: bureaucratic versus entrepreneurial, 80, 123

Careerist, 58, 62, 128-131. See also Corporado

Carter, Jimmy, 152, 239

Categorical grants, 18-19, 42

Chandler, Alfred D., Jr., 174, 175, 177, 268

Character: formation of, 58; new traits in American, 63, 124-130; fear and greed in, 131

Chicago, University of, 233

Cicero, 97

Civil rights, 44-45; Act, 142

Cloning, 120-130; clones, 144-145. See also Reproduction

Codetermination, 149

Commons, John R., 82, 84, 180-182. See also Institutionalism

Community Reinvestment Act, 241-242. See also Credit

Companies Act of 1844, 78

Competition, 64-65; perfect, 88; moribund, 173. See also Oligopolistic markets

Competition in regulatory laxity, 45, 79, 156

Concentration ratio, 214

Conglomerate movement, 65-68; for diversification, 173; and pricing power, 173; begins stagflation, 178, 183-186; as mini-capital market, 179. See also Milking

Conglomerate rationing, 183-185. See also Inflation; Milking; Unemployment

Congressional Budget and Impoundment Act, 189

Congressional Budget Office (CBO), 188-189, 196-197

Conspicuous consumption, 62-63; of drugs, 62

Consumer: demand in pre-industrial America, 61; in contemporary America, 62

Contamination of motives, 55-56, 60

Conventional wisdom, 82-83; retarded U.S. growth, 8; U.S. public spending, 8; crowding out, 9; on wage-price controls, 205, 211

Co-optation, 157-158. See also Regulator

Corporado, 58-59, 61-62, 257-258, 263, 271

Corporate revolution: in U.S., 79-80, 172-183; in administration, 173-178

Corporate taxes, 159-160

Corwin, Ronald, 123

Council of Economic Advisers (CEA), 188-189, 196-197

Countervailing power, 273

Credit, 201, 236, 240, 242. See also Money

Crowding out, 9, 249-250; and buyers inflation, 250

Cultural lag: in education, 140-142

Cut throat competition: regulation of, 69

Debt, federal government, 244-245

Decentralization, 18-19; and party politics, 19; and New Federalism, 18-19; costs of, 40-45

Defense, national, 253
Deficits, budget, 202, 243-244,
    248-251; President Reagan's,
    15; President Carter's, 15;
    stimulative, 16; pump priming,
    20; and Reaganomics, 20-21;
    and plant closings, 67; and
    conglomerate mergers, 68
Demand pull inflation, 212. *See also*
    Buyers inflation
Deregulation, 275; and Reaganomics,
    17-18; President Carter's, 17; and
    states' rights, 18; costs of, 45-46
Dewey, John, 135-136
Dickens, Charles, 100
Diversification, 214. *See also*
    Conglomerate
Division of labor, 101
Dixiecrats, 44-45, 247
Douglas, William O., 151
Dugger, Ronnie, 276

East India Company, 75-76
Economese, 82, 231, 250, 251
Economic democracy, 146
Economics, failure of, 268-272
Economic theory: gap with reality,
    3, 25, 81, 93, 212-215; as faulty
    science, 23-28; as economic
    praxeology, 91-92
Economies of scale and horizontal
    merger, 66
Education: enrollment in higher,
    9-10; state aid to, 43; educational
    institutions, 52; credentials, 116;
    filtering, 118-119, 135-142;
    careerists, 128; critique of,
    135-142; democratic, 135-137;
    for war, 136
Eichner, Alfred S., 85-86
Eisenhower, Dwight D., 205
Elasticity, 66 n
Emission standards: best existing
    practices, 194
Employment, 196; full, 89-90
Emulation, 56, 60, 129

Entrepreneur, 123, 129, 262.
    See also Career
Environment: planning, 186, 197;
    goals for, 191
Environmental Protection Agency
    (EPA), 193-194, 197, 275; as
    function-specific regulator, 70-71
Equal Employment Opportunity
    Commission (EEOC), 44, 187,
    197; as function-specific regulator,
    70-71; reform of, 142-144
Equality, 275, 276; international
    comparisons, 5-6; American
    ideal, 11, 169; costs of, 34-36;
    benefits of, 36-38; drive for, 133,
    168; in Japanese corporations,
    163; and wage-price controls,
    225-226
Eurodollar market, 236
Executive: social origins of, 121-122;
    wife of, 126
Expectations, 217
Externality, 82, 88

Family: corporate functions of,
    52-53
Fascism, 196, 198, 203
Fast-tracker, 127
Fear, 128
Federal charter for corporations,
    159-162; history of federal
    corporations, 165-166
Federal Corporate Administration
    (FCA): proposed, 149-151,
    160-162
Federalism, 155. *See also*
    New federalism
Federal Reserve System, 196, 201,
    231-235, 238-241, 258; co-opted,
    238; taming of, 255
Filtering, 115-120, 179; reform of,
    134-144
Final product market, 179
Financial intermediaries, 231-232,
    234, 241-242
Fiscal drag, 14, 255

Fiscal policy, 196, 202, 242-258;
President Reagan's, 14-16
Free enterprise, 195; American
counter-revolution, 19
Free inquiry, 135, 141, 269-270
Free will, 87
Friedman, Milton, 88-90, 92-93,
201, 230, 233
Friedman, Rose, 93
F-twist, 88-90. *See also*
Positivism
Functionally departmentalized
organization, 174-176
Funneling, 242

Galbraith, John Kenneth, 238; the
revised sequence, 52-53, 71; dual
economy, 85; technostructure,
129-130
Gamesman, 128-129, 163-164
Gerth, Hans, 123, 136
Gigantism, 114
Golden parachute, 59
Gold standard, 231
Government spending. *See*
International comparisons,
public spending
Greed, 63, 246, 257, 263, 273-274
Growth, economic, 187-188;
balanced, 190-191
Gubernatorial budgeting, 190
Guideposts, wage-price, 205-208,
211, 223

Haas, Eugene, 123
Habituation. *See* Roles
Hegemony, 54; defined, 49;
instruments of, 54-57;
corporate, 59-60
Hierarchy, 100-101
Hilton Hotels Corporation, 41
Hines, Thomas C., 41

Hiroshima, 252
History, 91, 167
Hofstadter, Richard, 137-139, 141
Hoover, Herbert, 225

Immigration restrictions, 219
Imports, 197
Incorporation: general laws of,
79-80
Individualism: frontier spirit, 3;
frustration of, 3, 130; and
supply-side economics, 20-21;
and frontier pluralism, 49; and
power, 50-61; and the illusion of
choice, 50, 60; methodological,
90-91
Inducements, 218-219
Industrial revolution, 29
Inequality: as a result of
Reaganomics, 33-34. *See
also* Equality
Inflation, 201, 203, 207; sellers,
158, 201, 213-215; in World
War II, 204-205; types of,
212-215; buyers, 212-215. *See
also* Conglomerate movement
Institution, 50-54, 83-84, 90; head
of, 59, 123-124
Institutionalism, 36, 71, 82, 86-87,
90, 180, 268; theory of the
labor market, 117-118; and the
AAUP, 140
Institutional resistance, 164-165
Instrumental value principle, 36, 39
Integration: horizontal and vertical,
64-66, 172-173
Interest rates, 191, 196, 235-236, 240
Intermediate product market, 179
Internalization of norms, 123
International comparisons, 4-5;
equality, 5-6; GNP, 6-7;
investment, 7-9; public spending,
8-9; social indicators, 9-10

Interventionist drift, 86
Invention and innovation, 31
Investment, 25; dependent on sales
    revenues, 25-28; and expected
    profits, 27; and the cost of credit,
    27. *See also* Capital
Investor city, 43
Investor state, 43

Jacksonian democrats, 166
Japan: corporate organization in,
    162-165
Jaw-boning, 206, 211, 218
Jencks, Christopher, 117, 120
Job competition, 120
Johns Hopkins University, 139
Johnson, Lyndon B., 205-206
Joint stock companies, 74-79;
    versus individual entrepreneurs,
    78; limited liability in, 78-79
Justice, 264

Kanter, Rosabeth Moss, 125-126
Kennedy, John F., 205-206
Keynes, John Maynard, 20, 230; and
    Say's law, 26
Keynesian economics, 82-83,
    86-87, 90
King, Martin Luther, Jr., 40, 167; 199
Kolko, Gabriel, 69

Labor market, 179; free, 114-115,
    117, 134; administered or
    bureaucratic, 114-118; external,
    115-116, 118-120; internal,
    115-116; institutional theory of,
    117; education and, 135-137
Laffer curve, 16
Laissez-faire, 29, 75, 131
Lange, Oskar, 89-90
Laws of supply and demand, 24-25

Leadership, 146; corporate, 163-165
Loopholes, tax, 253-254. *See also*
    Tax expenditures
Lowe, Adolph, 86, 90

Maccoby, Michael, 127-129, 162-165
Management: waves of administrative
    change, 173-178; the visible hand
    of, 175; replacing the market,
    179, 182
Marginal workers, 10-11; women,
    11; immigrants, 11
Market: administered, 85, 86-87,
    114-118
Market system, 261; and economic
    progress, 36-38; diminution of,
    64-67, 172-183; and filtering, 134
Marshall, Alfred, 80-81
Martin, William McChesney, Jr., 234
Mediocracy, 102
Megacorp, 40, 85, 86, 237
Mellon, Andrew, 225
Melman, Seymour, 80, 106
Mercantilism, 73
Mergers, 64-66; three waves of,
    172-173; reducing transactions
    costs, 183. *See also* Integration
Meritocracy, 102, 120
Methodology, 87-93
Militarization, 38-40
Military: spending 15, 39, 251-253,
    256; institutions, 52; hot versus
    cold war roles, 52; military
    industrial complex, 252, 267,
    273-274
Milking consumers, 62-63
Mills, C. Wright, 71, 100, 104, 123,
    124, 136
Minority workers, 219, 274
Mises, Ludwig von, 90-93
Missile gap, 252
Monetarism, 20-21. *See also*
    Monetary policy; Quantity theory
    of money

Monetarist school, 87-90, 92-93, 229-237, 268-269. *See also* Friedman, Milton
Monetary policy, 191, 196, 233-242, 258; President Reagan's, 16-17
Money: commodity, 230-231; commodity-reserve, 231; credit, 231-232; endogenous, 231-232; definitions of, 234-235
Moore, Wilbert, 125
Moral majority, 203
Morrill Act, 139
Mortgage credit, 236-237
Multidivisional organization, 174, 176-177
Multinational corporation, 40
Mystification, 57, 60. *See also* Economic theory

Nader, Ralph, 166
National economic budget, 190-191
National Economic Council: proposed, 188-190, 196
Neoclassical economics, 81-83; critique of, 83-87, 92-93; defense of, 87-93
New federalism, 247; as decentralization, 18-19; as party politics, 42-43; cause of community decay, 43; and old dixiecrats, 44-45, 272-273
New right, 13-14, 273
Nixon, Richard M., 202, 205, 233, 239; wage-price control program, 208-210

Occupational Safety and Health Administration (OSHA), 46, 17-18, 275; as function- specific regulator, 70-71; overregulation by, 157-158
Occupational structure, 106-107

O'Connor, James, 42
Office of Economic Stabilization, 204
Office of Management and Budget (OMB), 188-189, 196-197
Office of Price Administration, 204
Okun, Arthur, 34-36
Oligopolistic markets, 30; oligopoly, 174-175
O'Mahoney, Senator Joseph, 166
Ombudsman, 145-147
Opportunism, 264, 280; and appointees, 279-280
Organization of Petroleum Exporting Countries (OPEC), 210
Ouchi, William G., 162-165
Overproduction, 82

Paradox of thrift, 26-27
Parsons, Talcott, 125
Pathology: social, 203
Patriotism, 136
Pax Britannica, 73
Philanthropy, 56
Planning: within the firm, 64, 85; by government, 85-87; democratic, 86-87, 186-198; institutionalist imperative, 86-87; need for public, 185-188; vehicles, 188; bodies, 188-190; documents, 190-191; types of, 185-186; inducements, 192-194; and wage-price controls, 222-225
Planning process, proposed, 196-198
Plebiscite, 267
Pluralism: in America, 49-51; destroyed though subordination, 55
Polanyi, Karl, 45
Politics, failure of, 266-268; and campaign finances, 266-267; and lack of a labor party, 267
Polity: political roles in corporate America, 53-54
Poor nations, burdens of, 3

Positivism, 88, 93
Poverty, 263, 273-274; and
    Reaganomics, 28; incidence of, 37
Power: defined, 50; and institutions,
    50-51
Predictions, 88-89
Price mechanism, 81-82; in the
    labor market, 114--115
Private good, 251
Producer, 63-68; representative
    firm, 80-81. *See also* Megacorp;
    Conglomerate
Productivity: source, 36-37; and
    wage-price controls, 205-206,
    223-225
Profit appropriation, 227
Profit center, 177, 178
Promotion: reform of, 145-146.
    See also Reproduction
Proposition 13, 247
Protege as clone, 122-130
Public Directors on corporate boards:
    and wage-price controls, 221-222.
    See also Board of Directors
Public good, 251
Public school, 142, *See
    also* Education

Quantity theory of money,
    201, 230-233. *See also*
    Monetarist school
Quotas, job, 144. *See also*
    Recruitment, employee;
    Equal Employment
    Opportunity Commission

Racism, 130, 168, 187. *See also*
    Dixiecrats; Equality; Quotas;
    American dream
Rational expectations hypothesis, 21
Rationing, 213
Reaganomics, 14-22, 195; social
    costs of, 32-34

Reagan, Ronald, 13, 239, 266;
    Reaganomics, 14-28, 239;
    significance of his presidency,
    272-274
Recruitment: employee, 115-117;
    reforming, 134-144. *See
    also* Filtering
Redistribution, 34-36; and
    wage-price controls, 228; and
    monetary policy, 235-236
Red-lining, 242
Red tape, 102
Reform: grassroots movements,
    155-156; proposals, 168-169
Regionalism, 272-273
Registration Act of 1856, 79
Regulator, 68-71; early regulatory
    agencies, 68-69; as price-fixer,
    69; second-generation regulatory
    agencies, 69-71; industry-specific,
    69-70; function specific, 70-71;
    cooptation of, 69-70. *See also*
    different agencies
Reification, 62
Religion in corporate America, 54
Repression, 203
Reproduction: institutional,
    116-118, 120-130; homosocial,
    120-130; 179; homosexual,
    125-127; reform of, 144-152
Revolutionary drive, 28-29. *See
    also* Equality
Reynolds, Larry, 69
Right-to-work laws, 156. *See
    also* Investor state
Roles: socialization through, 58,
    84, 86; as institutions, 58
Roosevelt, Franklin Delano, 204
Russia Company, 74

Safety net programs: cuts in, 15
Salesmanship, 62
Sanctions, 218-219

Sarachek, Bernard, 123
Saving, 25; deadening effect
  on investment, 27
Savings and loan associations,
  236-237
Say's Law, 26, 82, 86, 88
Scapegoat, 265-266
Science and technology, 30-32
Selection: institutional, 118-120
Sexism, 130, 168, 187
Shannon, H.A., 79
Sherman Antitrust Act, 172
Significant other, 123. *See
  also* Sponsorship
Small business, 105, 235; goals for,
  191, 194
Small Business Administration,
  187, 197
Smith, Adam, 29, 64, 81; and the
  joint stock company, 73-77
Social control, 83-87, 91-92
Social indicators, 9-10
Social Security, 245
Sociology, 91
South Sea Company, 74-75;
  South Sea bubble, 75
Special interest group, 273, 279
Sponsorship, 122-124, 127. *See
  also* Reproduction
Stages of production, 63-64; and
  vertical integration, 65,
  171-172, 175
Stagflation, 10-11; and the
  conglomerate, 65-68, 265
Stanfield, J. Ron, 86,
State and local finance, 246-247
States' rights, 44, 272-273.
  See also Dixiecrats
Status, 62-63; occupational,
  117-118; inherited, 121-122,
  124; panic, 124-125, 263;
  corporate, 129
Stock jobbers, 75
S-twist, 88-89. *See also*
  Austrian school
Subjectivism, 90-92

Subordination, 55, 59
Supply-side economics, 19-22, 83,
  229, 270, 272; critique of, 23-32;
  and the paradox of thrift, 27;
  impact on demand, 28; social
  costs of, 32-47; and the market
  system, 36-37
Symbolism, 56

Taves, Marvin J., 123
Tax: on corporate income, 159-160;
  on dividends, 159-160;
  on retained earnings, 159-160;
  reform, 202, 254-255; burden,
  245-246; progressive, 254-255
Tax concessions: municipal, 41-45;
  state, 42-43
Tax evasion, 35
Tax expenditures, 244. *See
  also* Loopholes, tax
Tax revolt, 63
Technological progress. *See* Science
  and technology
Thatcher, Margaret, 265
Theory Z, 162-165
Thurmond, Strom, 44, 272
Thurow, Lester, 120, 160
Tight money, 191. *See also*
  Monetary policy
Tobin, James, 237-241, 258
Token, 269. *See also*
  Racism; Sexism
Tool, Marc, 36, 39
Transactions, 180-182
Trickle down theory, 32, 36-38;
  speed of trickle down effect, 37
Truman, Harry, 44
Trusts: as fabricated joint stock
  companies, 77. *See also* Antitrust

Underground economics, 28, 71,
  82-87, 270-271. *See also*
  Institutionalism

Unemployment rate, 203, 207; and
    stagflation, 11; and saving, 27;
    in World War II, 204-205; and
    wage guidelines, 224-225
Unions, 214; decline in, 51; and
    wage-price controls, 206
United States of America:
    founding of, 3-4; resources of, 3;
    international comparisons, 4-10.
    See also American dream
University: American, 55, 138-142,
    268-269; medieval, 137-138;
    german model, 139-140; first
    U.S., 139. *See also* Education

Veblen, Thorstein, 39, 55, 71, 82,
    84, 123, 129, 180, 182-183
Vietnam war, 205, 208, 244, 250
Vocational training, 137, 144, 264.
    See also Education
Volcker, Paul, 234, 236, 239, 258;
    and President Reagan, 17
Voter apathy, 267-268
Voting Rights Act, 44

Wage flexibility, 134
Wage-Price Commission, 220-223
Wage-price controls, 201-227; and
    the public director, 158-159;
    major programs, 203-212; and
    profits, 205-206, 226-227; and
    equality, 225-226; and freedom,
    226; and equity, 228
Wallace, George, 272
Warner, W. Lloyd, 121
Watt, James, 160; as
    leading deregulator, 17;
    anti-environmentalist, 17
Weber, Max, 103, 124-127, 145
Welfare, 257-258. *See also* Equality
Welfare state: liquidation of, 15
Williamson, Oliver E. 180, 182
Window of vulnerability, 252

Women: rising unemployment,
    10-11; homosexual reproduction,
    126. *See also* Equality; Sexism